THE UNITED STATES OF AMERICA

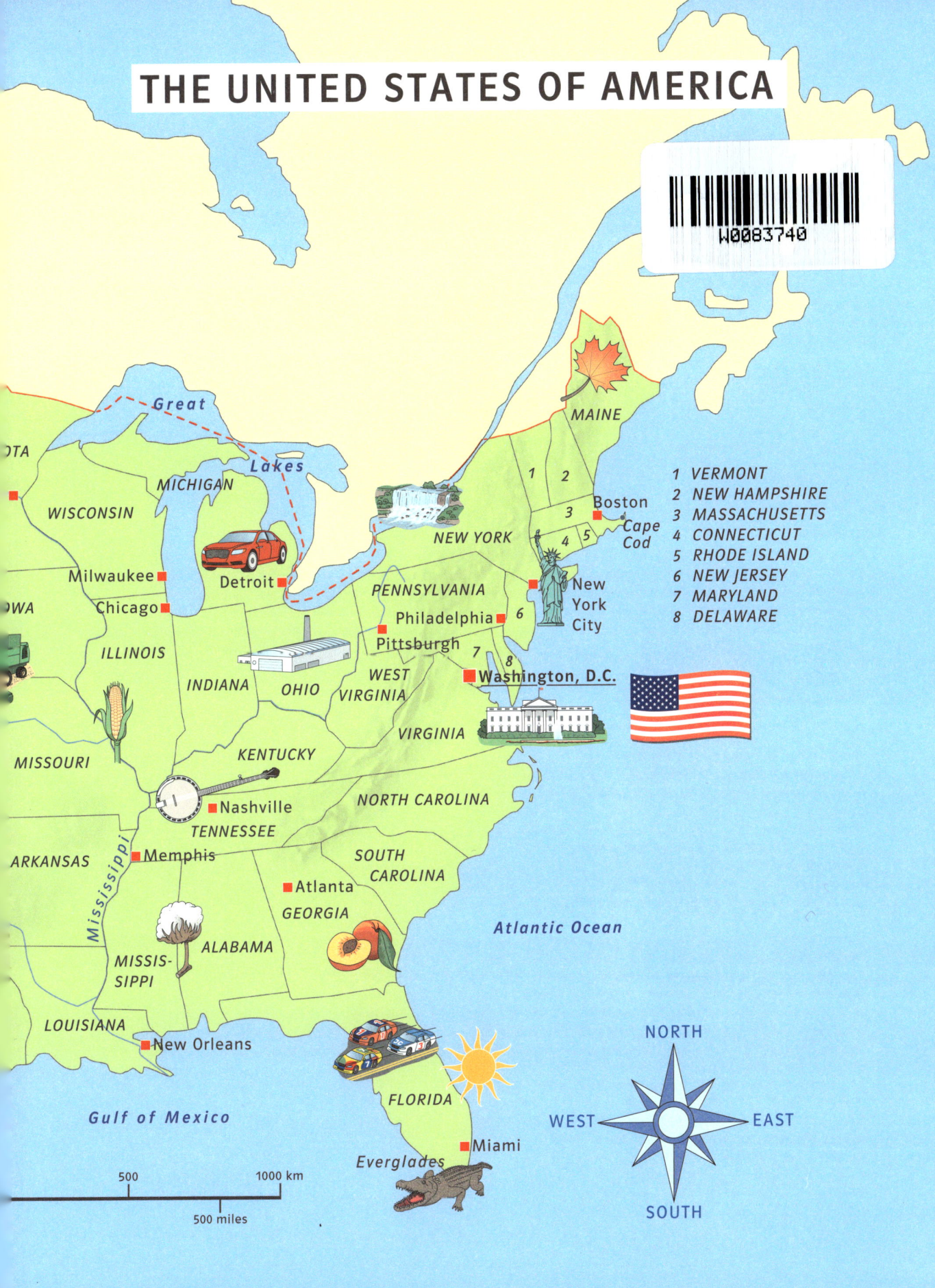

Great Lakes

MAINE

OTA

MICHIGAN

WISCONSIN

Milwaukee

Detroit

OWA

Chicago

ILLINOIS

INDIANA

OHIO

MISSOURI

KENTUCKY

ARKANSAS

Nashville

TENNESSEE

Memphis

Atlanta

GEORGIA

ALABAMA

MISSIS-
SIPPI

LOUISIANA

New Orleans

FLORIDA

Gulf of Mexico

Everglades

Miami

NEW YORK

PENNSYLVANIA

Philadelphia

Pittsburgh

WEST
VIRGINIA

VIRGINIA

NORTH CAROLINA

SOUTH
CAROLINA

1   2

3   Boston

4   5   Cape
Cod

6

7

8   Washington, D.C.

New
York
City

1   VERMONT
2   NEW HAMPSHIRE
3   MASSACHUSETTS
4   CONNECTICUT
5   RHODE ISLAND
6   NEW JERSEY
7   MARYLAND
8   DELAWARE

Atlantic Ocean

NORTH

WEST   EAST

SOUTH

500   1000 km

500 miles

W0083740

Blue Line 4

Ausgabe für Bayern (Mittelschulen) Klasse 8 R-Zug

Die Mediencodes (Beispiel: ⊕ Find more online: 9dk5x5) enthalten zusätzliche Unterrichtsmaterialien, die der Verlag in eigener Verantwortung zur Verfügung stellt.

Im Lernmittel wird in Form von Symbolen auf eine CD verwiesen. Diese enthält – bis auf die Hörverstehensübungen – ausschließlich optionale Unterrichtsmaterialien. Die CD unterliegt nicht dem staatlichen Zulassungsverfahren.

> Zusatzmaterial für Schülerinnen und Schüler u.a.:
> Blue Line 4 Bayern R-Zug Workbook mit Audio-CD (ISBN 978-3-12-548354-5)

1. Auflage

1 5 4 3 2 1 | 24 23 22 21 20

Alle Drucke dieser Auflage sind unverändert und können im Unterricht nebeneinander verwendet werden.
Die letzte Zahl bezeichnet das Jahr des Druckes.

Das Werk und seine Teile sind urheberrechtlich geschützt. Jede Nutzung in anderen als den gesetzlich zugelassenen Fällen bedarf der vorherigen schriftlichen Einwilligung des Verlages. Hinweis § 60 a UrhG: Weder das Werk noch seine Teile dürfen ohne eine solche Einwilligung eingescannt und in ein Netzwerk eingestellt werden. Dies gilt auch für Intranets von Schulen und sonstigen Bildungseinrichtungen. Fotomechanische oder andere Wiedergabeverfahren nur mit Genehmigung des Verlages.

© Ernst Klett Verlag GmbH, Stuttgart 2020. Alle Rechte vorbehalten. www.klett.de
Das vorliegende Material dient ausschließlich gemäß § 60b UrhG dem Einsatz im Unterricht an Schulen.

Herausgeber: Wolfgang Hamm, Marktredwitz
Autorinnen und Autoren: Daniel Shatwell, Hanau; Wolfgang Hamm, Marktredwitz sowie David Brimage, Brighton; Chris Caridia, London; Sara Conway, Stuttgart; Dr. Andrea Jessen, Tamm; Karen Seekings, London
Beratung: Michaela Cavallucci, München; Gaby Fruhmann, Parsberg; Michael Meisenzahl, Karlstadt; Lisa Schubert, Altdorf; Anna Weber, Taufkirchen
Externe Redaktion: Judith Pfeiffer-Ley, Mainz; Birgit Piefke-Wagner, Korntal-Münchingen

Entstanden in Zusammenarbeit mit dem Projektteam des Verlages.

Umschlaggestaltung und Gestaltungskonzept: know idea, Freiburg; Koma Amok, Stuttgart
Umschlagfotos: ShutterStock.com RF (Little_Desire), New York, NY; Alamy stock photo (Russ Bishop), Abingdon, Oxon
Illustrationen: Christian Dekelver, Weinstadt; Jaroslaw Schwarzstein, Hannover; Marcus Wilder, Hamburg; Sylvia Wolf, Wiesbaden; Steffen Wolff, Herzogenrath sowie Friederike Ablang, Berlin; Athos Boncompagni, Arezzo/Italien; Vera Brüggemann, Bielefeld; Martina Burghart-Vollhardt, Kamenz; Oliver Eger, Langenhringen; Jochen Ehmann, Stuttgart; Anke Fröhlich, Leipzig; Josef Hammen, Trierweiler; Steffen Jähde, Sundhagen; Hendrik Kranenberg, Drolshagen; Helga Merkle, Albershausen; Pawel Miedzinski, Kozieglowy/Polen; David Norman, Meerbusch; Axel Nicolai, Brauweiler; Liliane Oser, Hamburg; Katja Rau, Berglen; Myrtia Rockstroh, Berlin; Wolfgang Schaar, Grafing; Vera Schmidt, Remshalden-Grunbach; Wolfgang Slawski, Laboe; Birgit Tanck, Hamburg; Katja Wehner, Leipzig; Katrin Wolff, Wiesbaden; Dorothee Wolters, Köln
Satz: graphitecture book & edition; Fotosatz Kaufmann, Stuttgart
Reproduktion: Schwabenrepro GmbH, Stuttgart
Druck: Firmengruppe APPL, aprinta druck, Wemding

Printed in Germany
ISBN 978-3-12-548264-7

Inhalt

L = Listening   M = Mediation   R = Reading   S = Speaking   V = Viewing   W = Writing

So lernst du mit Blue Line

So lernst du mit deinem Buch.
Das Buch hat vier *Units* (Kapitel).
Jede *Unit* ist gleich aufgebaut.

Intro

Hier steigst du in das neue Thema ein.
Dazu gibt es auch einen kurzen Film.

Im gelben Kasten siehst du, was du in
der *Unit* lernen wirst.

Topics

In jeder *Unit* gibt es zwei *Topics*, in
denen du viele neue Dinge lernst.
Hier kannst du erkennen, wie schwer
eine Übung ist:

● schwer ◕ mittel ○ leicht

In der *Task* kannst du zeigen, dass du alles
verstanden hast, und deine eigenen Ideen
einbringen.

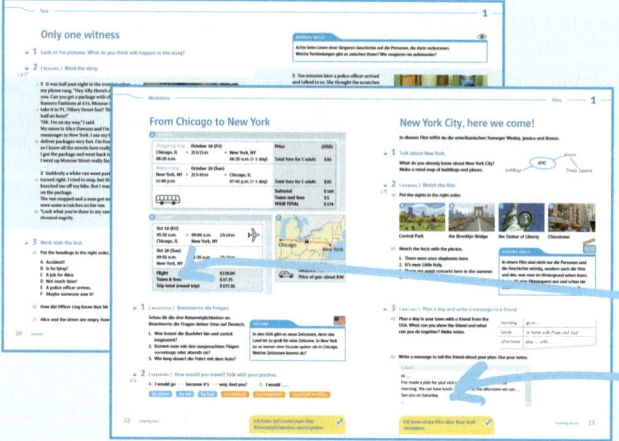

Text

Auf den *Text*-Seiten findest du spannende
Geschichten und andere Texte.

Mediation/Film

Auf der linken Seite geht es darum,
englische Informationen auf Deutsch
weiterzugeben.
Das nennt man *Mediation*.

Auf der *Film*-Seite geht es um einen
Film in englischer Sprache.

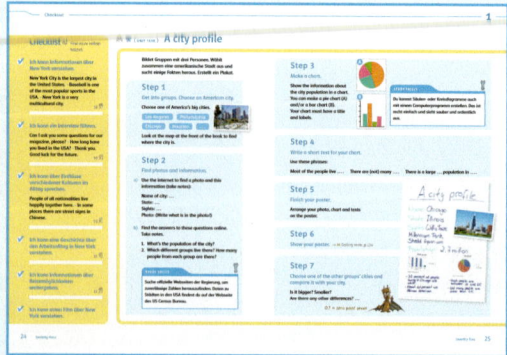

Checkout

Auf dieser Doppelseite kannst du zeigen, ob du
in der *Unit* alles verstanden hast.

Die Abschluss-Aufgabe (*Unit task*) könnt ihr meist
zu zweit oder in der Gruppe lösen.

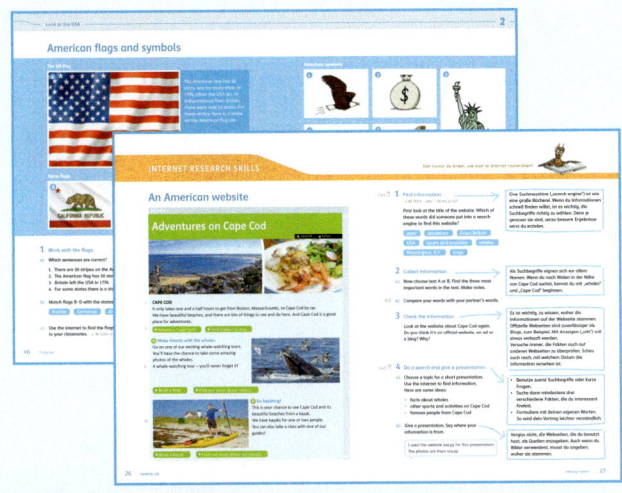

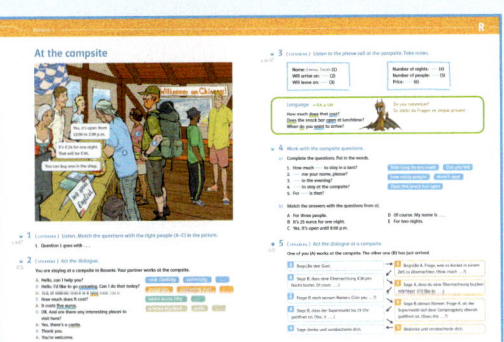

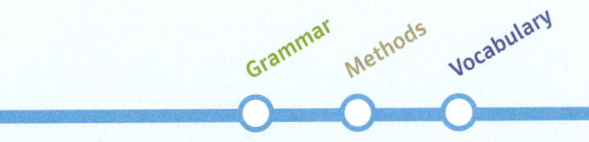

Look at the USA / Look at Canada

Hier kannst du die USA und Kanada weiter entdecken. Schau genau hin. Vieles kannst du verstehen oder erraten.

Skills

Auf jede *Unit* folgt eine Doppelseite, auf der du eine bestimmte Fertigkeit (*Skill*), Technik oder Lernstrategie besonders trainieren kannst.

Revision

Hier kannst du wiederholen, was du in den Klassen 5–7 bereits gelernt hast.

Symbol	Erklärung
○ ◐ ●	leicht/mittel/schwer (Niveaudifferenzierung)
✿	individualisierende Aufgabe (natürliche Differenzierung)
→ ○ p.96	Verweis auf leichtere Parallelübung auf der *Diff corner*-Seite
OR	Aufgabe zur Auswahl (Wahldifferenzierung)
⌐o	Entwicklung von Schlüsselkompetenzen für Ausbildung und Beruf
℗	Hier entsteht ein Produkt für das Portfolio.
4/6 ⎘	Verweis auf eine Übung im *Workbook*
→ **G1, p.106**	Verweis auf den Grammatikanhang (*Grammar*)
→ **M**	Verweis auf die Methodenseiten (*Methods*)
→ **V**	Verweis auf eine *Word bank* im Vokabular (*Vocabulary*)
◎◎	Partnerarbeit
◎◎	Gruppenarbeit
◎	Verweis auf die Lehrer-CD (Audio)
⌐	Verweis auf die Lehrer-DVD (Film)
⊕ Find more online: jv45yg	Code auf www.klett.de eingeben und Zusatzinformationen erhalten

Grammar   Methods   Vocabulary

Im Anschluss an die vier *Units* gibt es noch weitere nützliche Seiten:

Grammar: Hier findest du alle Regeln und Erklärungen zur Grammatik, Übungen und eine Liste der unregelmäßigen Verben.

Methods: Manche Übungen könnt ihr auf eine bestimmte Art und Weise bearbeiten. Das erkennst du an diesem Symbol: → M. Wie es genau funktioniert, kannst du hier nachlesen.

Vocabulary: Im *Vocabulary* findest du alle neuen Wörter in der Reihenfolge, in der sie in der *Unit* auftauchen, sowie *Word banks*, die dir bei der Bearbeitung der *Task* helfen. Im *Dictionary* sind die Wörter noch einmal alphabetisch aufgelistet: zuerst Englisch–Deutsch und dann Deutsch–Englisch.

Zoom in – The USA

This is one of the most beautiful places in the USA – Monument Valley.

1 Do the USA quiz with a partner.

1. What do Americans do on 4th July?
2. Who lives in the White House?
3. Which city is the capital of the USA?
4. What money do people use in the USA?
5. Who lived there before the Europeans?

6. In which state of the USA is Hollywood?
7. What animals can you see in Florida?
8. What is the name of the mountains in the west of the USA?

2

We always celebrate on 4th July. The USA got its independence from Britain on that day in 1776. There are always a lot of flags too!

3

The White House is where the president of the USA lives and works. It's in the capital, Washington, D.C.

4

We use dollars and cents in the USA. There are pictures of American presidents on the money.

5

The Native Americans lived here before the Europeans came.

Die Fragen 6–8 im Quiz sind für Profis. Um sie zu beantworten, sieh dir auch die Karte vorne im Buch an. Du kannst deine Antworten auf S. 202 überprüfen.

Welcome to New York!

New York City (NYC) is the largest city in the United States. There are five boroughs: The Bronx, Brooklyn, Manhattan, Queens and Staten Island. Here you can see Times Square in Manhattan. It's one of the most famous places in the city.

The United States is a country of immigrants. Many of them saw the Statue of Liberty when they arrived in the USA. The statue is on a small island near Manhattan. It was a present from France.

1 (SPEAKING) Look at the pictures.

What differences are there? Talk to a partner.

In picture 1 there is/are … .
There is/are … in picture … . But there isn't a … in picture … .
The people in picture … are … .

| stadium | water | restaurant | shops |

| … |

| standing | playing | working | … |

2 (READING) Which two sentences are right?

1. There are eight boroughs in New York City.
2. The Statue of Liberty is on a small island near France.
3. People in New York like baseball a lot.
4. Many young New Yorkers ride a bike in their job.
5. There are many museums in 'Little Italy' in Manhattan.

Am Ende dieser Unit kann ich ...
- Informationen über New York verstehen.
- ein Interview führen.
- über Einflüsse verschiedener Kulturen im Alltag sprechen.
- eine Geschichte über den Arbeitsalltag in New York verstehen.
- Informationen über Reisemöglichkeiten weitergeben.
- einen Film über New York verstehen.

3 Baseball is one of the most popular sports in the USA, and New Yorkers love it. Some players are really big stars.

4 The city is a very expensive place. A lot of young people there work as bike messengers or in cafés. Bike messengers often ride through Central Park, a large park in Manhattan. There are some lakes in the park too.

5 New York is a multicultural city. Many people went to live there from Italy, for example. There is still a large Italian population today. You can see many Italian restaurants in 'Little Italy' in Manhattan.

 3 (LISTENING) **Listen to the information about the Statue of Liberty.**

1,3
2/2

Choose the right answer.

1. The statue is **39 metres** • **93 metres** high.
2. The statue has 25 **windows** • **doors**.
3. There is a **museum** • **cinema** near the statue.
4. The statue has been in a lot of **films** • **games**.
5. The Statue of Liberty is open **every day** • **on Saturdays and Sundays**.

Mit „New York" bezeichnet man sowohl die Stadt als auch den Bundesstaat New York. Die Stadt heißt auch „New York City" (oder „NYC"). Im Jahr 2017 wohnten ca. 8,6 Millionen Menschen in NYC. Was ist die größte Stadt in Deutschland?

Ich kann Informationen über New York verstehen. ✔

Living the dream?

1 (READING) **Read the interview with José Blanco.**

1,4
3/1

1 Interviewer: Hello José. Can I ask you some questions for our magazine, please?
José: Hi. Sure.
Interviewer: You're a new star on one of New
5 York's best baseball teams. Where are you from?
José: My family is from Cuba.
Interviewer: How long have you lived in the USA?
10 José: I've lived here for 13 years.
Interviewer: Your parents left their home country. Was that easy?
José: No, it was a difficult decision. But they were very poor. My father couldn't find work
15 in Cuba. My parents wanted to give my sister and me the best opportunities.
Interviewer: What were the first years like for your family?
José: It was difficult because my parents
20 couldn't speak English well. But other people from Cuba helped them. Later my parents opened a small store.

Interviewer: How did you feel?
José: I was a new arrival. Everything was very
25 new and exciting. Later I was sad because I was homesick. But I got used to life here. I haven't been homesick for a long time.
Interviewer: You're 23 now. How long have you played baseball?
30 José: I've played baseball for eight years. I've had lots of opportunities since 2015. That's when I became the star of my school team.
Interviewer: You've had a successful career!
José: Yes, I have. My story is a great example
35 of the American Dream. I was a new arrival and I wanted to be successful. I have been an American citizen since December last year. For most people it's much harder.
Interviewer: So, what about your plans?
40 José: Well, I often talk to people in Cuba, and I'd like to help them.
Interviewer: Thank you, José. Good luck for the future.

CULTURE

Die Idee des amerikanischen Traums ist, dass jeder hart arbeiten und so ein besseres Leben erreichen kann. Manche Einwanderer wurden sogar Millionäre, z. B. der Jeans-Hersteller Levi Strauss, der aus der Nähe von Bamberg kam. Was denkst du über den amerikanischen Traum?

2 Work with the text.

a) What is the text about? Choose the best sentence. → ◯ p.90

A José talks about baseball and how he came to Los Angeles.
B José talks about his life, his family and the American Dream.
C José talks about his family and his favourite music.

b) Copy and complete the fact card. → M Think – pair – share, p.127

Name: ——	People in family:
From: —	——
Lives in: ——	Career/job: ——
How long in USA: ——	Happy/sad?: ——

Halte deine Notizen so kurz wie möglich. Schreibe nur die wichtigsten Wörter („Schlüsselwörter") auf.

3 Life in a different country

3/2

a) Match the parts of the sentences. → ◯ p.91

1. José's parents left Cuba
2. They were poor and they couldn't find
3. It was difficult in the USA
4. Some people from Cuba
5. Later they opened
6. José soon got used to
7. Last year he became

a. work in Cuba.
b. American life.
c. helped them.
d. because they couldn't speak English well.
e. and went to live in the USA.
f. an American citizen.
g. a small store.

b) Imagine you have to live in a different country. Make your own sentences.

| I will miss . . . . | I will be . . . . | I will get help from . . . . | I won't know/like . . . . | . . . |

4 (LISTENING) Listen to the interview with Malee.

1,5
3/3

Malee is an immigrant from Thailand. Take notes to complete the sentences.
You don't need all of the words.

1. Malee went to live in the USA when she was —— .
2. She lived with her —— and his family in Brooklyn.
3. It was —— to make friends at school.
4. She has a job in a —— now.
5. Her uncle had an accident —— years ago.
6. She wants to have her own —— in the future.

| café | store | easy | restaurant | two |
| uncle | ten | three | hard | brother |

4/4–5

5 (SPEAKING) **Talk to your partner.** → **M** Milling around, p.124

a) Make questions and take turns. → ○ p.91

A: Have you ever lived in a different country?
B: Yes, I have. / No, I haven't.

B: Have you ever …?
A: Yes, I have. / No, I haven't.

1. live in a different country?
2. play basketball?
3. visit the USA?
4. talk to an American?
5. be homesick?
6. help on a farm?

Language → **G1**, p.106
I've visited Berlin three times.
Have you ever played baseball?
My brother has worked hard.
Have you ever been to Cuba?

b) Write two sentences about you and two sentences about your partner.

I have/haven't ….   My partner has/hasn't ….   He/She ….

Language detectives → **G1**, p.106

I've lived here for 13 years.
I haven't been homesick for a long time.
I've had lots of opportunities since 2015.
I have been an American citizen since December.

Mit welchem englischen Wort für „seit"
wird ein Zeitpunkt und mit welchem eine
Zeitspanne ausgedrückt?

6 (WRITING) **Look at these words.**

a) For or since? Put the words and phrases in the right list.

for	since

2017   three days   three o'clock   April
two weeks   Saturday   six months
an hour   two years   December

b) Find three more phrases for each list.

7 **Make sentences about José and Malee. Use since or for.**

4/6

1. José has lived in New York for 13 years.
2. His father has worked in the store —— 2004.
3. His aunt has not worked —— last year.
4. Malee has lived in the USA —— she was ten.
5. Her uncle has had a cat —— nine months.
6. She has not seen her family in Thailand —— five years.

5/7 **8** (SPEAKING) **How long?**

a) Talk to your partner. Use your own ideas. → ○ p. 91

I haven't	watched …	visited …	bought …	**since ….**
	played …	seen …	…	**for ….**

A: I haven't watched TV for two weeks. And you?
B: Really? I've watched TV a lot this week!

b) Tell the class. How long have you …?

I've lived in …. I've been a student at …. I've been a fan of …. …

9 **Match the questions and answers to make an interview.**

1. Can I ask you some questions, please?
2. How long have you been in Germany?
3. Why did you want to come here?
4. Did you know anybody in Germany?
5. How long has your aunt lived there?
6. What are your plans for the future?

a. Yes, we did. My aunt lives in Berlin.
b. I'd like to finish school here.
c. She has lived there since 2004.
d. My parents and I arrived here a year ago.
e. Yes, of course!
f. We wanted to have a better life.

Language → **G 2, p. 107**

My parents and I <u>arrived</u> here a year ago.

✳ **10** (TASK) **Interviewing a new arrival** → V Interviewing a new arrival, p. 130

5/8

a) There is a new student at your school. The student has come from a different country.
You want to know more about him/her. Prepare an interview with a partner.

Think about these points:

* where the student is from
  (Where are you from?)
* how long the student has been here
  (How long have you been …?)
* why the student came to Germany
* the student's plans for the future
* what the student knows about Germany
  and Bavaria

SPEAKING SKILLS

Denke daran, dein Interview höflich zu beginnen und zu beenden. Verwende „Please", „Thank you" und „You're welcome". Zeige Interesse. Wenn du etwas nicht verstehst, sage: „Sorry, can you repeat that, please?" Versuche zu helfen, wenn jemand stecken bleibt.

b) Interview your partner. Take notes from the interview. Think of more questions.

c) Present your interview to the class.

Schau dir die Fragen in Übung 9 an. Sie können dir weiterhelfen!

Ich kann ein Interview führen. ✔

In the city

1 (READING) **Read a magazine article about teenagers in New York.**

1,6

We talked to four young people about life in New York. This is what they told us …

1
Jian: I live in the borough of Queens with my parents and my sister. We moved here when I was four. People of all nationalities live happily together here. There are Chinatowns in Manhattan, Brooklyn
5 and Queens. In some parts of Queens there are street signs in Chinese.

Tamila: I was born in Jamaica, but my family moved to Brooklyn in 2010. Brooklyn is a fantastic place. There are so many cool stores with clothes and shoes. One of my favorite days is Labor Day, in September. There is a parade in Brooklyn on that day. The people in the parade
10 always play music very loudly.

Nikolai: We're from Russia, but we've lived in the USA for ten years. Our apartment is in Harlem, a part of Manhattan. Everyone walks quickly here – Harlem is an awesome place, but it isn't a place for slow people! The food is amazing. There are many different restaurants –
15 Italian, Turkish, Japanese and Spanish. They cook really well here!

Angela: I'm from the Bronx. I was born here, and I've lived here all my life. I live with my mom, my uncle and my cousin. My mom came here from Cuba in the 1980s. She speaks English badly, so we speak Spanish at home. I love it here, but life isn't always easy. People work
20 hard, and some parts of town aren't safe at night. Sometimes we visit the zoo in the Bronx. It's near our apartment.

CULTURE

„Labor Day" ist am ersten Montag im September und ein Feiertag in den USA. Viele verabreden sich mit Freunden oder grillen gemeinsam. Was unternimmst du an Feiertagen wie dem 1. Mai?

2 **Match the headings with the teenagers. (You don't need all of the headings.)**

A A lot of different restaurants
B Born in the Bronx
C Tall buildings

D Cool stores and a parade
E People from around the world in one place

3 **Work with the text.** → **M** Bus stop, p.122

a) Right, wrong or not in the text? → ◯ p.92

1. Jian moved to New York when he was 14.
2. New York has more than one Chinatown.
3. The stores in Brooklyn are cool.
4. Tamila has two brothers.
5. Nikolai came to the USA nine years ago.
6. He has a skateboard.
7. Angela has always lived in the Bronx.
8. Her mother came to New York from Italy.

b) Complete the sentences.

1. Some of the street signs where Jian lives are in —— .
2. Tamila moved to Brooklyn with —— .
3. The food is very good —— .
4. Angela's mother has lived in the Bronx since —— .
5. Angela speaks Spanish at home because her mother speaks —— .

4 (SPEAKING) **Match the nationalities with the flags.**

6/1

 Italian ·  Chinese · Spanish ✓ · 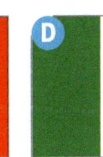 Japanese ·  Turkish

A   B   C   D   E

1. A: That's the <u>Spanish</u> flag.

5 **Work with words.**

a) Find the opposites. (Which word has two opposites?) → ◯ p.93

| easy ✓ · quiet · interesting · cheap ·
slow · good · happy · safe | boring · bad · fast · dangerous
sad · hard ✓ · quick · loud · expensive |

1. easy – hard

b) Look at the texts on page 16 again. Find three words that mean the same as 'great'.

6 (SOUNDS) **Listen, read and say.**

1,7
6/2
7/3

1. We‿moved‿here | when‿I‿was‿four.
2. Our‿apartment‿is‿in‿Harlem.
3. My‿town‿is‿a‿fantastic‿place.
4. I've‿lived‿here | all‿my‿life.
5. Some‿parts‿of‿town‿aren't‿safe.

Höre dir die Sätze genau an und versuche, sie nachzusprechen. Achte darauf, wie die Wörter beim Sprechen miteinander verbunden werden.

Language detectives → G 3, p.108

Times Square is a <u>loud</u> place.
The <u>food</u> is <u>amazing</u> in Harlem.

They <u>play</u> music very <u>loudly</u>.
Everyone <u>walks</u> quickly here.

Mit einem <u>Adjektiv</u> beschreibst du, <u>wie etwas ist</u>. Mit einem <u>Adverb</u> sagst du,
<u>wie jemand etwas tut</u>. Die Endung für Adverbien ist <u>-ly</u>. Wie ist das im Deutschen?

7/4–6 **7 How do they do it?**

a) Put in the right words. There are two words which you don't need. → ○ p.93

> badly   easily   happily   loudly ✓   dangerously
>
> slowly   quietly   carefully

1. People in Harlem restaurants often talk <u>loudly</u>.
2. Angela's mother speaks English ——.
3. New Yorkers never walk ——.
4. People from different cultures live —— together here.
5. You have to walk across the roads in Manhattan very ——.
6. Speak to American people and you can learn English ——.

b) Which words didn't you need in a)? Write a sentence with each word.

*Sei vorsichtig bei Wörtern
wie „careful" und „happy"!*
→ carefully
→ happily

8/7 **8 New York life**

a) Complete the sentences. → ○ p.93

1. Everything happens <u>quickly</u> in New York. (quick)
2. It's a great place for music. You can find clubs ——. (easy)
3. Bike messengers have to ride their bikes very ——. (fast)
4. People work very —— here. They never stop! (hard)
5. But in Central Park you can sit down and read ——. (quiet)
6. And it's easy to eat —— in Harlem. (good)

Language → G 3, p.108
Beachte: Diese drei Adverbien sind
unregelmäßig!
a <u>hard</u> player → she plays <u>hard</u>
a <u>fast</u> player → he runs <u>fast</u>
a <u>good</u> chef → he cooks <u>well</u>

b) Choose the right words to complete part of an internet page about Manhattan.

> **INTERNET**
>
> You can see New York very **easy** • **easily** (1) when
> you walk. Most of the city is **good** • **well** (2) for
> trips on foot. But think about your trip **careful** •
> **carefully** (3) before you leave. New York people like
> to walk **quick** • **quickly** (4). Are you **slow** • **slowly**
> (5) on foot? Then stay on the right, or a New Yorker
> will shout at you **angry** • **angrily** (6)!

9 (GAME) What am I doing?

Choose a word from each group. Act the activity in that way. Your friends must guess the activity and how you are doing it.

Are you
+
eating   washing   singing
riding a bike   running
walking   swimming
+
loudly?   fast?   slowly?
happily?   carefully?
angrily?   sadly?

A: Are you swimming slowly?   B: That's right. / No, that's wrong. Try again!

10 Complete the text about Central Park. Choose the right words.

Central Park is **at · in · on** (1) the middle of Manhattan. They **opened · opens · start** (2) the park more than 150 years ago. Today there are tall **build · builds · buildings** (3) near the park. New Yorkers love to visit Central Park on Sunday afternoons and talk **quiet · quietly · quite** (4) with friends, or just eat ice cream. There is **after · all · also** (5) a zoo in the park **what · when · where** (6) visitors can see many interesting animals. Central Park is the most **famous · famously · large** (7) city park in the USA!

11 (TASK) Different cultures where you live → V Talking about culture, p.131

Prepare a short presentation about the cultures where you live. → M 1-minute-presentation, p.122

a) Which nationalities are there at your school? Make a list. Use a dictionary if you need to.

b) What can you find from the different nationalities around your school? Make notes:

shops   food   clothes
restaurants   signs   music
important days   dance   …
Turkish   Italian   Chinese   …

STUDY SKILLS

Sammle Informationen und mache dir Notizen. Teile deine Präsentation in klare Schritte ein. Stelle dein Thema vor: Denke an einen interessanten Einstieg (Bild, Lied) oder einen Einleitungssatz. Beantworte mögliche Fragen nach der Präsentation.

c) Give your presentation. → M Tip top, p.127

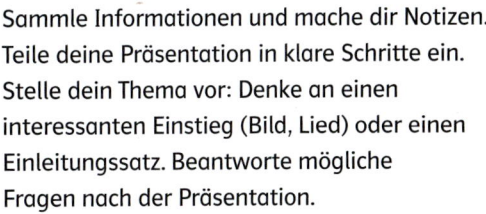

I live in …. It's ….
There are many Turkish/Italian/… there.
Most of them like to buy …/go to ….

You can often see …. My favourite is ….
People celebrate / play music / dance …ly.

Ich kann über Einflüsse verschiedener Kulturen im Alltag sprechen. ✔

Only one witness

1 Look at the pictures. What do you think will happen in the story?

2 (READING) Read the story.

1,8

1 **1** It was half past eight in the evening when
my phone rang. "Hey Ally, there's a job for
you. Can you get a package with clothes from
Romero Fashions at 616, Monroe Street and
5 take it to 91, Tillary Street fast? They need it in
half an hour!"
"OK. I'm on my way," I said.
My name is Alice Dawson and I'm a bike
messenger in New York. I use my bike and I
10 deliver packages very fast. I'm from Brooklyn,
so I know all the streets here really well.
I got the package and went back to my bike.
I went up Monroe Street really fast.

2 Suddenly a white van went past me and
15 turned right. I tried to stop, but the van
knocked me off my bike. But I was lucky. I fell
on the package.
The van stopped and a man got out. There
were some scratches on his van.
20 "Look what you've done to my van!" the man
shouted angrily.

I was angry too. "You turned right and didn't
signal!" I answered. "I'm calling the police!"
"You can say what you like!" the man said.
25 "You don't have any witnesses!"
I knew that he was right. There was no one in
the street at this time of the evening.

3 Work with the text.

a) Put the headings in the right order.

   A Accident!
   B Is he lying?
   C A job for Alice
   D Not much time!
   E A police officer arrives.
   F Maybe someone saw it!

b) How did Officer Ling know that Mr Mancini was lying?

4 Complete the sentences.

1. Alice delivers packages very fast.
2. The van k—— Alice off her bike.
3. The driver turned right and didn't s——.
4. Alice's bike was w——.
5. She thought she saw someone in the w——.
6. Mr Mancini saw the a——.
7. He wasn't telling the t——.

Need help? Look at lines 54–55 again.

c) Alice and the driver are angry. How could they make the situation better? Talk with a partner.

Achte beim Lesen einer längeren Geschichte auf die Personen, die darin vorkommen. Welche Verbindungen gibt es zwischen ihnen? Wie reagieren sie aufeinander?

3 Ten minutes later a police officer arrived and talked to us. She thought the scratches
30 on the van weren't too bad, but my bike was wrecked.
The driver got in his van and drove off. Police officer Ling said, "Well, the problem is that you don't have any witnesses."
35 "Yes, but I think I saw someone in the window in that building," I said. "I think it was a man."
"In the first floor apartment? OK, let's look."

4 The name on the door said Mancini. We rang the doorbell. Then a man opened
40 the door. He was about 50 and he was in a wheelchair.
"What do you want?" the man said excitedly. He had a strong Italian accent.
"There was an accident in the road near your
45 apartment," Officer Ling answered.
"What are you talking about?" Mr Mancini asked.
I said, "A driver knocked me off my bike. I saw you in the window."
50 "No, no. That's wrong," said Mr Mancini.

"Have you ever seen this lady?" Officer Ling asked him.
"No, I haven't."
"And did you see the driver?"
55 "No, I didn't. I didn't see the man in the van."
"You're lying!" I shouted. "I saw you!"
"OK, prove it!" the man answered.
"I think we can, Mr Mancini," Officer Ling said quietly. "I know that you're not telling the
60 truth."

9/1–4

5 **Choose one of the tasks.**

a) Alice told her best friend about the evening. Write her message.

Hi Mandy,
Guess what? I had an accident on my bike …

had a new job … • van turned … and didn't … • bike was wrecked … • didn't have any … • called the … • rang the … • talked to … • didn't tell … • knew because he said "I …"

OR

b)   Prepare a short presentation about bike messengers in New York. Find a good photo on the internet and look for this information. (The tips on page 19 can help you.)
→ M 1-minute-presentation, p.122

– What do bike messengers deliver?
– How fast do they ride? Is their job safe or dangerous? What do they wear?
– And you? (Would you like this job?)

Give your presentation.

Ich kann eine Geschichte über den Arbeitsalltag in New York verstehen.

From Chicago to New York

A INTERNET

Outgoing trip	October 18 (Fri)		Price	(USD)
Chicago, IL > 21h15m > New York, NY				
08:20 a.m. 06:35 a.m. (+ 1 day)			Total fare for 1 adult:	$84
Return trip	**October 20 (Sun)**			
New York, NY > 21h45m > Chicago, IL				
11:00 p.m. 07:45 p.m. (+ 1 day)			Total fare for 1 adult:	$85
			Subtotal	$169
			Taxes and fees	$5
			YOUR TOTAL	$174

B INTERNET

Oct 18 (Fri)			
05:50 a.m.	> 09:00 a.m.	2h10m	
Chicago, IL	New York, NY		
Oct 20 (Sun)			
09:55 a.m.	> 11:35 a.m.	2h40m	
New York, NY	Chicago, IL		
Flight		$130.00	
Taxes & fees		$47.35	
Trip total (round trip)		$177.35	

C

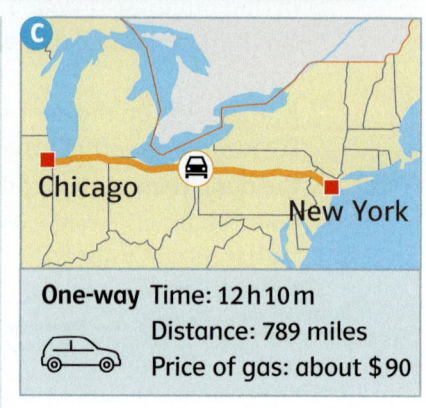

Chicago   New York

One-way   Time: 12h10m
Distance: 789 miles
Price of gas: about $90

1 (MEDIATION) **Beantworte die Fragen.**

Schau dir die drei Reisemöglichkeiten an.
Beantworte die Fragen deiner Oma auf Deutsch.

1. Was kostet die Busfahrt hin und zurück insgesamt?
2. Kommt man mit den ausgesuchten Flügen vormittags oder abends an?
3. Wie lang dauert die Fahrt mit dem Auto?

CULTURE

In den USA gibt es neun Zeitzonen, denn das Land ist zu groß für eine Zeitzone. In New York ist es immer eine Stunde später als in Chicago. Welche Zeitzonen kennst du?

2 (SPEAKING) **How would you travel? Talk with your partner.**

A: I would go —— because it's —— way. And you?   B: I would ….

by plane   by car   by bus   the fastest   the cheapest   the most exciting

Ich kann Informationen über Reisemöglichkeiten weitergeben. ✔

New York City, here we come!

In diesem Film triffst du die amerikanischen Teenager Wesley, Jessica und Ronan.

1 **Talk about New York.**

What do you already know about New York City?
Make a mind map of buildings and places.

2 (VIEWING) **Watch the film.**

2⌧

a) Put the sights in the right order.

Central Park   the Brooklyn Bridge   the Statue of Liberty   Chinatown

b) Match the facts with the photos.

1. There were once elephants here.
2. It's near Little Italy.
3. There are great concerts here in the summer.
4. It can get very hot in here.

> **VIEWING SKILLS**
>
> In einem Film sind nicht nur die Personen und die Geschichte wichtig, sondern auch die Orte und das, was man im Hintergrund sehen kann. Suche dir eine Filmsequenz aus und schau sie ohne Ton an. Was passiert im Hintergrund?

3 (WRITING) **Plan a day and write a message to a friend.**

a) Plan a day in your town with a friend from the USA. What can you show the friend and what can you do together? Make notes.

morning:	go to …
lunch:	at home with Mum and Dad
afternoon:	play … with …

b) Write a message to tell the friend about your plan. Use your notes.

> **E-MAIL**
>
> Hi …,
> I've made a plan for your visit on Saturday. We can … in the morning. We can have lunch … with …. In the afternoon we can ….
> See you on Saturday,
> …

> Ich kann einen Film über New York verstehen. ✔

Checklist Find more online: 9dk5x5

✓ **Ich kann Informationen über New York verstehen.**

New York City is the largest city in the United States. • Baseball is one of the most popular sports in the USA. • New York is a very multicultural city.

10

✓ **Ich kann ein Interview führen.**

Can I ask you some questions for our magazine, please? • How long have you lived in the USA? • Thank you. Good luck for the future.

10

✓ **Ich kann über Einflüsse verschiedener Kulturen im Alltag sprechen.**

People of all nationalities live happily together here. • In some places there are street signs in Chinese.

10

✓ **Ich kann eine Geschichte über den Arbeitsalltag in New York verstehen.**

11

✓ **Ich kann Informationen über Reisemöglichkeiten weitergeben.**

11

✓ **Ich kann einen Film über New York verstehen.**

(UNIT TASK) A city profile

Bildet Gruppen mit drei Personen. Wählt zusammen eine amerikanische Stadt aus und sucht einige Fakten heraus. Erstellt ein Plakat.

Step 1

Get into groups. Choose an American city.

Choose one of America's big cities.

Los Angeles   Philadelphia

Chicago   Houston   . . .

Look at the map at the front of the book to find where the city is.

Step 2

Find photos and information.

a) Use the internet to find a photo and this information (take notes):

Name of city: …
State: …
Sights: …
Photo: (Write what is in the photo!)

b) Find the answers to these questions online. Take notes.

1. What's the population of the city?
2. Which different groups live there? How many people from each group are there?

STUDY SKILLS

Suche offizielle Webseiten der Regierung, um zuverlässige Zahlen herauszufinden. Daten zu Städten in den USA findest du auf der Webseite des US Census Bureau.

Step 3

Make a chart.

Show the information about the city population in a chart. You can make a pie chart (A) and/or a bar chart (B). Your chart must have a title and labels.

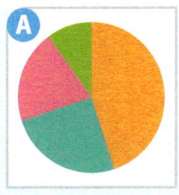
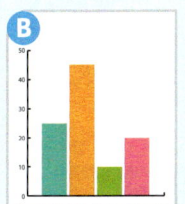

STUDY SKILLS

Du kannst Säulen- oder Kreisdiagramme auch mit einem Computerprogramm erstellen. Das ist recht einfach und sieht sauber und ordentlich aus.

Step 4

Write a short text for your chart.

Use these phrases:

Most of the people live ….   There are (not) many ….   There is a large … population in ….

Step 5

Finish your poster.

Arrange your photo, chart and texts on the poster.

Step 6

Show your poster. → M Gallery walk, p.124

Step 7

Choose one of the other groups' cities and compare it with your city.

Is it bigger? Smaller?
Are there any other differences? …

0.7 = zero point seven

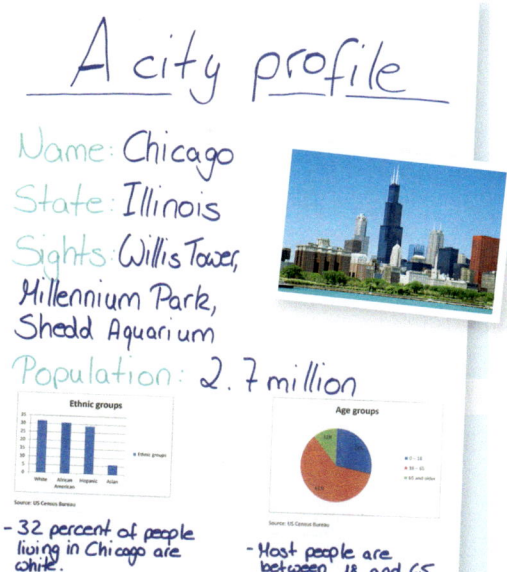

A city profile

Name: Chicago
State: Illinois
Sights: Willis Tower, Millennium Park, Shedd Aquarium
Population: 2.7 million

- 32 percent of people living in Chicago are white.
- About 31 percent are African American.

- Most people are between 18 and 65.
- Not many people are older than 65.

An American website

INTERNET

Adventures on Cape Cod

Q SEARCH   ≡ MENU

1   **CAPE COD**
It only takes one and a half hours to get from Boston, Massachusetts, to Cape Cod by car.
We have beautiful beaches, and there are lots of things to see and do here. And Cape Cod is a great
place for adventures.

5   ▶ Where is Cape Cod?   ▶ Find a place to stay.

A **Make friends with the whales.**
Go on one of our exciting whale-watching tours.
You'll have the chance to take some amazing
photos of the whales.

10   A whale-watching tour – you'll never forget it!

▶ Book a tour.   ▶ Find out more about whales.

B **Go kayaking!**
This is your chance to see Cape Cod and its
beautiful beaches from a kayak.
We have kayaks for one or two people.

15   You can also take a class with one of our
guides!

▶ Book a kayak.   ▶ Find out more about our classes.

Hier kannst du lernen, wie man im Internet recherchiert.

14/1 **1 Find information.**

→ **M** Think – pair – share, p.127

First look at the title of the website. Which of these words did someone put into a search engine to find this website?

park   adventure   Great Britain

USA   sports and activities   whales

Washington, D.C.   dogs

> Eine Suchmaschine („search engine") ist wie eine große Bücherei. Wenn du Informationen schnell finden willst, ist es wichtig, die Suchbegriffe richtig zu wählen. Denn je genauer sie sind, umso bessere Ergebnisse wirst du erzielen.

2 Collect information.

a) Now choose text A or B. Find the three most important words in the text. Make notes.

b) Compare your words with your partner's words.

> Als Suchbegriffe eignen sich vor allem Nomen. Wenn du nach Walen in der Nähe von Cape Cod suchst, kannst du mit „whales" und „Cape Cod" beginnen.

3 Check the information.

Look at the website about Cape Cod again. Do you think it's an official website, an ad or a blog? Why?

> Es ist wichtig, zu wissen, woher die Informationen auf der Webseite stammen. Offizielle Webseiten sind zuverlässiger als Blogs, zum Beispiel. Mit Anzeigen („ads") soll etwas verkauft werden.
> Versuche immer, die Fakten auch auf anderen Webseiten zu überprüfen. Schau auch nach, mit welchem Datum die Information versehen ist.

14/2 **4 Do a search and give a presentation.**

a) Choose a topic for a short presentation. Use the internet to find information. Here are some ideas:

- facts about whales
- other sports and activities on Cape Cod
- famous people from Cape Cod

> • Benutze zuerst Suchbegriffe oder kurze Fragen.
> • Suche dann mindestens drei verschiedene Fakten, die du interessant findest.
> • Formuliere mit deinen eigenen Worten. So wird dein Vortrag leichter verständlich.

b) Give a presentation. Say where your information is from.

> I used the website xxx.yy for this presentation. The photos are from xxx.yy.

> Vergiss nicht, die Webseiten, die du benutzt hast, als Quellen anzugeben. Auch wenn du Bilder verwendest, musst du angeben, woher sie stammen.

At the campsite

Yes, it's open from 12:00 to 2:00 p.m.

It's € 24 for one night. That will be € 96.

You can buy one in the shop.

Willkommen am Chiemsee!

We speak English.

C

B

A

1 (LISTENING) **Listen. Match the questions with the right people (A–C) in the picture.**

1,9

1. Question 1 goes with ....

2 (SPEAKING) **Act the dialogue.**

You are staying at a campsite in Bavaria. Your partner works at the campsite.

A: Hello, can I help you?
B: Hello. I'd like to go canoeing. Can I do that today?
A: Yes, of course. There is a lake near here.
B: How much does it cost?
A: It costs five euros.
B: OK. And are there any interesting places to visit here?
A: Yes, there's a castle.
B: Thank you.
A: You're welcome.

rock climbing   swimming   ...
mountain   swimming pool   ...
seven euros fifty   ...
science museum   park   ...

1,10

3 (LISTENING) Listen to the phone call at the campsite. Take notes.

Name: Emma Smith (1)
Will arrive on: —— (2)
Will leave on: —— (3)

Number of nights: —— (4)
Number of people: —— (5)
Price: —— (6)

Language → G4, p.109

How much **does** that **cost**?
Does the snack bar **open** at lunchtime?
When **do** you **want** to arrive?

Do you remember?
So stellst du Fragen im simple present.

4 Work with the campsite questions.

a) Complete the questions. Put in the words.

1. How much —— to stay in a tent?
2. —— me your name, please?
3. —— in the evening?
4. —— to stay at the campsite?
5. For —— is that?

How long do you want   Can you tell

how many people   does it cost

Does the snack bar open

b) Match the answers with the questions from a).

A For three people.
B It's 25 euros for one night.
C Yes. It's open until 8:00 p.m.

D Of course. My name is ....
E For two nights.

5 (SPEAKING) Act the dialogue at a campsite.

One of you (A) works at the campsite. The other one (B) has just arrived.

A Begrüße den Gast.

→ **B** Begrüße A. Frage, was es kostet in einem Zelt zu übernachten. (How much …?)

A Sage B, dass eine Übernachtung € 20 pro Nacht kostet. (It costs ....)

B Sage A, dass du eine Übernachtung buchen möchtest. (I'd like to ....)

A Frage B nach seinem Namen. (Can you …?)

B Sage B deinen Namen. Frage A, ob der Supermarkt auf dem Campingplatz abends geöffnet ist. (Does the …?)

A Sage B, dass der Supermarkt bis 19 Uhr geöffnet ist. (Yes, it ....)

B Bedanke und verabschiede dich.

A Sage danke und verabschiede dich. ←

One country – different states

Hi! I'm Jane and I'm from Alaska. Alaska is the largest state in the USA, but it's far away from the rest of the country. Many towns in Alaska are far away from roads. You need a plane or boat to get to them. The largest city in Alaska is Anchorage.

Alaska

Not many people live in Alaska. Visitors can see many wild animals there. Denali National Park is in Alaska. Denali, the highest mountain in the USA, is in the park.

1 (SPEAKING) **Talk about the photos.**

Choose a photo and describe it to your partner.

There is/are ….
In the foreground there is/are ….
In the background there is/are ….
You can see … in the middle / on the left / on the right.

beach   bear   bridge   farm

fruit   mountain   river   …

2 (READING) **Read the texts. Which state?**

16/1

a) Which state is it? Alaska or California?

1. There is a city with many hills here.
2. It has the USA's highest mountain.
3. They make a lot of films in this state.
4. It is far away from the rest of the USA.
5. This is great for fruit and vegetables.

b) Which state would you like to visit? Say why.

Am Ende dieser Unit kann ich ...
- Informationen über die USA verstehen.
- eine E-Mail schreiben.
- ein Problem am Flughafen lösen.
- einen Text über Erdbeben verstehen.
- Informationen im Hotel weitergeben.
- einen Film über Berufswünsche verstehen.

3

California is in the west of the USA. It has many sunny beaches, and surfing is a popular sport there. One of the biggest cities in California is Los Angeles (LA). Hollywood, the capital of the world's movie industry, is near LA.

4

San Francisco is also in California. The Golden Gate Bridge is one of the city's landmarks. San Francisco has many hills, and there is a famous cable car. There are sometimes earthquakes in San Francisco and other cities.

5

California

Of all the states in the USA, California produces the most fruit and vegetables. Many of the workers on the farms are Hispanics. They came from other countries, like Mexico, and they speak Spanish.

---

 3 (LISTENING) **Listen to a radio report. Find the right words.**

1,12
16/2

1. Laura Price is an actor in a new ——.
2. She had her first lessons when she was ——.
3. When she was 13, her family moved to ——.
4. She lives with her parents, her sister and their little ——.
5. She would like to make a film in ——.

| Alaska | dog | ten | Los Angeles | 15 |

| eight | movie | New York | cat | play |

Ich kann Informationen über die USA ✔
verstehen.

Going to California

1 (READING) **Read the e-mails.**

1,13

1 Jane and Chris are cousins. Jane lives in Anchorage, Alaska. Chris moved from Alaska to Los Angeles with his parents.

E-MAIL

Hi Chris,

I hope everyone is well in LA. I'm looking forward to my trip! We're all fine here in
5 Anchorage. Last week we visited Denali National Park. The guide was nice. He introduced himself to us and told us about the animals and birds in the park. (We saw a grizzly bear in the woods later!) Then we went rock climbing. It looked dangerous, but we didn't hurt ourselves. We sat by the lake and had a picnic. I took a photo of myself. We had a great day! Can we go surfing in LA? Do people have lessons or do they teach themselves? Have you ever seen any
10 famous people at the beach? Grandma says hi. Guess what? She bought a laptop yesterday. She's teaching herself how to use it. Maybe she'll send an e-mail to you! Do you miss Alaska?
See you soon,
Jane

E-MAIL

Hi Jane,

15 Thanks for your e-mail! It's great to hear that you're well. We're fine too. It sounds like you enjoyed yourselves at Denali! You asked about surfing. I didn't teach myself – I had lessons. (I'm still not very good at it now!) We can go to Venice Beach. The waves aren't too big there. If we don't go into the water, you can just take a photo of yourself on the beach. I haven't seen a famous person at the beach yet. Maybe we'll meet a star while you're here!
20 I sometimes miss Alaska. I'd love to go rock climbing or canoeing at Denali again.
Say hi to Grandma from me. I'm sure she'll learn quickly! When does your flight arrive on Saturday? Dad and I can meet you at the airport. It'll be great to see you!
Bye,
Chris

CULTURE

Alaska hat seine eigene Zeitzone: Alaska Standard Time. In Alaska ist es eine Stunde früher als in Kalifornien. Es liegen 3766 km – oder 2340 Meilen – zwischen Anchorage und Los Angeles (Luftlinie). Ein Flug dauert etwa fünf Stunden. Wo könntest du in fünf Stunden von München aus hinfliegen?

2 **What will happen? Choose the best sentence.**

A Chris will visit Jane in Alaska soon.
B Jane will visit Chris in California soon.
C Jane and her dad will visit Chris in California soon.

3 Find the four true statements. → M Peer correction, p.125

1. Jane went to Denali two weeks ago.
2. They went rock climbing there.
3. Jane wants to go canoeing in LA.
4. Grandma has a laptop now.
5. They can go to a beach with large waves.
6. Chris saw a film star yesterday.
7. He doesn't miss Alaska every day.
8. Jane will arrive in California on Saturday.

17/1 ## 4 Work with words from the text.

a) What are the words? → ○ p.94

A —— can be very dangerous.

There are many —— in Alaska.

The —— are high today.

We can sit by the ——.

The —— to LA lasts five hours.

—— is a popular sport in LA.

b) What is it? Complete the sentences.

1. A guide …
2. A picnic …
3. A laptop …
4. Canoeing …

a. is a small ….
b. is an activity on a river or a ….
c. shows a place to ….
d. is a … outside.

5 (SOUNDS) Which words rhyme?

17/2 a) Make pairs.

| guide | wood | so | wave |
| dear | now |

| here | gave | could | how |
| know | ride |

1,14 b) Listen and check your answers.

6 (SPEAKING) Would you like to …? Talk about the activities with a partner.

17/3-4

I would like to … because it is …. I wouldn't like to … because it is … / because I ….

| go rock climbing | meet a grizzly bear |
| go surfing | have a picnic | … |

| exciting | cool | dangerous | scary |
| like / don't like … | … |

Language detectives → G 5, p.110

I took a photo of <u>myself</u>.
You can take a photo of <u>yourself</u>.
We didn't hurt <u>ourselves</u>.
Do <u>they</u> teach <u>themselves</u>?

Wie sagt man, dass man etwas selbst oder für sich selbst tut? Schau dir die Einzahl- und Mehrzahlformen an. Was fällt dir auf?

7 What did they say at Denali? Put in <u>myself</u> or <u>yourself</u>.

18/5

1. "I'd like to introduce <u>myself</u>. I'm Steve. I'm your guide."
2. "You're good at rock climbing! Did you teach —— ?"
3. "This is cool! I'm really enjoying —— !"
4. "You don't need to be scared, Tim. Tell —— : 'I can do it!'"
5. "What happened, Mark? Did you hurt —— ?"
6. "Can you wait, please? I want to take a photo of —— ."

8 What are they doing?

18/6–7
19/8

a) Complete the sentences. → ○ p.94

himself   herself   ourselves   yourselves   themselves

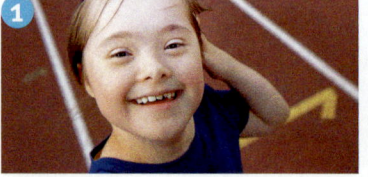

She is taking a photo of ——.   He is looking at ——.   They are introducing ——.

"We are teaching —— some new tricks."

"Did you and your friends enjoy —— ?" "Yes, we did!"

I → myself
you → yourself
he → himself
she → herself
we → ourselves
you → yourselves
they → themselves

b) Match the sentences which mean the same thing.

1. We had a great time.
2. The teacher told us her name.
3. Jane wore two pullovers on the trip.
4. Grizzly bears are large, strong animals.
5. Chris's dad is learning Spanish without a teacher.

a. He's teaching himself.
b. She kept herself warm.
c. They can look after themselves.
d. She introduced herself.
e. We really enjoyed ourselves.

9 What did Chris tell his dad?

19/9

a) Choose the right words.

Chris: Jane **sends** · **is sending** · <u>sent</u> (1) an e-mail yesterday. She and her friends really enjoyed **they** · **themselves** · **them** (2) at Denali. They **are going** · **went** · **have gone** (3) there last week. Grandma is teaching **she** · **her** · **herself** (4) how to use a computer. She'll send an e-mail to **we** · **us** · **ourselves** (5) soon. Jane wants to go to the beach with **me** · **my** · **myself** (6). Maybe we'll see **much** · **any** · **some** (7) stars there.

Achte auf die Signalwörter! Bei „yesterday" und „last week" brauchst du das simple past!

b) Put in <u>at</u>, <u>on</u> or <u>in</u>.

1. Jane will arrive —— Saturday.
2. Can we meet her —— the airport?

3. Her flight arrives —— 4:00 p.m.
4. I'm sure Jane will enjoy herself —— LA.

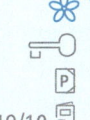

10 (TASK) An e-mail to a friend → V A trip to the country, p.132 → M Writers' conference, p.127

19/10

Read Sophie's e-mail and answer it. Tell her about your last trip.

E-MAIL

Hi,
It's great to hear that you're well!
You asked about our trip to the north of California. We really enjoyed ourselves. We had sunny weather and we saw a lot of raccoons and rabbits. There were very big trees too. Many of them are over 500 years old! We took a lot of photos of ourselves in front of them.
What about you? What did you do on your last trip?
Bye,
Sophie

WRITING SKILLS

1. Denke an eine Anrede. (Hi xxx, Dear xxx,)
2. Zeige Interesse an Sophies E-Mail. (It's great to hear that …, It sounds like you enjoyed yourself in …, …)
3. Beantworte Sophies Frage. (You asked about …)
4. Beschreibe den Ausflug. (We went to …, We went …, We saw …, We enjoyed ourselves, …)
5. Denke an einen Schluss. (See you soon, Bye, …)

Ich kann eine E-Mail schreiben. ✔

One of those days

1 Look at the photo. Where would you see this person?

2 (READING) Read about Jane's journey to LA.

1,15

1 Jane arrives at the airport in Anchorage at eleven o'clock.

Check-in agent: Hi. Can I see your ticket and passport, please?

5 **Jane:** Hi. I'm flying to LA. The flight leaves at 12:30 p.m.

Check-in agent: I'm afraid your flight is delayed.

Jane: Oh no!

10 **Check-in agent:** I'm very sorry. The plane is coming from Chicago and they've had strong winds. Your flight will leave four hours late.

Jane: Is there anything you can do about it?

Check-in agent: There's a flight to LA at

15 2:30 p.m. I can book you on that flight now.

Jane: Oh yes, please. What time does it land?

Check-in agent: At 8:25 p.m. It departs from gate 43 at 2:30 p.m. The boarding time is 2:00 p.m. Here's your boarding card. Have a

20 good flight!

Jane: Thank you. Goodbye!

The plane lands safely in LA. But there is another problem and Jane has to complain.

Jane: Hi. I've just arrived from Anchorage, but
25 my suitcase isn't here. What can I do about it?

Employee: Well, I can help you with that. But you must tell us what your suitcase looks like and where you're staying.

Jane: I don't believe it! First my flight was
30 delayed, now my suitcase isn't here. I hope the suitcase didn't get lost.

Employee: I'm really sorry, but we'll find your suitcase quickly. We can usually get a suitcase to a passenger the next day, so you don't need
35 to worry. Will you be in LA tomorrow?

Jane: I'll be at my uncle's house in …

3 Which is Jane's boarding card?

A	
2 OCT	11:00
Boarding time: **10:30**	
Seat: 21B	
Gate: 43	

B	
2 OCT	19:25
Boarding time: **18:55**	
Seat: 14D	
Gate: 30	

C	
2 OCT	14:30
Boarding time: **14:00**	
Seat: 27A	
Gate: 43	

Schau dir die Uhrzeiten im Text gut an. Vergiss nicht:
a.m. = vormittags, p.m. = nachmittags.

4 Work with the text.

a) Match the sentence parts. → ○ p.95

1. Jane's flight is delayed
2. It isn't a problem
3. When Jane arrives in LA,
4. The employee can help
5. Jane doesn't need to worry

a. because she will get her suitcase tomorrow.
b. there is another problem.
c. because there are strong winds.
d. because there is another flight.
e. but she needs some information.

b) Talk about one of the other boarding cards in exercise 3.

The flight is … at … .
The boarding time is … .
… seat is … … leaves from … .

CULTURE

Wenn du dich auf Englisch über ein Problem beschweren möchtest, bleib ruhig und stelle Fragen wie diese: „Is there anything you can do about it?" oder: „What can I do about it?"

20/1 **5 Work with the airport words.**

a) Jane tells her friend about her flight in an e-mail. Put in the words. → ○ p.96

| delayed | suitcase | complained | landed | flight | booked | airport ✓ |

E-MAIL

Hi Carrie,
I'm in LA but I didn't have a very good trip. ☹ I arrived at the airport (1) in Anchorage at 11 o'clock.
My flight was ── (2). But there was another ── (3) and they ── (4) me on that.
When I ── (5) in LA, my ── (6) wasn't there! I ── (7) to an employee and I will get it tomorrow.
See you soon,
Jane

b) Write Carrie's e-mail to Jane. Use these phrases.

| Thanks for … . | I'm sorry that your … . | That sounds … . | I hope you … . |

6 (LISTENING) Listen to the announcements. Choose the right answers.

1,16
20/2

1. Passengers on the flight to New York should go to gate **70** • **17**.
2. The flight to Chicago is delayed because there is **bad weather** • **a problem with the plane**.
3. Susan is flying to **Washington, D.C.** • **LA.**
4. Jackie is trying to find her **father** • **mother**.
5. Passengers for flight **BL 818** • **BL 858** to Washington, D.C. should go to gate 23.

LISTENING SKILLS

Wenn du Durchsagen am Flughafen hörst, konzentriere dich auf die Hauptinformationen: An- und Abflugzeiten, Flugnummern, das Gate … Diese werden immer wiederholt.

7 **Put the words and phrases into groups.** → M Peer correction, p.125

| at 2:30 p.m. | quickly | at the airport ✔ | in LA | the next day | at the beach |

| carefully | tomorrow | from Chicago | loudly | every morning | well |

Where?	When?	How?	
at the airport	...	...	

Language detectives → G 6, p.111

Jane arrives at the airport at eleven o'clock. The flight departs from gate 43 at 2:30 p.m. We'll find your suitcase quickly.

Welche Wörter benutzt du, um zu sagen, wo, wann und wie etwas geschieht? Wo stehen die Wörter im Satz?

21/3–4

8 **Complete the sentences about Jane's week in LA.**

a) Put the adverbs in the right order. → ○ p.96

1. Jane's suitcase arrived in LA the next day. (the next day / in LA)
2. She had surfing lessons .... (every morning / at the beach)
3. Jane and Chris had an ice cream .... (at a café / on Tuesday afternoon)
4. They didn't see any stars .... (in LA / yesterday)
5. Before she left, Jane packed .... (carefully / her suitcase)
6. She said ... to Chris .... (sadly / goodbye)

b) Choose the right order.

1. Jane .... (quickly / to the gate / went)
2. Her plane .... (at 11:00 a.m. / left / LA)
3. It .... (in Alaska / at 3:00 p.m. / landed)
4. Her mother .... (met / at the airport / her)

9 (SPEAKING) **An interview about a flight**

22/5

a) Match the questions with the answers.

1. Where did you fly to?
2. Who did you sit next to?
3. How long did the flight last?
4. Was the flight delayed?
5. Did you have any food on the flight?
6. Did you watch a film?

a. Yes, I did. I had a cheese sandwich.
b. No, I didn't. I listened to music.
c. I sat next to my little brother.
d. It lasted three hours.
e. We flew to LA.
f. Yes, it was. It was an hour late!

b) Act the dialogue with a partner.

10 (LISTENING) Listen to four dialogues. Which sentences are right?

1,17

1. The plane leaves at 1:50 p.m.
2. The flight from LA lands at 11:25 a.m.
3. The plane to Frankfurt leaves at 12:15 p.m.
4. The plane lands at 6:45 p.m.

Language → G 7, p.112

The flight <u>departs</u> at 2:30 p.m.
What time <u>does</u> the plane <u>land</u>?

LISTENING SKILLS

Konzentriere dich beim Zuhören und achte gezielt auf die Uhrzeiten in den Gesprächen. Entscheide dann, ob die Uhrzeit im Satz richtig ist. Du musst die anderen Informationen in den Dialogen nicht wörtlich verstehen.

11 (TASK) A role play: At the airport → V At the airport, p.133

22/6

a) Act a role play. Partner A is a check-in agent at the airport. Partner B is a passenger.

Check-in agent

1 (Du möchtest das Flugticket und den Reisepass sehen.)
Hi. Can I see your ticket and passport, please?

3 (Der Flug hat leider eine Verspätung von vier Stunden.)

5 (Entschuldige dich. Du kannst den Passagier auf einen anderen Flug buchen. Die Abflugzeit ist 12 Uhr.)

7 (Der Flug landet um 15:30 Uhr.)

9 (Die Gatenummer ist B43 und die Einsteigezeit ist 11:30 Uhr. Verabschiede dich und wünsche dem Passagier einen guten Flug.)

Passenger

2 (Du fliegst um 9:45 Uhr nach San Francisco.)
I'm flying to San Francisco. The flight leaves at ....

4 (Bleibe ruhig und frage: Was kann er/sie tun?)

6 (Frage: Wann kommt der Flug an?)

8 (Nimm das Angebot an.)

10 (Bedanke und verabschiede dich.)

These phrases can help:

I'm very sorry.
There's a flight to ... at .... I can book you on that flight now.
It lands at .... Have a good flight!

Oh no! / I don't believe it!
Is there anything you can do about it?
When does it land?
Oh yes, please!

b) Act your role play in class. → M Dramatic reading, p.123

Ich kann ein Problem am Flughafen lösen.

When the earth shakes

1 (SPEAKING) **Talk with a partner.**

Think: How many earthquakes are there every year?

2 (READING) **Read the text about earthquakes.**

1,18

1 **1 What is an earthquake?**
  In an earthquake the earth shakes for a
  short time. We don't always feel them, but
  earthquakes happen more often than we think.
5 There are about 500,000 earthquakes in the
  world every year. One hundred of them cause
  damage.
  In California there are usually two or three
  serious earthquakes a year. But earthquakes
10 can happen in other parts of the USA too.

2 What causes an earthquake?
  The earth's crust has about 20 different plates.
  These plates move very slowly.
  When the plates push hard against each other,
15 the earth moves and there is an earthquake.

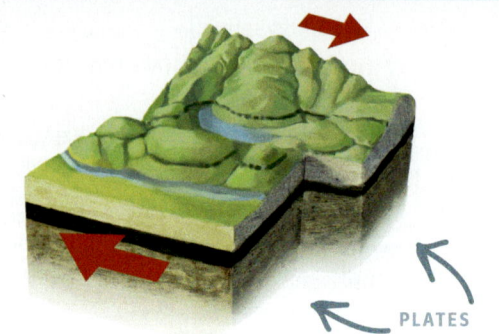

PLATES

3 Complete the sentences.

1. About 500,000 earthquakes happen in the world ....
2. There are usually two or three ... a year ....
3. There is an earthquake when the plates push hard ....
4. Earthquakes can destroy ....
5. Engineers can make buildings ... during an earthquake.
6. People buy first-aid items, ...
7. During an earthquake you should ... and hold ....

Lies zuerst den Satz in der Aufgabe. Überfliege den Text und suche gezielt nach den unterstrichenen Schlüsselwörtern. Diese verraten dir die Lösung (z.B. 500,000).

READING SKILLS

Viele Wörter im Text kannst du aus dem Zusammenhang erschließen. Oft/Manchmal gibt es auch ein ähnliches Wort im Deutschen. Was könnte zum Beispiel „the earth's **crust**" heißen (Zeile 12)? Oder „**first-aid** items" (Zeilen 30–31)?

3 How dangerous are earthquakes?

Large earthquakes can cause many problems. They can destroy buildings and bridges. They can also cause fires or tsunamis (very large
20 waves). A lot of people can get hurt or die. Today engineers design buildings so that they are safer during an earthquake.
The Richter scale shows how strong an earthquake is. Earthquakes above 6 on the
25 Richter scale are very dangerous.

4 What can people do?

People in earthquake areas all around the world make plans for earthquakes and tsunamis. At school children learn what to
30 do during an earthquake. People buy first-aid items, blankets, food in cans and bottles of water. When you feel an earthquake, it is best to sit under a strong table and hold one of the legs.

4 Choose one of the tasks.

23/1–3

a) Give a short presentation. Use the internet to find out about one of these earthquakes:

1906   2009   2011

Your presentation should have these points:

– In which country/city was the earthquake?
– How dangerous was it?
– Find a photo and describe the scene.

→ **M** 1-minute-presentation, p.122

 OR

b) Make a poster about what to do in earthquake areas. Look at text 4 for ideas. Write tips and add pictures.

Think about these points:

– What should you buy and have at home?
– What should you do during an earthquake?

→ **M** Gallery walk, p.124

Ich kann einen Text über Erdbeben verstehen.

Finding out about a hotel

HOTEL LUXOR
LOS ANGELES

Amenities:
- underground parking lot
- near to famous sights
- air-conditioned rooms
- café
- high-speed internet
- use of fitness center
- shuttle service to airport
- pets not allowed

1 (MEDIATION) **Pass on information at a hotel.**

In einem Hotel in Kalifornien hilfst du einem deutschen Touristen, der wenig Englisch kann. Vermittle zwischen ihm und der Mitarbeiterin im Hotel.

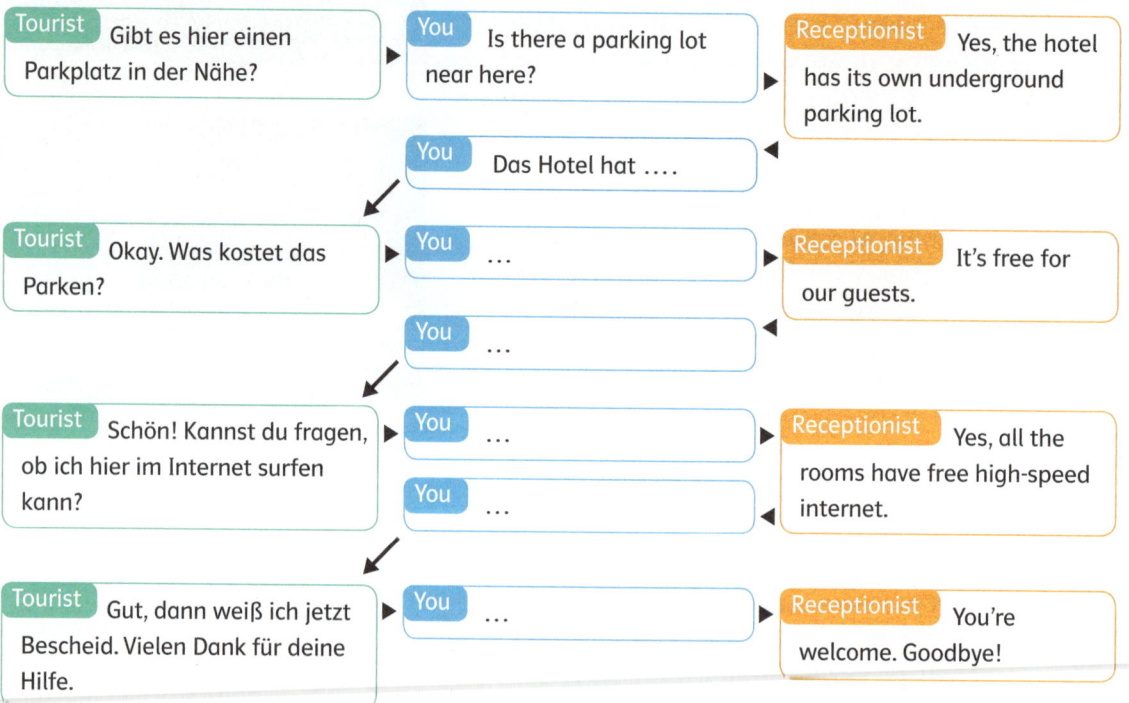

Tourist Gibt es hier einen Parkplatz in der Nähe?

▸ **You** Is there a parking lot near here?

▸ **Receptionist** Yes, the hotel has its own underground parking lot.

You Das Hotel hat ....

Tourist Okay. Was kostet das Parken?

▸ **You** ...

▸ **Receptionist** It's free for our guests.

You ...

Tourist Schön! Kannst du fragen, ob ich hier im Internet surfen kann?

▸ **You** ...

▸ **Receptionist** Yes, all the rooms have free high-speed internet.

You ...

Tourist Gut, dann weiß ich jetzt Bescheid. Vielen Dank für deine Hilfe.

▸ **You** ...

▸ **Receptionist** You're welcome. Goodbye!

2 (SPEAKING) **Act more dialogues.**

Nutzt die Informationen zu den anderen Dienstleistungen im Hotel oben und spielt zu dritt weitere Gespräche.

CULTURE

Britisches und amerikanisches Englisch können unterschiedlich sein. Einige Wörter werden anders geschrieben oder ausgesprochen. Was sind die amerikanischen Wörter für „car park" und „centre"?

Ich kann Informationen im Hotel weitergeben. ✔

Talking about jobs

In diesem Film triffst du Wesley, Jessica und Jessicas Cousin Ronan wieder.

1 (SPEAKING) **Talk about jobs.**

Talk with a partner. What would/wouldn't you like to do? (Say why or why not.)

work in a shop? | work with computers? | work with animals? | work at a café? | . . .

2 (VIEWING) **Watch the film.**

a) Watch the film until 02:08. Choose the right answers.

1. Wesley would like to work
   with animals · at a café.
2. Last year Jessica worked at
   a burger bar · a supermarket.
3. Ronan works at
   a swimming pool · a store.
4. Wesley wants to save money for
   a car · a new bike.

Wesley   Jessica

b) Complete the sentences (02:08 to the end).
You don't need one answer.

1. Wesley wants to —— .
2. Jessica would like to —— .
3. Ronan wants to —— .

design computer games | be an actor

have a restaurant | work with horses

> **CULTURE**
>
> Im Silicon Valley bei San Francisco haben viele der wichtigsten Hightech-Unternehmen ihren Sitz. Die meisten haben als sehr kleine Firmen angefangen, bevor sie sehr erfolgreich wurden. Welche Hightech-Unternehmen gibt es in der Nähe deines Wohnorts oder in Deutschland?

3 (SPEAKING) **Talk about the jobs in the film.**

Which of the jobs in 2b) would/wouldn't you like to do? Say why.

A: I'd like to .... I like ....
B: Really? I wouldn't like to do that! I ....

Ich kann einen Film über Berufswünsche verstehen. ✔

Checklist 🌐 Find more online: 9dk5x5

✔ **Ich kann Informationen über die USA verstehen.**

Alaska is the largest state in the USA. • It's far away from the rest of the country. • California is in the west of the USA.

24 📱

✔ **Ich kann eine E-Mail schreiben.**

Hi …, • I hope everyone is well. • Say hi to … for me. • I took a photo of myself. • See you soon, …

24 📱

✔ **Ich kann ein Problem am Flughafen lösen.**

What can I do about it? • There's a flight to LA at 2:30 p.m. • We can usually get a suitcase to a passenger the next day.

24 📱

✔ **Ich kann einen Text über Erdbeben verstehen.**

25 📱

✔ **Ich kann Informationen im Hotel weitergeben.**

25 📱

✔ **Ich kann einen Film über Berufswünsche verstehen.**

✻ (UNIT TASK) # A holiday blog

Schreibe einen Internetblog über einen besonderen Tag in den Ferien. Suche Bilder und zeige den Blog deinen Klassenkameraden.

Step 1

Think of an interesting day in your last holidays.

Choose one special event like a party or a day trip that you had in your last holidays. It can also be about a visit from a friend. Who did you meet? What did you do?

Step 2

Ask your friends and family about your special day.

Think about places, food and activities. Talk to people who were there with you if you aren't sure about names, places and times. You can also look at photos of the event.

Step 3

Make notes about the event or visit.

- What time did it start? When did it finish?
- Who was there?
- What did you do and see?
- How did you feel?
- Did you eat something special?
- What was the weather like?
- Anything else?

Step 4

Use your notes to write a draft.

Say what happened in the beginning, in the middle and at the end of your special event. Find some photos and write captions for them. Describe how you felt about the day. These examples will give you some ideas:

First …. Then …. After that ….
I didn't know that ……. was new to me.

It was amazing/funny/awful ….

I was excited/surprised/sad/angry/ ….

INTERNET

"I played games with my grandfather in the afternoon."

"I played basketball with my team. We were so excited!"

"It was very cold when we went bike riding, but we had a lot of fun!"

Step 5

Check your draft. → M Peer correction, p.125

Wenn du nicht sicher bist, wie ein Wort geschrieben wird, schau im Wörterbuch nach. Nutze auch die Checkliste auf Seite 129.

WRITING SKILLS

In einem Blog schreibst du deine eigene Meinung. Vergiss also nicht zu sagen, was du denkst.

Step 6

Present your blog. → M Gallery walk, p.124

Show your blog to the other students. Decide which blog is the most interesting. Say why.

American flags and symbols

The US flag

The American flag has 50 stars, one for every state. In 1776, when the USA got its independence from Britain, there were only 13 states. For these states there is a stripe on the American flag too.

State flags

1 **Work with the flags.**

a) Which sentences are correct?

1. There are 50 stripes on the American flag.
2. The American flag has 50 stars and 13 stripes.
3. Britain left the USA in 1776.
4. For some states there is a star *and* a stripe.

b) Match flags B–D with the states.

Florida   California   Alaska

CULTURE

In amerikanischen Klassenzimmern hängt immer eine US-Flagge. Viele Amerikaner haben auch eine Flagge vor dem Haus oder im Vorgarten. Es gibt auch eine Flagge für jeden Bundesstaat. Was könntest du einem amerikanischen Freund über die bayrische Flagge erzählen?

c) Use the internet to find the flags of other states of the USA and make a poster. Present the poster to your classmates. → M Gallery walk, p.124

American symbols

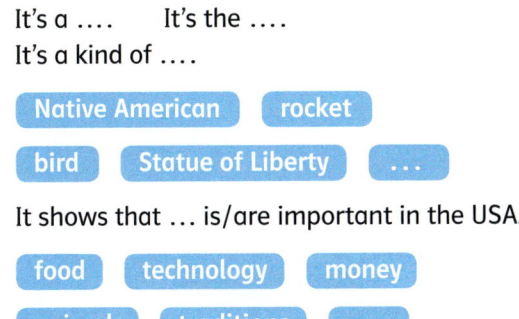

1 🦅	**2** 💰 $	**3** 🗽
4 🏈	**5**	
6 🍔🍟	**7** 🚀	

🗣🗣 **2** (SPEAKING) **Talk about the symbols with a partner.**

It's a ....   It's the ....
It's a kind of ....

> Native American   rocket

> bird   Statue of Liberty   ...

It shows that ... is/are important in the USA.

> food   technology   money

> animals   traditions   ...

CULTURE 🇺🇸

Der Weißkopfseeadler („bald eagle") ist ein amerikanisches Symbol. Er kommt in vielen Gebieten Nordamerikas vor. Der Vogel wurde als Symbol für die USA gewählt, weil er schön, stark und frei ist. Welche Symbole anderer Länder oder Regionen kennst du?

Alaska – wild and beautiful

Denali National Park
wild and beautiful

Be 'bear careful'!

1 Alaska is a wild and beautiful state with very different seasons. It is famous for its long, cold winters and short, but warm summers. You can see amazing animals in the USA's largest state. You shouldn't miss Denali National
5 Park, the home of Denali (6,190 m). It's the highest mountain in the country!

Many tourists come to Denali National Park to see the grizzly bears. The bears have a good sense of smell and they are often hungry too. That's why visitors on campsites
10 in Denali National Park must keep their food away from the bears, for example in their cars.

There are also Alaskan huskies in Denali National Park. Rangers in Denali keep huskies because they make life easier in the park in the winter months. The rangers look
15 after the dogs from when they are born. They train them to pull sleds. Huskies are strong animals – they can pull things that are much heavier than themselves. In very cold weather the dogs are a great help. They transport food and supplies for the rangers.

Denali   Huskies

28/1 **1 Look at the dictionary entry.**

Look at the entry for 'keep'. Find the right German word(s) in these sentences.

1. Rangers **keep** huskies because they make life easier.
2. Visitors on campsites must **keep** their food **away** from the grizzly bears.

> **keep** [kiːp]
> I. *n* (1) *no pl* (Lebens)unterhalt *m*
> II. *vt* <kept, kept> (hold onto) behalten; *bills, receipts* aufheben; to ~ **keep one's sanity** sich geistig gesund halten
> III. *vi* <kept, kept> (1) *(stay fresh) food* sich halten (2) *(wait)* Zeit haben; *your questions can ~ until later* deine Fragen können noch warten (3) *(continue) don't stop*, ~ **walking** bleib nicht stehen, geh weiter; *don't ~ asking silly questions* stell nicht immer so dumme Fragen
> **keep away** I. *vi* **to keep away** *(from sb)* sich (von jdm) fernhalten; *I just can't seem to ~ away from chocolate (hum)* irgendwie kann ich Schokolade einfach nicht widerstehen *fam* II. *vt* **to ~ sb away** jdn fernhalten

Einen Eintrag in einem Wörterbuch nennt man „entry". Jedes Wort wird in seiner Grundform angegeben. Suche zuerst immer danach.

Hier erfährst du, wie du das Wort aussprechen sollst.

Hier siehst du, ob das Wort ein Verb oder Nomen ist.

Viele englische Wörter haben mehr als nur eine Bedeutung. Deshalb findest du jeweils eine Nummer für jede Bedeutung.

Achte auf Präpositionen. Hier siehst du, dass ein Verb eine andere Bedeutung haben kann, wenn eine Präposition folgt.

28/2 **2 Work with a dictionary.**

a) Find the right German meaning for the underlined words. Use a dictionary.

1. Grizzly bears have a good <u>sense</u> of <u>smell</u>.
2. <u>Rangers</u> in Denali keep Alaskan huskies.
3. They train them to pull <u>sleds</u>.
4. They transport food and <u>supplies</u>.

b) Choose the right German meaning from a dictionary.

1. You shouldn't <u>miss</u> Denali National Park.
   a. verpassen   b. vermissen
2. It's the highest mountain in the <u>country</u>!
   a. ländliche Gegend   b. Land
3. The dogs are a <u>great</u> help.
   a. großartig   b. groß

Manchmal brauchst du ein Wort nicht nachzuschlagen; vielleicht klingt es ähnlich wie das deutsche Wort oder ein Fremdwort: z. B. „Alaskan" oder „transport".

Du kannst natürlich auch Online-Wörterbücher benutzen. Auch hier gilt: Nimm nicht gleich die erste Bedeutung. Lies immer erst den gesamten Eintrag.

Southern life

The American South

1

New Orleans is the most famous city in the American South. It's on the Mississippi River. You can get on a steamboat in New Orleans and ride on the river. The Mississippi is about 2,350 miles long!

2

The American South has many traditions. Family meals are very important, for example. Many people are proud to be from the South. And many African Americans live there.

1 (SPEAKING) **Work with the photos.**

Tell your partner about one of the photos.

In the picture there is/are …. You can see ….

| family | beach | waves | concert |

| ship | singer | sunny | … |

| is travelling | are eating and talking |

| is singing | is working | … |

2 (READING) **Find the words.**

32/1 ↗

1. New Orleans is a famous city on a very long —— .
2. The people in the American South often have family —— .
3. The Caribbean has a warm —— .
4. The people in Jamaica speak —— .
5. Many people like Bob Marley's —— .
6. There aren't many jobs, so some people have to —— the Caribbean.

Am Ende dieser Unit kann ich ...
- Informationen über Lebensweisen in zwei Regionen verstehen.
- mit einem Problem umgehen.
- über Zukunftspläne sprechen.
- eine längere Geschichte verstehen.
- Informationen über eine Tradition weitergeben.
- einen Film über Thanksgiving verstehen.

The Caribbean

3

There are thousands of islands in the Caribbean. The islands are not part of the USA. Tourists enjoy the beautiful beaches and the warm climate on islands like Barbados and Jamaica.

4

Bob Marley was a famous reggae singer. He was born in Jamaica, one of the islands in the Caribbean where the people speak English. Bob Marley's music is still popular all around the world.

5

The Caribbean is a beautiful place. There are jobs in the tourist industry, but life isn't easy there. Some people have to leave the Caribbean because there aren't enough jobs. Many go to the USA, Canada or Great Britain.

3 (LISTENING) **Listen to the interview. Choose the right answers.**

2,2
32/2

1. Greg worked with Bob Marley in the **1980s** · **1970s**.
2. Marley wrote songs about **young** · **poor** people.
3. Greg met Marley at a **concert** · **friend's house**.
4. Marley was **easy** · **difficult** to work with.
5. He wasn't very interested in **money** · **football**.
6. He died in **1981** · **1991**.

In diesem Radio-Interview geht es um den Reggae-Sänger Bob Marley und seine Musik.

Ich kann Informationen über Lebens-weisen in zwei Regionen verstehen. ✔

An argument at Thanksgiving

1 (SPEAKING) **Talk about special meals in your family.** → M Round robin, p.126

| When do you have the meal? | Who comes? | What food do you eat? | ... |

2 (READING) **Read the dialogue.**

2,3

1 The Millers from New Orleans are at home for the Thanksgiving holiday. Janet and Mark Miller are with their son Jacob (15), Janet's older sister Sherrie, and Mark's mom Brenda.

5 **Mark:** Were you able to get here OK yesterday?
Brenda: Yes. There was so much traffic! But my bus from Memphis was only a few minutes late!
10 **Janet:** OK, everyone. The food is ready now. I hope you're hungry. Take a seat, Brenda.
Mark: Would you like some turkey, Sherrie?
Sherrie: No thanks, Mark. I don't eat any meat now. I've been a vegetarian for a few months.
15 And I only eat a little cheese.
Janet: What? Why didn't you tell me? I'll have to cook something different now!
Sherrie: I told you on the phone last week.
Janet: Are you sure about that?
20 **Sherrie:** Yes, I'm sure.
Brenda: Please don't be annoyed, Janet. You've been very busy. Maybe you forgot. And there are so many vegetables. Don't you think so, Sherrie?
25 **Sherrie:** You're right. I really don't mind. I'd love some corn and potatoes. But just a little butter, please.

Mark: How many potatoes would you like?
Sherrie: Two, please, Mark.
30 **Janet:** I'm sorry, Sherrie. Next time we talk on the phone, I'll listen more carefully.
Sherrie: It's OK, Janet. I understand. I'd like to say a few words before we eat. You've done so much work for this weekend. I'm really
35 thankful for all this great food! I'm lucky to have you as my sister, Janet.
Mark: Happy Thanksgiving, everyone!
Everyone: Happy Thanksgiving!
Jacob: Are we allowed to eat now? I'm
40 hungry!

CULTURE

„Thanksgiving" ist ein wichtiger Feiertag in den USA. Er ist immer am vierten Donnerstag im November. Das erste Mal wurde Thanksgiving 1621 gefeiert, als einige amerikanische Ureinwohner die europäischen Siedler einluden, mit ihnen zu essen. Viele US-Amerikaner reisen weite Strecken, um das lange (Thanksgiving-)Wochenende mit ihrer Familie zu verbringen. Was ist der wichtigste Feiertag in deiner Familie?

3 Correct the names.

Mark   Janet   Jacob   Brenda   Sherrie

1. Sherrie came to New Orleans yesterday. (5–7)
   <u>Brenda</u> came to New Orleans yesterday.
2. Mark is a vegetarian now. (13–14)
3. Brenda is worried because she didn't cook a meal for Sherrie. (16–17)
4. Jacob can eat corn and potatoes. (25–26)
5. Janet is very thankful. (34–36)
6. Mark wants to eat now. (39)

Schau im Text nach, wenn du nicht sicher bist! Die Angaben in Klammern sagen dir, in welcher Zeile sich die Lösung befindet.

33/1 ## 4 Work with the words from the text.

a) Match the words with the pictures. (There is one more picture than there are words!) → ○ p.97

1. turkey
2. chicken
3. strawberries
4. cheese
5. corn
6. potatoes
7. bacon

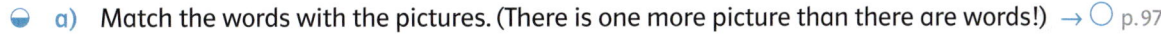

b) Find the words in the dialogue.

1. She doesn't have much time at the moment. She's very —— .
2. I'm very —— for your beautiful present.
3. That wasn't very nice of you. I'm —— !
4. He doesn't eat any meat. He's a —— !

5 Match the English phrases with the German. → M Bus stop, p.122

33/2

1. I really don't mind.
2. That's a good idea.
3. It's OK. I understand.
4. Don't you think so?
5. I'm sorry.
6. Please don't be annoyed.
7. You're right.
8. Take a seat, please.

a. Du willst sagen, dass … dir etwas leid tut.
b. … jemand recht hat.
c. … etwas dir nichts ausmacht.
d. … du etwas für eine gute Idee hältst.
e. … etwas kein Problem ist: du verstehst.
f. … jemand sich setzen soll.
g. … jemand sich nicht ärgern soll.
h. Du willst fragen, ob jemand die Sache auch so sieht.

6 (SOUNDS) Listen, read and say.

2,4
34/3

1. I only eat a little **cheese**.
2. I told you on the **phone** last week.
3. There are so many **vegetables**. |
   Don't you **think** so, | Sherrie?
4. I really **don't mind**.
5. I'm really **thankful** for all this great **food**.

SPEAKING SKILLS

Fällt dir auf, dass manche Wörter beim Sprechen stärker betont werden als andere? Achte auch darauf, dass im Englischen manche Silben in Sätzen zusammengezogen werden.

Language detectives → G8, p.113

There was so much traffic.
How many potatoes would you like?
Just a little butter, please.
The bus was only a few minutes late.

Hier geht es um Mengenangaben.
Wann verwendest du much und many?
Wann verwendest du a little, wann a few?
Denke dabei an Einzahl und Mehrzahl.

7 Put the words into two groups. → M Peer correction, p.125

34/4

a) Make a table and sort the words. → ○ p.97

How much …?	How many …?
cheese	strawberries
…	…

cheese ✔ strawberries ✔ work vegetables
food games butter meat meals
sandwiches minutes turkey rice

b) Add these words to the table. (Use a dictionary if you are not sure!)

children water people time pizza feet pizzas

8 (SPEAKING) Work with a partner. Would you like …? → M Double circle, p.123

a) Make dialogues. → ○ p.97

34/5

A: Would you like
a little
a few

bread strawberries rice

+

potatoes bacon salad

with your burger?
with your egg?
with your ice cream?
with your fish?
with your chicken?
in your sandwich?
…

B: Yes, please. I'd like ….
No, thanks. I don't like …./I don't eat ….

b) Ask about these things to eat and drink. butter cheese chips orange juice

9 Choose the right answers. Much or many, a few or a little?

34/6
35/7

The first Thanksgiving was **many** • **much** (1) years ago, in 1621. The European people in America only had **a few** • **a little** (2) food. Some Native Americans invited them to share a meal. (The Europeans still didn't have **many** • **much** (3) food after that, but they were very thankful!) Today people travel **many** • **much** (4) miles to be at home for Thanksgiving. They have a big meal and watch American football on TV. Thanksgiving is only **a few** • **a little** (5) weeks before Christmas. The day after the holiday is 'Black Friday', when **many** • **much** (6) Americans start their Christmas shopping.

The first Thanksgiving

10 (TASK) A Thanksgiving dialogue → V Ideas and suggestions, p.134

35/8–9

a) Read about the Miller family after the meal. What could the problem be?

Jacob wants to watch the football game.
Brenda wants to go to the park with her family.
Sherrie wants a nice holiday with her family.

Vergiss nicht! Brenda ist Jacobs Oma (und zu Besuch). Sherrie ist seine Tante.

b) Work in groups of three. Read the dialogue. Use the phrases on the right to make a new dialogue.

Jacob: The football game starts in a few minutes. We can watch it on TV!
Brenda: Why don't we go to the park?
Jacob: What? But it's an important game!
Brenda: Yes, Jacob. But it's a beautiful day!
Sherrie: Please don't be annoyed, Jacob. Grandma just wants to spend time with you. Why don't we just go for a short walk?
Jacob: That's a good idea. I'm sorry, Grandma!
Brenda: It's OK, Jacob. I understand.
Sherrie: Then we can all watch the last part of the game together. Don't you think so?
Brenda: You're right, Sherrie. A little football is OK!

I missed the last game

we always watch football at Thanksgiving

...

it's only a few miles

a walk is good for you after a meal

...

Grandma came all the way from Memphis, remember?

You only see Grandma once a year.

...

c) Practise and act the dialogue. → M Dramatic reading, p.123

Ich kann mit einem Problem umgehen. ✔

Hier lerne ich, über Zukunftspläne zu sprechen.

Young Caribbeans

1 (READING) Read Tara's blog.

2,5

BLOG

1 **Leaving Jamaica**   17/06/2020
by Tara Clarke (18)

I heard the noise of a gun in our street again last night. 'That's Kingston,' I thought. I'm really happy
because I'm going to leave Jamaica next month. I'm going to train as a nurse in Canada. Isn't that
5 exciting? What are your plans? Are you going to stay in Jamaica? Tourists think that Jamaica is
beautiful. They spend their time in expensive hotels and on sunny beaches. They think that everyone
is happy, but I disagree. Life isn't always easy in Kingston. There's a lot of violence and there are a lot
of problems with drugs. But there are also some good things here – like my family! They help me to
stay strong, and I can always rely on them. My family will be part of my life forever.

10 **Comments**

Layla: 18/06/2020 at 08:09 a.m.
I'm fed up with the violence here too, Tara. You can't avoid it. I'm going to train as a vet's assistant in
Florida in September. I really love animals. My sister is going to move to the USA in September too.
She's going to train as an engineer in Texas. We are going to chat online every day.

15 Aman: 18/06/2020 at 12:15 p.m.
Where are you going to live in Canada, Tara? Family is important to me too. That's why I'm not going
to leave the island. My uncle is a hairdresser in Kingston. I'm going to work in his hairdressing salon
next year. I like talking to people, so it's the right job for me! My brother is going to stay in Jamaica
too. He's going to train as a hotel manager in a few months.

CULTURE

Die Familie ist für die meisten Menschen in Jamaika sehr wichtig. Es gibt oft Großfamilien mit vielen
Tanten, Onkeln, Cousinen und Cousins. In jamaikanischen Familien ist man nie zu alt, um
zurechtgewiesen zu werden oder Ratschläge von älteren Familienmitgliedern zu bekommen. Wie
wichtig ist Familie für dich und deine Freunde?

2 Work with the text.

a) Choose the right answers. → ◯ p. 98

1. Tara has found a job in **Canada** · **California** · **Kingston**.
2. Kingston has problems with **dirty beaches** · **guns and drugs** · **dogs**.
3. Tara will never forget her **family** · **dog** · **best friend**.
4. Layla and her sister want to work in **Great Britain** · **the USA** · **Canada**.
5. Aman wants to work with **a friend** · **his father** · **his uncle**.
6. Aman's brother wants to work at a **hotel** · **shop** · **restaurant**.

b) Where is it in the text? Read the sentences and say the lines.

1. Somebody says that tourists don't know what Jamaica is really like.
2. Somebody says how she will keep in touch with her family.
3. Somebody says why he wants to be a hairdresser.

36/1 3 Work with the job words.

a) Match the jobs with the places. You don't need all of the places.

1. a nurse – <u>hospital</u>
2. a vet's assistant
3. a caretaker
4. an actor
5. a hairdresser
6. a (shop) assistant

supermarket   theatre

animal rescue shelter   restaurant

hospital ✓   airport   school

hairdressing salon

b) Find jobs for the two places that you didn't need in a).

4 (LISTENING) Listen to the young people's plans for the future.

2,6

What's the job? You don't need all of the jobs.

hotel manager   hairdresser

chef   vet's assistant

1. Tamila wants to be a ....
2. Raheem wants to be a ....
3. Shamar wants to be a ....

> **LISTENING SKILLS**
>
> Schau dir die Berufsbezeichnungen an, bevor du dir den Beitrag anhörst. Überlege dir, welche Wörter im Text vorkommen könnten, die mit den Berufen zu tun haben. Bei „chef" (Koch) könnte das zum Beispiel „restaurant" oder „food" sein.

5 (SPEAKING) Talk about jobs with a partner. → M Double circle, p. 123

A: Maybe I can be a <u>chef</u>.
B: Why?
A: I like working with <u>food</u>. And you?
B: …

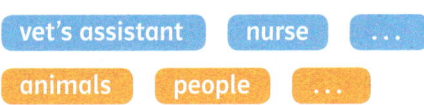

vet's assistant   nurse   ...

animals   people   ...

Language detectives → **G 9**, p.114

I'm going to leave Jamaica next month.
My sister is going to move to the USA in September.
I'm not going to leave Jamaica.

Hier handelt es sich um Pläne für die Zukunft. Wie bildest du diese Form des Futurs? Achte auch auf die Signalwörter!

---

6 Put Tara's sentences about her plans in the right order.

36/2
37/3

1. as a nurse • train • I'm going to
   I'm going to train as a nurse.
2. stay • I'm not going to • in Jamaica
3. in a big hospital • work • I'm going to

4. with my family • I'm going to • chat online
5. my new life • enjoy • in Canada • I'm going to
6. forget • I'm not going to • my friends
7. the violence • I'm not going to • here • miss

37/4 **7** What are the plans?

a) Complete the sentences. → ◯ p.99

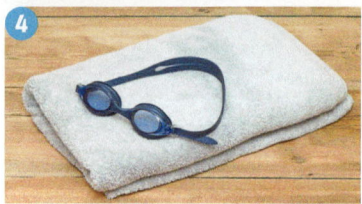

1. Aman is going to play basketball on Saturday.
2. Tara —— her blog on Sunday.
3. Layla's cousins —— to the USA next year.
4. Layla and her sister —— next week.
5. Aman —— his mother later today.
6. Tara and her brother —— a cake tomorrow.

is going to write   is going to call
is going to play ✓   are going to make
are going to go swimming
are going to travel

b) Complete Danielle's comment about Tara's blog.

BLOG

DANIELLE: 18/06/2020 at 12:15 p.m.
I'm going to work (1, to work) in my father's hotel in Kingston when I leave school. I —— (2, not to leave) my family! My brothers —— (3, to stay) in Jamaica too. My sister —— (4, to move) to Canada next year, like you. She —— (5, to train) as a chef! But she —— (6, not to live) in Canada forever!

8 (SPEAKING) Interview your partner about his or her plans.

37/5

	meet friends	tomorrow?
	visit family	at the weekend?
A: Are you going to	watch a film	in the holidays?
	+ make a cake	+ next week?
	work as a …	one day?
	…	…?

B: Yes, I am. ☺
No, I'm not. ☹

Language → G 9, p.114
Are you going to play basketball next week?

38/6 **9** (WRITING) Match the questions and answers.

a) Complete the questions and find the answers. There are more answers than you need. → ○ p.99

1. What … next year? (do)
   What are you going to do next year?
2. Where …? (live)
3. Why … that job? (do)
4. When …? (start)
5. … home often? (come)

a. Because I like working with people.
b. In September next year.
c. I'm going to train as a hotel manager.
d. Yes, I am. My family is important to me!
e. She's going to train as a chef.
f. I'm going to live in another city.

b) Write three more questions about the future.

10 (TASK) Your plans for the future → V Jobs, p.135

38/7–8

a) Think about these questions. Make notes.

1. What are you going to do when you leave school? Say why.
2. Where are you going to live?
3. What other things are important to you?

Du musst keine ganzen Sätze schreiben. Achte aber darauf, dass du deine Notizen lesen kannst. Du wirst sie in Teil b) brauchen.

b) Give a short talk about your plans.
Use your notes. → M 1-minute-presentation, p.122

I'm going to … .   I'd like to … .   I'm not going to … .   … is very important to me.

…

Your classmates can ask questions.

Are you going to …?   Why are you going to …?   …

39

Ich kann über Zukunftspläne sprechen. ✔

Jazz funerals in New Orleans

INTERNET

On the way to heaven

1 The 'jazz funeral' was brought to New Orleans
by African slaves about 300 years ago.
The people at the funeral were sad. But they
celebrated the end of slavery for the dead
5 person too. They wanted to help them find
their way to heaven. There were funerals like
this for poorer African Americans and later
also for musicians. Today there are jazz
funerals for other people, and people
10 organize funerals like this in other parts of the
USA too.

There is always a parade with a band at a jazz
funeral. On the way to the cemetery the band
plays slow, sad songs. But after the funeral
15 there is happy music. A famous song at jazz
funerals is 'When the saints go marching in'.
One of the biggest jazz funerals in New Orleans
took place on August 29, 2006. The
communities remembered the people who
20 died during Hurricane Katrina in August 2005.
More than 1,800 people lost their lives in the
hurricane.

1 (MEDIATION) **Beantworte die Fragen.**

Dein Freund, der sich für New Orleans interessiert, hat diesen Text im Internet gefunden. Da sein
Englisch nicht so gut ist, bittet er dich um Hilfe. Beantworte seine Fragen auf Deutsch.

1. Was feierten die Menschen bei den ersten „Jazz-Beerdigungen"?
2. Für wen gab es solche Beerdigungen? Wie ist es heute?
3. Was steht im Text über die Musik bei den Beerdigungen?
4. An welches Ereignis erinnerte die Beerdigung am 29. August 2006?

CULTURE

Eine Jazz-Beerdigung zeigt, dass man gleichzeitig über den Tod eines Familienmitglieds oder Freundes
traurig sein und das Leben feiern kann. Was denkst du über diese Art von Beerdigung?

Ich kann Informationen über eine
Tradition weitergeben.

Trouble at Thanksgiving

In diesem Film triffst du Jessica, ihre Eltern und Jessicas Cousin Ronan wieder.

1 (SPEAKING) **Talk about the photo from the film.**

Look at the photo. Think about these questions.

1. Where are Jessica and her dad?
2. What are they doing?

2 (VIEWING) **Watch the film.**

a) Choose the right answers.

1. Jessica can't make a **pecan pie** · **pizza**.
2. Ronan has just played **baseball** · **football**.
3. Jessica's sister is **visiting friends** · **working**.
4. Ronan's **mum** · **brother** is stuck in traffic.

5. Dad wants to watch **the football game** · **a film**.
6. There is a problem with the **turkey** · **salad**.

b) Watch the film again and take notes. Which one of these things *don't* we see?

a pecan pie   a turkey   volunteer work   an airport

some awful traffic   the family dog   a football game   a big parade

CULTURE

Seit den 1940er-Jahren wird dem US-Präsidenten jedes Jahr ein Truthahn geschenkt und ins Weiße Haus gebracht. Der Präsident veranlasst stets, dass der Truthahn nicht geschlachtet wird. Danach lebt das Tier auf einer Farm in Virginia. Welche Feiertagstraditionen gibt es in deinem Land?

3 **Read Jessica's e-mail to her friend. Put in the words.**

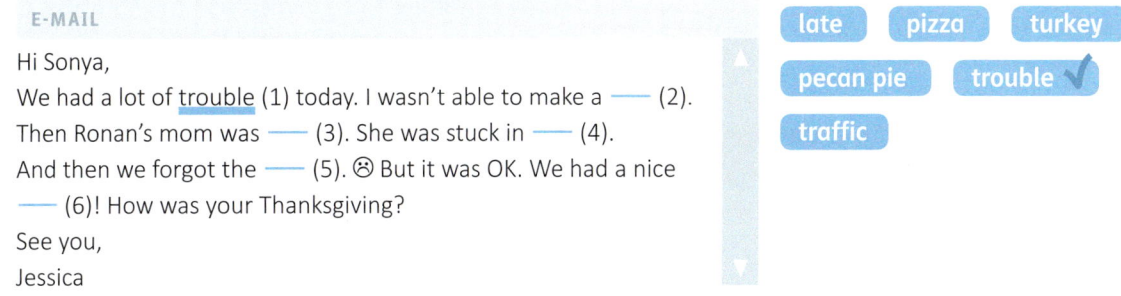

E-MAIL

Hi Sonya,
We had a lot of <u>trouble</u> (1) today. I wasn't able to make a —— (2).
Then Ronan's mom was —— (3). She was stuck in —— (4).
And then we forgot the —— (5). ☹ But it was OK. We had a nice
—— (6)! How was your Thanksgiving?
See you,
Jessica

late   pizza   turkey
pecan pie   trouble ✔
traffic

4 (WRITING) **Write an e-mail to an American friend.**

Write about a special day or meal in your family. You can use Jessica's e-mail for help.

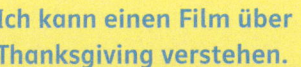
Ich kann einen Film über Thanksgiving verstehen.

Checklist 🌐 Find more online: 9dk5x5

✔ **Ich kann Informationen über Lebensweisen in zwei Regionen verstehen.**

The American South has many traditions. • The Caribbean is beautiful, but life isn't easy there.
40 ⤢

✔ **Ich kann mit einem Problem umgehen.**

Were you able to get here OK yesterday? • My bus from Memphis was only a few minutes late. • I only eat a little cheese. • I really don't mind. • It's OK. • I understand.
40 ⤢

✔ **Ich kann über Zukunftspläne sprechen.**

I'm going to leave Jamaica next month. • Are you going to stay in Jamaica? • I'm not going to leave the island. • My brother is going to train as a hotel manager.
40 ⤢

✔ **Ich kann eine längere Geschichte verstehen.**
41 ⤢

✔ **Ich kann Informationen über eine Tradition weitergeben.**
41 ⤢

✔ **Ich kann einen Film über Thanksgiving verstehen.**

👥 ❋ (UNIT TASK) # A place to visit

Bildet Gruppen mit drei bis vier Schülerinnen und Schülern. Jede Gruppe stellt einen interessanten Ort oder ein interessantes Reiseziel vor. Sucht euch einen Ort in den Südstaaten oder in der Karibik aus.

Step 1

Choose an interesting place to visit.

It could be a town or city in the American South. It could also be an island in the Caribbean. Here are some ideas:

New Orleans   Memphis   ...
Jamaica   Barbados   ...

Step 2

Get organized.

What do you already know about the place? Make notes: What can you do there? What is it famous for?

Step 3

Make a mind map about the place.

Find information on the internet, or ask your family. You can also visit the library or a travel agent's. Make a mind map and add the information.

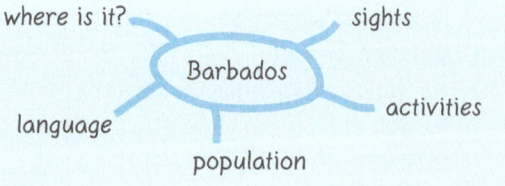

where is it?   sights
Barbados
language   activities
population

Step 4

Organize your information.

Talk about the information that your group has found.
Find a good order for the different pieces of information
and make a list with points that you can talk about.

> where
> population
> language
> sights
> activities

Step 5

Write the presentation.

a) Write two or three key words for each point on your list.
Decide who is going to talk about which point.

b) Use your notes to write your part of the presentation.

Step 6

Practise your presentation.

Use your notes when you practise. You can also use the phrases on page 89.

*Übe deine Präsentation vor dem Spiegel, einem Familienmitglied oder
Freund. Du bist dann entspannter, wenn du die Präsentation hältst.
Es hilft dir auch, wenn du die meisten Informationen auswendig weißt.*

Step 7

Give your presentation. → M Tip top, p.127

Give your presentation. Listen to other presentations. Which one did you like best? Why?
You can use these phrases to give feedback:

The presenters spoke clearly.
The information about … was very interesting.
I enjoyed the part about ….
I didn't know that ….
The presenters used the time well.
The presenters answered all of the questions.

Mark's decision

1 On September 14, 2018 Hurricane Florence hit Wilmington, a city in the American South. There was damage to many buildings and bridges.

5 Thousands of people had to leave their homes. They had to sleep at local schools or stay at a friend's house in another city. For three days people couldn't make phone calls or use the internet.

10 Mark Wilson, a 34-year-old teacher, lives in Wilmington. He said in an interview yesterday: "I was lucky to have a boat. That's more useful than a car after a hurricane. So I took my two kids, Brian and Lisa. We wanted 15 to go to the local school."

But on the way they saw a movement in the window of a house. "It was a young woman with her daughter," Mark said. "I was worried about my kids, but I decided to help."

20 So Mark went to the house in the boat. "I carefully pulled them into our boat," he said. "They were cold and unhappy. It was impossible to leave them there."

Mark took the woman and her daughter to 25 the school, where they got food and warm clothes. Two days later they were able to go back to their home.

Now the woman has invited the Wilsons to visit her next week. "I'm really thankful. It 30 was a big decision to stop the boat to save us. It will be great to meet Mark and his family again and say thank you for his help," she said in an interview on national radio.

The Wilsons are very happy about the 35 invitation. Now they want to help other families too. That's why they have given money to a project to rebuild playgrounds in Wilmington.

Hier kannst du lernen, wie man mit Wortfamilien arbeitet.

44/1 **1** **Read the text.**

Choose the right answer.

> Lies zunächst den ganzen Text. Welcher der drei Sätze fasst zusammen, worum es geht?

A   A man and his daughter had an accident after a hurricane.
B   A man helped a woman and her daughter after a hurricane.
C   A woman helped a man and his daughter after a hurricane.

44/2 **2** **Work with the words from the text.**
→ M Think – pair – share, p.127

a)   Look at these words. Which is the 'root word'? What do the words mean in German?

building;   to **build**;   to re**build**

> Jedes Wort gehört zu einer Wortfamilie. Das Grundwort (auf Englisch „root word") ist ein einfaches Wort ohne Endung oder Vorsilbe. Wenn du die Bedeutung des Grundwortes kennst, kannst du die Bedeutung eines unbekannten Wortes oft erschließen.

b)   Copy the table with the words from the text. Write the root words and the German meanings. Use a dictionary for help.

	root word	German
1. **teach**er	to teach	Lehrer/in, unterrichten
2. un**happy**	…	…
3. im**possible**	…	…
4. **dec**ision	to …	…
5. **invit**ation	to …	…
6. **worr**ied	to …	

> Achte auf die Endungen und Vorsilben der Wörter in der ersten Spalte. Nomen, Adjektive und Verben haben oft bestimmte Endungen oder Vorsilben, die dir einen Hinweis auf die Bedeutung der Wörter geben können.
>
> teacher (Lehrer, Lehrerin) → Personen
> impossible (unmöglich)   → Gegenteile

44/3 **3** **Make a word from the same family.**

1.   to act → actor
2.   to sing
3.   nation
4.   to call
5.   help

`-er` `-ful`
`-or`  `-al`
`-er`

> Du kannst selbst weitere Wörter derselben Wortfamilie bilden. Denke an verschiedene Wortarten, zusammengesetzte Wörter und Gegenteile. Benutze dein Wörterbuch. Auf den „Dictionary Skills"-Seiten in deinem Buch kannst du nachschauen, wie ein Eintrag im Wörterbuch aufgebaut ist.

At the summer camp

1 (LISTENING) **Listen to the dialogue at the summer camp.**

2,9

Find out which person has which suitcase or bag (A–D).

Amy   Pascal   Sophie   Max

1. Amy has ….

Lies die Namen und schau dir die Gepäckstücke im Bild an. Hör dir dann den Text an. Wem gehört welches Gepäckstück?

2 (WRITING) **Find the right picture. Copy the sentences and complete the words.**

1. You can go sw****** at the summer camp.
2. Ca****** is a very popular activity.
3. Wear a helmet if you go r*** c*******.

4. Visitors often play b********* at the summer camp too.
5. You can go ho*** r***** here.

3 (LISTENING) **Listen to Pascal and Amy at the summer camp.**

2,10

Which two sentences are right?

1. Amy thinks that canoeing is more exciting than basketball.
2. There is a river where she lives in the USA.
3. Pascal wants to try horse riding.
4. Amy's sister hurt her leg last year.

Language → G10, p.115

I think horse riding is <u>safer than</u> canoeing.
Rock climbing is <u>the easiest</u> activity.
I'd like to try something <u>more exciting</u>.
That's <u>the most dangerous</u> thing ever!

Do you remember?
So vergleichst du zwei Dinge oder
Aktivitäten. Achte auf die verschiedenen
Formen bei kurzen und langen Adjektiven.

---

4 (SPEAKING) **Find a summer camp activity with your partner.**

You and your partner are at the summer camp. Act the dialogue.

A Sage, dass du es nicht erwarten kannst, zum Klettern zu gehen. (I can't wait to ....) →

B Sage, dass du das langweilig findest. Du möchtest Kanufahren gehen. (I think that's .... I'd like to go ....)

A Sage, dass du Klettern spannender als Kanufahren findest. (I think ... is more ....) →

B Sage, dass du Kanufahren interessanter findest. (I think ....)

A Sage, dass du auch reiten möchtest. Das gefällt dir gut. (I'd like to go ....) →

B Sage ja, aber es ist teurer. Sage, dass du gern da drüben Basketball spielen möchtest. (Yes, but that's ....)

A Sage ja, das ist am einfachsten und am billigsten. Sage, dass du auch spielen möchtest. (Yes, that's ....) →

B Sage: Okay! Das machen wir. (Let's ....)

Working in Canada

Hi! My name is Josh and I live in Toronto. I'm a big ice hockey fan. The Toronto Maple Leafs are my team. Ice hockey is the most popular sport in Canada – we usually call it 'hockey'.

1

2

Canada is the second largest country in the world. Immigrants from many different countries live and work there. Most people live in big cities near the US border, like Toronto. That's where most of the jobs are.

---

1 (SPEAKING) **Talk about the photos.**

a) Work with a partner. What's in the photos?

There is …. / There are ….

a wild animal	a boy in a helmet
city buildings	warm clothes
signs	a flag	…

b) What would/wouldn't you like to see or do in Canada? You can use the words from a).

2 (READING) **Complete the sentences.**

46/1

1. Canada's most popular sport is ….
2. Most of the jobs in Canada are in ….
3. Grizzly bears and moose live in ….
4. In the past France and Britain both had ….
5. The signs in Quebec are ….
6. Nunavut, in the north of Canada, is where ….

Am Ende dieser Unit kann ich ...
- Informationen über Kanada verstehen.
- über Freizeit und Medien sprechen.
- mich auf einen Job bewerben.
- Stellenanzeigen und Lebensläufe verstehen.
- Informationen über Teilzeitjobs weitergeben.
- einen Film über ein Bewerbungsgespräch verstehen.

There are high mountains, big rivers and thousands of lakes in Canada's wilderness. Tourists can see wild animals, like grizzly bears and moose. But winters are hard in Canada.

Britain and France both had colonies in Canada in the past. Many people in Quebec speak French, and the signs are in that language. But most Canadians speak English.

The Inuit are a group of people who lived in Canada before the Europeans came. The Inuit have their own language, but many speak English. Most Inuit live in the north of Canada, in Nunavut.

3 (LISTENING) Listen: Which four sentences are right?

2,12
46/2

1. Lara often goes surfing in the summer.
2. Healthy food is expensive in Nunavut.
3. She plays with her brothers and sisters in the winter.
4. Scott speaks the Inuit language well.
5. He can't watch TV in the Inuit language.
6. He makes his own clothes.
7. He is proud to be Inuit.

In diesem Hörtext sprechen zwei Inuit-Teenager über das Leben in Nunavut.

Ich kann Informationen über Kanada ✔ verstehen.

It's not fair!

1 (READING) Read the dialogue.

2,13

1 Josh is at school in Toronto. It's break. He and his friends Emma and Alex are talking about how they use social media.

Josh: My parents say I spend too much time
5 online. I often get updates about Ontario hockey teams on my app. I sometimes watch TV series on my phone too. But my mum and dad watch TV every day. It's not fair!

Alex: I know what you mean. I put some
10 photos online yesterday and my mum got angry. But what's the problem with a few selfies? I'm very careful. I never share information with people who aren't my friends.

15 Emma: I posted selfies a lot but now I think they're boring. I made a video at the weekend.

Alex: A video? How did you do it?

Emma: I had a film with some birds which were very beautiful. I made it in Banff
20 National Park last summer. I used a song which I really like. I uploaded the video to a music website yesterday.

Josh: Wow! I'd like to do that!

Alex: Yes, it sounds cool.

25 Emma: It isn't difficult. There is free software which is very good. But you have to be careful with songs. They have copyright on them.

Alex: Do you have many followers on the music website?

30 Emma: No, I don't. But I said thanks to a girl who commented on my video. She's from Vancouver. She liked it a lot.

Alex: Videos sound like a lot of work to me! I like watching tutorials – you know, videos
35 that show you how to do something. I used one when I repaired my bike yesterday. The tutorial was great. I think a lot of TV series are too long. They have too many episodes. I often just chat with friends. Or I share funny photos
40 and videos with them on my phone. Oh, it's time to go. What's our next lesson?

Josh: Er, sorry?

Alex: Hey, you don't need your phone now, Josh! Let's go!

2 Match the photos with the kinds of social media in the dialogue.

CULTURE

Ottawa, die kanadische Hauptstadt, liegt in der Provinz Ontario. Die größte Stadt in Ontario ist Toronto. Sie hat 2,7 Millionen Einwohner. Der Nationalpark von Banff ist der älteste Nationalpark in Kanada. Er liegt in einem sehr schönen Gebirge. Welche Nationalparks in Bayern kennst du? Warst du schon einmal dort? Warum sind diese Parks so wichtig?

3 Who is it? → **M** Peer correction, p.125

a) Put in the names. → ◯ p.100

1. <u>Alex</u> only shares information with friends.
2. —— gets updates about hockey.
3. —— used a tutorial about bikes yesterday.
4. —— made a video about a trip.
5. —— would like to make a video.
6. —— thinks selfies are boring.
7. —— spends too much time online (maybe!).

b) Who do you think is right, Alex or his mother? Is it always OK to post pictures of yourself?

47/1-2 **4** Work with the words from the text.

a) Put in the right words. (There is one word that you don't need.) → ◯ p.101

| commented | online | episodes | chat | tutorial ✓ | uploaded | share |

1. A <u>tutorial</u> shows you how to do something.
2. Emma —— a video to a website yesterday.
3. A girl —— on the video.
4. People often —— funny photos and videos.
5. Alex uses his phone to —— with friends.
6. TV series often have a lot of —— .

b) Find the words in the text.

1. This is a piece of news or information.
2. This has news about a star or a team.
3. This is a place on the internet.
4. This is a kind of fan on the internet.

5 (SPEAKING) Talk to a partner. How often do you use social media? → **M** Double circle, p.123

47/3

| I + | often
sometimes
occasionally
never | + | post my own photos.
watch TV series.
use tutorials.
upload videos.
chat with friends.
comment on photos and videos. | + And you? |

SPEAKING SKILLS

Höre deinem Partner/deiner Partnerin gut zu und mache dir Notizen. Wenn du etwas nicht verstehst, frage nach: „Can you repeat that, please?"

6 (SOUNDS) Read, say and listen.

48/4

a) The words below all have the letter 'a' but it sounds different. Make a chart. Say the words with a partner. Put the words into the right group in the chart.

app ✓   game ✓   angry   update

made   chat   way   thanks

/æ/	/eɪ/
app	game

2,14   b) Listen to the words and check your chart.

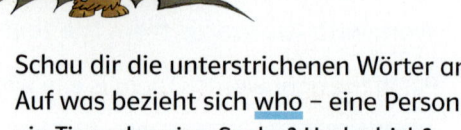

Language detectives → **G 12**, p.117

I never share information with people who aren't my friends.
I said thanks to a girl who commented on it.
I used a song which I really like.
There is free software which is very good.
I had a film with some birds which were very beautiful.

Schau dir die unterstrichenen Wörter an. Auf was bezieht sich who – eine Person, ein Tier oder eine Sache? Und which?

7 Put in who or which.

48/5–6

1. Josh has an app which gives him news about hockey.
2. He's a boy —— spends a lot of time online.
3. Alex used a tutorial —— was great.
4. Emma said thanks to a girl —— commented on her video.
5. Ten people liked the video —— she made.

8 (SPEAKING) What are the people and things? → **M** Bus stop, p.122

a) Find the word and put in who or which. → ○ p.101

1. a person —— comes from Canada
   A Canadian is a person who comes from Canada.
2. an animal —— lives in the wilderness
3. a city —— is near the US border
4. a person —— works at a restaurant
5. someone —— works at a hospital
6. a place —— is in the north of Canada

a chef   a nurse

a moose   Nunavut

a Canadian ✓   Toronto

Du kannst „that" immer anstelle von „who" und „which" benutzen:
It's a thing that ....
It's a person that ....
It's an animal that ....

b) Make a quiz for your partner.

It's a person … works at …. It's an animal … lives in …. It's a thing … you find in ….

49/7–8 **9** (WRITING) **Write about photos from a trip to Bavaria.**

a) Write sentences for these photos from a social media site. → ○ p.102

the bus • took us to the youth hostel

the guide • showed us the sights

a photo • I took on the second day

a shop • sells cool T-shirts

a Canadian girl • we met

a castle • is very old

1. This is the bus <u>which</u> took us to the youth hostel.

b) Find five photos from your last class trip. Write sentences about each one.

10 (TASK) **A poster about social media in your free time** → **V** Social media and technology, p.136; → **V** Sports and activities, p.137

49/9

a) Make a list of websites and apps which you use in your free time.

b) Talk about your ideas in a group. Choose a website, app or activity that you want to present. → **M** Placemat, p.125

Think about these questions:
What do you use it for? How long do you use it every day?
What is good or not so good about it? Who can use it?

Wenn du keine sozialen Medien benutzt, kannst du auch ein Poster über eine andere Freizeitaktivität gestalten.

c) Make a poster about your website, app or activity. Use screenshots or photos.

d) Present your poster. → **M** 1-minute-presentation, p.122

This is our favourite ….
With this … you can chat/learn about/….
We use it … hours every day.

We love/like the app/website because ….
It's not so good that ….
Young/older people/… can use it.

Ich kann über Freizeit und Medien sprechen. ✔

A job in Toronto

1 (READING) **Read the job ad (A) and the application (B).**

2,15–16

A

Receptionist, Chelsea Hotel

1 We are one of the largest hotels in Toronto.

Are you able to:
- work in a team,
5 - help guests from different countries,
- work weekends and holidays?

We are looking for someone:
- with experience in customer service,
- with good computer skills,
10 - who speaks English well.

We offer:
- a good salary and training in an amazing city (not many Canadian cities are as amazing as Toronto!)

15 Please send your CV and letter of application to Mr F. Roberts at xx@xx.ca

B E-MAIL

Dear Mr Roberts,

I would like to apply for the job as a receptionist at the Chelsea Hotel.

20 I have two years of experience. When I was 16, I did an internship at a travel agent's in Cork, Ireland. I learned a lot about customer service there. I also worked in a bed and breakfast in Ireland. At the moment I am working in

25 Canada at the Park Hotel in London, Ontario. It is nearly as big as your hotel. Now I am looking for a job in a more interesting city.

I was born in Ireland, so English isn't a problem. I am a confident and reliable worker,

30 and I am good at working with people from other countries. I like working in a team.

You will find more information in my CV. I look forward to hearing from you.

Yours sincerely,

35 Julie Wynner

Language → G 11, p.116

I <u>was born</u> in Ireland.

2 **Complete the sentences.**

1. The hotel is looking for a <u>receptionist</u>.
2. The person will help guests who come from —— .
3. The person will get training and a good —— .
4. Julie did an internship at a —— .
5. Toronto is a more —— city than London, Ontario.
6. Julie was born in Ireland so she speaks —— well.
7. She sends her —— with the e-mail.

50/1 **3** What's the word?

a) What is it? (There is one word that you don't need.) → ○ p.102

apply ・ salary ✓ ・ receptionist ・ travel agent's ・ internship ・ guest ・ CV

1. A <u>salary</u> is the money that someone gets for a job.
2. A —— has more information about a person who wants a job.
3. An —— is a job for a few weeks or months.
4. When you ——, you write and say that you want a job.
5. A —— is a person who answers phone calls and helps at a hotel.
6. A —— is a shop which sells flights and holidays.

b) Match the sentences.

1. Mia doesn't worry about her work.
2. Jade likes working with other people.
3. Simon doesn't take long to do his work.
4. If Taylor says she will do something, she will do it.

a. She's very reliable.
b. He's a fast worker.
c. She's very confident.
d. She's good at working in a team.

50/2 **4** (WRITING) Work with a letter of application.

a) Copy the letter of application. Complete the words. → ○ p.103

E-MAIL

Dear Mrs Walker,

I would like to <u>apply</u> (1) for the job as a chef at Monte Carlo Restaurant.

I finished sch—— (2) one and a half years ago and did an in—— (3) at a café. Then I trained as a ch—— (4) at a restaurant. I got a lot of ex——(5) there.

I am a rel—— (6) person and I like working in a t—— (7).

You will find more in—— (8) in my CV.

I look for—— (9) to hearing from you.

Yours sin—— (10),

Martin Henderson

b) Where can these extra sentences go in the letter?

1. I also learned a lot about customer service.
2. I also have good computer skills.
3. I read about the job on your website.

CULTURE

Förmliche Briefe beginnen im Englischen immer mit dem Wort „Dear". Als Grußformel am Ende schreibt man oft „Yours sincerely". Wie ist das im Deutschen?

5 (LISTENING) **Listen to the job interview.**

2,17
50/3

a) Listen and choose the right answers.

1. The job is at a **hotel** · **computer store**.
2. Vicky plays **baseball** · **computer games**.
3. She worked at a **café** · **hotel** last year.
4. The woman offers Vicky some **tea** · **water**.
5. Vicky can **find out more about the store** · **go shopping** later.

> **LISTENING SKILLS**
>
> Wenn du einen Dialog zum ersten Mal hörst, mache dir Notizen zu den W-Fragen: Wer? Was? Wann? Wo? Warum? Achte beim zweiten Hören gezielt auf die gesuchten Informationen.

b) What do you think? Will Vicky get the job? Why (or why not)?

6 (SPEAKING) **Act part of a job interview with a partner.**

51/4

a) Match the sentences.

Partner A
1. Good morning! Take a seat, please.
2. Why did you apply for this job?
3. Have you worked at a hotel before?
4. Can you work Saturdays and Sundays?
5. You say that you are a reliable person. Can you give me an example?

Partner B
a. Yes, of course. I have time at weekends.
b. Yes, I can. I look after my sister every week.
c. Good morning. Thank you.
d. I wanted to get some experience at a hotel.
e. No, I haven't. But I did an internship at a supermarket last year.

b) Act the interview with a partner. You can change some details.

Language detectives → G 13, p.118

The Park Hotel is nearly <u>as big as</u> your hotel. <u>Not</u> many Canadian cities are <u>as amazing as</u> Toronto.

Wie drückst du aus, dass Personen oder Dinge <u>gleich</u> oder <u>nicht gleich</u> sind?

---

7 **What do the people say?**

Use <u>as … as</u> (☺) or <u>not as … as</u> (☹).

1. Martin: The Monte Carlo Restaurant is —— the restaurant where I trained. (big, ☺)
   The Monte Carlo Restaurant is <u>as big as</u> the restaurant where I trained.
2. A hotel manager: My new car looks great. And it's —— the old one too. (reliable, ☺)
3. Amy: I like rock climbing. It's —— it looks! (easy, ☹)
4. An American woman: Toronto is a cool place, but it's —— New York City! (interesting, ☹)
5. Vicky: I'm —— my older sister. But I'm learning! (confident, ☹)
6. Mrs Wilson: The computer games in our store are —— they are online. (cheap, ☺)

8 (SPEAKING) Work with a partner. Make comparisons.

a) Compare the jobs. Use <u>as … as</u> or <u>not as … as</u>. → ○ p.103

51/5
52/6

❶ Helen, hairdresser

❷ Lisa, assistant

❸ Marc, receptionist

	Helen, hairdresser	Lisa, assistant	Marc, receptionist
journey to work (long)	15 minutes	45 minutes	15 minutes
team (large)	6 people	6 people	8 people
salary (high)	+	++	++

1. Helen's journey to work / Marc's
   Helen's journey to work is <u>as long as</u> Marc's.
2. Lisa's team / Marc's

3. Helen's salary / Lisa's
4. Lisa's team / Helen's
5. Marc's journey to work / Lisa's
6. Lisa's salary / Marc's

b) Compare these things with a partner.

1. Bamberg – Munich (big)
2. football – ice hockey (exciting)

3. horse riding – rafting (dangerous)
4. TV series – computer games (interesting)

A: I think Bamberg is not as big as Munich.
B: You're right. I think … .

9 (TASK) A letter of application → V Job applications, p.138

a) Look at the jobs. Choose the one that's best for you.

52/7

`hairdresser`   `police officer`
`assistant`   `…`

b) Write a letter of application for the job. You can use the phrases on the right. Use a dictionary if you need to. → M Writers' conference, p.127

E-MAIL

Dear Mr / Mrs …,
I would like to apply for the job as a … .
I … . (What experience do you have?)
I am … . (What kind of person are you?)
You will … . (Where can they find more information?)
I look forward to hearing from you.
Yours sincerely,
…

WRITING SKILLS

Überprüfe deinen Entwurf sorgfältig. Ein Partner oder eine Partnerin kann dir Feedback geben. Es ist auch eine gute Idee, den Entwurf eine Stunde später noch mal anzuschauen. Ist er okay oder kannst du noch etwas hinzufügen, um ihn besser zu machen? Nutze auch die Checkliste auf Seite 129.

Ich kann mich auf einen Job bewerben. ✔

The right job for you?

1 How many jobs can you remember in English? → M Think – pair – share, p.127

2 (READING) Read the job ads and the CV.

2,18

A

CUSTOMER SERVICE ASSISTANT
for railway stations in Ottawa, Ontario

1

5 **Are you a confident and reliable person?
Do you like working with people?
Are you flexible with working hours?**

We are looking for assistants to work at our railway stations.

10 You will check tickets, answer questions and help customers with their problems.

You will need to work different hours between 6:00 a.m. and 10:00 p.m.

You should:

15 • have a secondary school leaving certificate,
• have some experience in customer service,
• be friendly and flexible.

B

Job as a **travel agent**
in Toronto, Ontario

20

We are looking for a friendly travel agent who wants to see the world and help other people do the same.

25 You will:
• organize, plan and sell flights and vacations,
• give information about different countries and help customers plan their vacation,

30
• make reservations and book tours.

You should:
• have a qualification in Tourism,
• have experience as a travel agent,
35 • have good computer skills,
• be a careful and efficient worker.

3 Complete the sentences.

Job A
1. The person will work at … in ….
2. He or she will help ….
3. He or she must be ….
Job B
4. He or she will help customers ….
5. He or she must have experience as ….
6. The person must be a … worker.

The CV
7. Anja left school in ….
8. During the summer holidays she ….
9. Her hobbies are ….
10. She speaks ….

Ein englischer Lebenslauf enthält normalerweise kein Foto. Du kannst dein Geburtsdatum angeben, musst aber nicht. „References" sind Informationen über dich, die der Arbeitgeber von Menschen bekommt, die dich gut kennen. Wie sieht ein deutscher Lebenslauf aus?

2,19

Name: Anja Fischer
Address: Graf-Zeppelin-Str. 1xx,
9xxxx Regensburg, Germany

Phone: + 49 123 456 7890
55 **E-mail:** abz@xy.de
Date of birth: 12th August 2004

40 A flexible and confident person who likes working with people

EDUCATION:
2014–2020: Mittelschule Regensburg
(secondary school)
45 2010–2014: Grundschule (primary school)

QUALIFICATIONS:
2020: Mittlerer Schulabschluss
(secondary school leaving
certificate)

50 **SKILLS:**
Good computer skills, good at working
in a team; languages: German, English,
Russian

EXPERIENCE:
2018–2020: I helped at a local supermarket
during the summer holidays.
60 April 2019: Internship at an animal rescue
shelter

INTERESTS:
Cooking and basketball (I play in a team for
my local club.)

65 **REFERENCES:**
Available on request

4 Choose one of the tasks.

a) Choose one of the jobs. Why should you get the job? Prepare a short presentation for your classmates.
→ M 1-minute-presentation, p.122

53/1–2

OR

b) Write your CV in English. Use a computer.

Du kannst Anjas Lebenslauf als Vorlage für deinen eigenen benutzen. Vergiss nicht, auch deinen deutschen Lebenslauf zu überprüfen.

Make notes about:
– your experience,
– what you are good at,
– your languages,
– what kind of person you are,
– other information that could help.

Give the presentation. Will you get the job?

Ich kann Stellenanzeigen und Lebensläufe verstehen. ✔

Looking for part-time work

Find your student job!

A

We are looking for a
BABYSITTER who can take care
of our kids (ages 3 + 5).
The hours are from 8:00 p.m.
and later on Friday and Saturday
evenings.
Earn C$ 16 per hour.
– Jill and Pete Carter

B

DOG WALKER needed for
weekday evenings.
You can work near your home
and be outside (also when the
weather is bad).
Earn C$ 14 per hour.

– Sonia Dickens and family

C

GARDEN HELPER
Do you like hard work?
Do you want to work outside?
Earn C$ 15 per hour.
Work in the afternoon and at
weekends.

– Matt Jolly and family

1 (MEDIATION) **Ergänze die Informationen auf Deutsch.**

1. Welche drei Jobs werden angeboten?
   Bei Familie A muss man <u>sich um die Kinder kümmern</u> (1), bei Familie B —— (2), und bei Familie
   C —— (3).
2. Welche Arbeitszeiten werden erwartet?
   Die Gartenarbeit soll an den Wochenenden und am —— (4) gemacht werden.
   Famile A braucht jemanden, der am —— (5) und Samstag ab 20 Uhr oder etwas später auf die
   Kinder aufpasst.
   Der Hund muss jeden —— (6) am Abend ausgeführt werden.
3. Wie werden die Jobs bezahlt?
   Der bestbezahlte Job ist bei Familie —— (7); am wenigsten bekommt man bei Familie —— (8).

2 (WRITING) **Copy the form and fill it in.**

APPLICATION FORM

Last name: ███████████   First name(s): ███████████

E-mail: ███████████   Which job are you applying for? ███████

When can you start? ████ / ████ / ████

Send

Ich kann Informationen über
Teilzeitjobs weitergeben.   ✔

Working at a US summer camp

In diesem Film triffst du Amy, ihre jüngere Schwester Jessica und ihren Cousin Ronan wieder.

1 (SPEAKING) **Talk about your holidays.**

What did you do in your last summer holidays?
Talk with a partner.

I stayed in .... I played ....
I spent time in ... with ....
I went to .... I visited ....

CULTURE

Die Sommerferien in den USA und Kanada sind oft länger als in Deutschland. Viele Kinder gehen in dieser Zeit in Feriencamps. In vielen Camps ist Sport (z. B. Reiten) sehr wichtig oder Computerspiele. Gibt es Feriencamps, wo du wohnst? Würdest du gerne eines besuchen?

2 (VIEWING) **Watch the film.**

a) Choose the right answer.

1. Amy gets **an e-mail** • **a letter**.
2. Ronan wants to go to **summer camp** • **Science camp**.
3. Amy has already worked **with old people** • **with children**.
4. Chris says that Amy **can have the job** • **must have a second interview**.

b) Watch the film from 01:31 to 01:55 again. Which sport **doesn't** Silverley offer?

3 (SPEAKING) **Talk about the job.**

a) Watch the interview again (from 03:17 to 05:32).

b) Would you like to work as a camp counselor?

I'd like to ....
I wouldn't like to ....

work with small children sleep in a tent

work with people from different countries

have (no) time for myself . . .

VIEWING SKILLS

Achte darauf, wie Chris, der das Bewerbungsgespräch durchführt, auf Amy eingeht (indem er sie z. B. anlächelt).
Wie kann eine Person in einem Gespräch sonst noch auf ihren Partner oder ihre Partnerin eingehen?

Ich kann einen Film über ein Bewerbungsgespräch verstehen. ✔

Checklist 🌐 Find more online: 9dk5x5

✔ **Ich kann Informationen über Kanada verstehen.**

Ice hockey is the most popular sport in Canada. • Canada is the second largest country in the world. • Most Inuit live in the north of Canada, in Nunavut.

54 ↗

✔ **Ich kann über Freizeit und Medien sprechen.**

I often get updates. • I never share information with people who aren't my friends. • There is free software which is very good.

54 ↗

✔ **Ich kann mich auf einen Job bewerben.**

I would like to apply for the job as a receptionist at the Chelsea Hotel. • I am looking for a job in a more interesting city. • You will find more information in my CV.

54 ↗

✔ **Ich kann Stellenanzeigen und Lebensläufe verstehen.**

55 ↗

✔ **Ich kann Informationen über Teilzeitjobs weitergeben.**

55 ↗

✔ **Ich kann einen Film über ein Bewerbungsgespräch verstehen.**

�֍ (UNIT TASK) # My dream job

Denk über deinen Traumberuf nach. Was würdest du gern werden? Stelle ihn drei Minuten lang vor.

Step 1

Choose your dream job.

What would you really like to do? Here are some ideas …

chef (at a restaurant in LA?)

hairdresser (for a star?) . . .

Step 2

Think about what you need for the job.

Make a mind map about your dream job. The mind map can look like this:

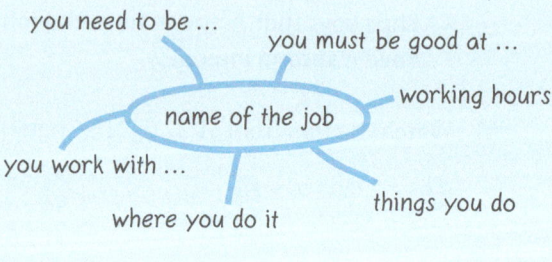

you need to be …   you must be good at …

name of the job   working hours

you work with …

where you do it   things you do

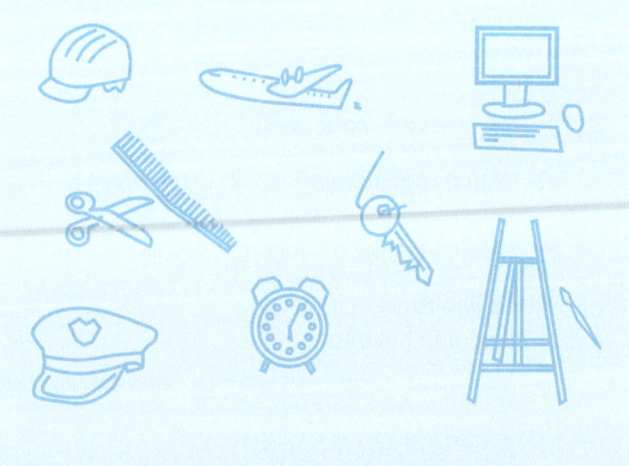

Step 3

Find out more details about your job.

Add new details to your mind map.

Du kannst natürlich auch ein Wörterbuch verwenden. Vergiss nicht, dass viele englische Wörter mehrere Bedeutungen haben. Die erste Bedeutung ist nicht immer die, die du brauchst!

Step 4

Plan your presentation.

Make sure your presentation has:

- an introduction
  Say what you are going to talk about. You can start with a picture.

- a main part
  This should have all the information about your dream job.

- a conclusion
  Name the dream job again. Finish the presentation in a friendly way.

> I'd like to tell you about ..../I'm going to present ....

> The first thing I'd like to tell you about my dream job is ....

> So that's ..., my dream job!/I hope you liked my presentation./Thanks for listening!

Step 5

Practise your presentation.

Ask your family and friends to listen when you practise the presentation. They can ask you questions and give you feedback.

Step 6

Give your presentation.

Speak slowly and clearly. Give the others time to ask questions at the end and ask them for feedback. → M Tip top, p.127

You can give feedback like this:

I enjoyed the part about ....
I didn't understand .... What did you mean?

You spoke slowly and clearly.
The presentation was/wasn't too short/long ....

Sights and signs in Canada

Most Canadians love ice hockey. It's an exciting game!

The Canadian flag is red and white.

This statue is in the west of Canada.

There are bears in the Canadian wilderness.

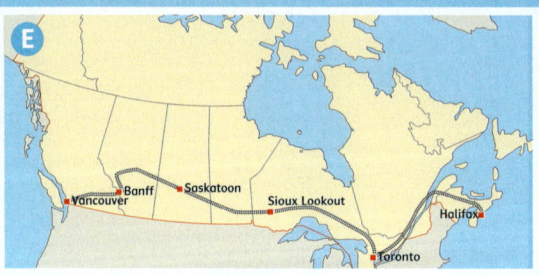

You can travel by train from one side of Canada to the other.

The journey takes five days!

1 (SPEAKING) **Work with the photos.**

a) Talk about the photos with a partner.

There is …   a statue   a bear   a train   a game of …   a flag   a map of …
In the background I can see …   mountains   trees   people   buildings

b) Which of the things would you like to see and do in Canada?

I'd like to   see … watch …
I wouldn't like to   play … meet …
                travel …

1 ARRIVÉES

TRAIN	ARRIVING FROM	TIME
36	OTTAWA	17:56
69	NEW YORK	19:10
38	OTTAWA	19:56
64	TORONTO	20:16
27	QUEBEC	20:56
66	TORONTO	21:43

2 DANGER FOR SUR 60 KM

3 INUIT ART — AND — SOUVENIRS — FOR SALE —

4 Vancouver whale-watching Tours
Winter times: 8:30 a.m. 11:30 a.m. 2:30 p.m.
Trips last 2 hrs.

5 PAY FARE AHEAD
Bridge to Canada ONLY
EXIT 275
USA Port Huron
EXIT ONLY

6 DEPARTURES

Time	Flight	Destination	Gate
12:00	OD 1961	TORONTO	06
12:15	PN 0034	VANCOUVER	18
12:20	T3 0529	MONTREAL	32
12:30	PN 2415	CALGARY	14
12:50	GI 1872	OTTAWA	09
12:55	T3 0944	HALIFAX	27
13:20	SF 2778	EDMONTON	20
13:45	OD 0061	WINNIPEG	31
13:50	BK 1532	YELLOWKNIFE	04
14:05	OD 3487	VICTORIA	12
14:30	PN 0194	REGINA	03

2 Beantworte die Fragen auf Deutsch.

1. Wann kommt der Zug aus Quebec an? (Foto 1)
2. Warum sollten Autofahrer hier vorsichtig sein? (Foto 2)
3. Was können Touristen hier kaufen? (Foto 3)
4. Du möchtest Wale beobachten, musst aber um 13 Uhr zurück in Vancouver sein. Welche Tour solltest du machen? (Foto 4)
5. Was solltest du beachten, wenn du über die Brücke nach Kanada einreist? (Foto 5)
6. Von welchem Gate startet der nächste Flug nach Ottawa? (Foto 6)

A topic-based talk

Topic 1: Canada

- second largest country in the world
- more than 37 million people live there
- capital: Ottawa
- other important cities: Toronto, Vancouver
- wilderness and animals (moose, bears, …)

Topic 2: Jobs

- can find jobs (ads on internet, in newspapers)
- should write a letter of application and a CV
- should do internships
- skills: As a … you should be ….
- salary

Topic 3: New York City

- largest city in the USA
- more than 8.5 million people live there
- famous sights (Statue of Liberty, Times Square, …)
- Central Park: more than 4 km long
- lots of immigrants live in the city

Hier kannst du lernen, wie man eine Kurzpräsentation zu einem Thema hält.

1 Choose a topic.

First read about the three topics.
Which topic do you want to talk about?

> Welches Thema interessiert dich am meisten? Weißt du genug über dein Thema oder brauchst du noch detailliertere Informationen?

58/1 ## 2 Collect more information.

→ **M** Think – pair – share, p.127

Find other students with the same topic.
Think about ideas together. Make notes and compare them.

> Du kannst auch eine „mind map" anlegen.
>
> people — cities
> Canada — sports
> sights
> animals — facts

58/2 ## 3 Prepare your talk.

a) Use your notes to make a plan for your talk. You should talk about three or more aspects of the topic.

b) Practise your talk at home or with a partner.

> Folgende Wendungen kannst du in deiner Präsentation verwenden:
> – Today I'm going to talk about ....
> – I am very interested in ... because ....
> – I can give you an example: ....
> – Did you know that ...?
> – The last part is about ....
> – That's the end of my presentation.
> – Thank you for listening. Do you have any questions?

58/3 ## 4 Give your talk.

→ **M** 1-minute-presentation, p.122

Give your talk to the other students.
They can give you feedback.

> I didn't know that ....
> I didn't understand the part about ....
> Can you say the part about ... again, please?

> Lies deine Notizen nicht einfach vom Blatt ab. Versuche, dich an die wichtigsten Fakten zu erinnern. Vergiss nicht, deine Sätze mit Wörtern wie „first" und „after that" zu verbinden.

Unit 1, page 13

○ **2** **Work with the text.**
1,4 ☞

1 Interviewer: Hello José. Can I ask you some
questions for our magazine, please?
José: Hi. Sure.
Interviewer: You're a new star on one of New
5 York's best baseball teams. Where are you
from?
José: My family is from Cuba.
Interviewer: How long have you lived in the
USA?
10 José: I've lived here for 13 years.
Interviewer: Your parents left their home
country. Was that easy?
José: No, it was a difficult decision. But they
were very poor. My father couldn't find work
15 in Cuba. My parents wanted to give my sister
and me the best opportunities.
Interviewer: What were the first years like for
your family?
José: It was difficult because my parents
20 couldn't speak English well. But other people
from Cuba helped them. Later my parents
opened a small store.

Interviewer: How did you feel?
José: I was a new arrival. Everything was very
25 new and exciting. Later I was sad because
I was homesick. But I got used to life here.
I haven't been homesick for a long time.
Interviewer: You're 23 now. How long have
you played baseball?
30 José: I've played baseball for eight years. I've
had lots of opportunities since 2015. That's
when I became the star of my school team.
Interviewer: You've had a successful career!
José: Yes, I have. My story is a great example
35 of the American Dream. I was a new arrival
and I wanted to be successful. I have been
an American citizen since December last
year. For most people it's much harder.
Interviewer: So, what about your plans?
40 José: Well, I often talk to people in Cuba, and
I'd like to help them.
Interviewer: Thank you, José. Good luck for
the future.

a) What is the text about? Choose the best sentence.

A José talks about baseball and how he came
to Los Angeles.
B José talks about his life, his family and the
American Dream.
C José talks about his family and his favourite music.

Suche im Text nach den Wörtern, die markiert sind. Wenn du sie alle finden kannst, hast du den richtigen Satz.

Unit 1, page 13

3 Life in a different country

a) Match the parts of the sentences.

1. José's parents left Cuba and went to live
2. They were poor and they couldn't find work
3. It was difficult in the USA because they couldn't speak
4. Some people from Cuba
5. Later they opened a small
6. José soon got used to American
7. Last year he became an American

a. in Cuba.
b. life.
c. helped them.
d. English well.
e. in the USA.
f. citizen.
g. store.

Unit 1, page 14

5 (SPEAKING) Talk to your partner. → M Milling around, p.124

a) Make questions and take turns.

A: Have you ever lived in a different country?
B: Yes, I have. / No, I haven't.

B: Have you ever …?
A: Yes, I have. / No, I haven't.

1. lived in a different country?
2. played basketball?
3. visited the USA?
4. talked to an American?
5. been homesick?
6. helped on a farm?

Language → G 1, p.106

I've visited Berlin three times.
Have you ever played baseball?
My brother has worked hard.
Have you ever been to Cuba?

Unit 1, page 15

8 (SPEAKING) How long?

a) Talk to your partner.

	:	watched TV	:	
	:	played football	:	**since** last year / two weeks ago / yesterday.
I haven't	+	visited my friend	+	**for** a year / two weeks / a day.
	:	seen my cousin	:	
	:	bought a new T-shirt	:	

A: I haven't watched TV for two weeks. And you?
B: Really? I've watched TV a lot this week!

_____ **Unit 1, page 17**

○ **3** **Work with the text.** → M Bus stop, p.122

1,6 ⊚

We talked to four young people about life in New York. This is what they told us …

1 Jian: I live in the borough of Queens with my parents and my sister. We moved here when I was four. People of all nationalities live happily together here. There are Chinatowns in Manhattan, Brooklyn and Queens. In some parts of Queens there are street

5 signs in Chinese.

Tamila: I was born in Jamaica, but my family moved to Brooklyn in 2010. Brooklyn is a fantastic place. There are so many cool stores with clothes and shoes. One of my favorite days is Labor Day, in September. There is a parade in Brooklyn on that day. The people in the parade

10 always play music very loudly.

Nikolai: We're from Russia, but we've lived in the USA for ten years. Our apartment is in Harlem, a part of Manhattan. Everyone walks quickly here – Harlem is an awesome place, but it isn't a place for slow people! The food is amazing. There are many different restaurants –

15 Italian, Turkish, Japanese and Spanish. They cook really well here!

Angela: I'm from the Bronx. I was born here, and I've lived here all my life. I live with my mom, my uncle and my cousin. My mom came here from Cuba in the 1980s. She speaks English badly, so we speak Spanish at home. I love it here, but life isn't always easy. People work

20 hard, and some parts of town aren't safe at night. Sometimes we visit the zoo in the Bronx. It's near our apartment.

a) Right, wrong or not in the text?

1. Jian moved to New York when he was 14.
2. New York has more than one Chinatown.
3. The stores in Brooklyn are cool.
4. Tamila has two brothers.
5. Nikolai came to the USA nine years ago.
6. He has a skateboard.
7. Angela has always lived in the Bronx.
8. Her mother came to New York from Italy.

Schau dir die unterstrichenen Sätze im Text genau an. Sie helfen dir, die Lösungen zu finden.

Unit 1, page 17

5 Work with words.

a) Find the opposites.

1. easy ↔ hard
2. quiet ↔ l——
3. interesting ↔ b——
4. cheap ↔ e——
5. slow ↔ f——

6. slow ↔ q——
7. good ↔ b——
8. happy ↔ s——
9. safe ↔ d——

boring   bad   fast
dangerous   sad
hard ✔   loud
expensive   quick

Unit 1, page 18

7 How do they do it?

a) Put in the right words.

badly   happily   loudly ✔   slowly   easily   carefully

1. People in Harlem restaurants often talk loudly.
2. Angela's mother speaks English b——.
3. New Yorkers never walk s——.
4. People from different cultures live h—— together here.
5. You have to walk across the roads in Manhattan very c——.
6. Speak to American people and you can learn English e——.

Sei vorsichtig bei Wörtern wie „careful" und „happy"!
→ carefully
→ happily

Unit 1, page 18

8 New York life

a) Complete the sentences.

quietly   well   quickly ✔   hard   fast   easily

1. Everything happens quickly in New York.
2. It's a great place for music. You can find clubs e——.
3. Bike messengers have to ride their bikes very f——.
4. People work very h—— here. They never stop!
5. But in Central Park you can sit down and read q——.
6. And it's easy to eat w—— in Harlem.

Language → G3, p.108

Beachte: Diese drei Adverbien sind unregelmäßig!

a hard player → she plays hard
a fast player → he runs fast
a good chef → he cooks well

Unit 2, page 33

○ **4 Work with words from the text.**

a) What are the words?

Surfing   waves   bear ✓   flight   woods   lake

1

A <u>bear</u> can be very dangerous.

2

There are many —— in Alaska.

3

The —— are high today.

4

We can sit by the ——.

5

The —— to LA lasts five hours.

6

—— is a popular sport in LA.

Unit 2, page 34

○ **8 What are they doing?**

a) Complete the sentences.

himself   herself   ourselves   yourselves   themselves

1

<u>She</u> is taking a photo of ——.

2

<u>He</u> is looking at ——.

3

<u>They</u> are introducing ——.

4

"<u>We</u> are teaching —— some new tricks."

5

"Did <u>you</u> and your friends enjoy —— ?" "Yes, we did!"

I → myself
you → yourself
he → himself
she → herself
we → ourselves
you → yourselves
they → themselves

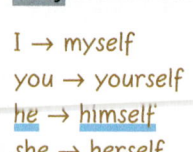

Unit 2, page 37

○ **4 Work with the text.**

1,15 ⌾

1 Jane arrives at the airport in Anchorage at eleven o'clock.

Check-in agent: Hi. Can I see your ticket and passport, please?

5 **Jane:** Hi. I'm flying to LA. The flight leaves at 12:30 p.m.

Check-in agent: I'm afraid your flight is delayed.

Jane: Oh no!

10 **Check-in agent:** I'm very sorry. The plane is coming from Chicago and they've had strong winds. Your flight will leave four hours late.

Jane: Is there anything you can do about it?

Check-in agent: There's a flight to LA at

15 2:30 p.m. I can book you on that flight now.

Jane: Oh yes, please. What time does it land?

Check-in agent: At 8:25 p.m. It departs from gate 43 at 2:30 p.m. The boarding time is 2:00 p.m. Here's your boarding card. Have a

20 good flight!

Jane: Thank you. Goodbye!

The plane lands safely in LA. But there is another problem and Jane has to complain.

Jane: Hi. I've just arrived from Anchorage, but

25 my suitcase isn't here. What can I do about it?

Employee: Well, I can help you with that. But you must tell us what your suitcase looks like and where you're staying.

Jane: I don't believe it! First my flight was

30 delayed, now my suitcase isn't here. I hope the suitcase didn't get lost.

Employee: I'm really sorry, but we'll find your suitcase quickly. We can usually get a suitcase to a passenger the next day, so you don't need

35 to worry. Will you be in LA tomorrow?

Jane: I'll be at my uncle's house in …

a) Match the sentence parts.

1. Jane's flight is delayed
2. It isn't a problem
3. When Jane arrives in LA,
4. The employee can help
5. Jane doesn't need to worry

a. because she will get her suitcase tomorrow.
b. there is another problem.
c. because there are strong winds.
d. because there is another flight.
e. but she needs some information.

Die unterstrichenen Sätze im Text helfen dir, die Lösungen zu finden.

Unit 3, page 57

2 Work with the text.

2,5

BLOG

1 **Leaving Jamaica**   17/06/2020
by Tara Clarke (18)

I heard the noise of a gun in our street again last night. 'That's Kingston,' I thought. I'm really happy
because I'm going to leave Jamaica next month. I'm going to train as a nurse in Canada. Isn't that
5 exciting? What are your plans? Are you going to stay in Jamaica? Tourists think that Jamaica is
beautiful. They spend their time in expensive hotels and on sunny beaches. They think that everyone
is happy, but I disagree. Life isn't always easy in Kingston. There's a lot of violence and there are a lot
of problems with drugs. But there are also some good things here – like my family! They help me to
stay strong, and I can always rely on them. My family will be part of my life forever.

10 **Comments**

Layla: 18/06/2020 at 08:09 a.m.
I'm fed up with the violence here too, Tara You can't avoid it. I'm going to train as a vet's assistant in
Florida in September. I really love animals. My sister is going to move to the USA in September too.
She's going to train as an engineer in Texas. We are going to chat online every day.

15 Aman: 18/06/2020 at 12:15 p.m.
Where are you going to live in Canada, Tara? Family is important to me too. That's why I'm not going
to leave the island. My uncle is a hairdresser in Kingston. I'm going to work in his hairdressing salon
next year. I like talking to people, so it's the right job for me! My brother is going to stay in Jamaica
too. He's going to train as a hotel manager in a few months.

a) Choose the right answers.

1. Tara has found a job in **Canada** · **Kingston**.
2. Kingston has problems with **dirty beaches** · **guns and drugs**.
3. Tara will never forget her **family** · **best friend**.
4. Layla and her sister want to work in **Great Britain** · **the USA**.
5. Aman wants to work with **his father** · **his uncle**.
6. Aman's brother wants to work at a **hotel** · **shop**.

*Die unterstrichenen Sätze im Text
helfen dir, die Lösungen zu finden.*

Unit 3, page 58

○ **7** **What are the plans?**

a) Complete the sentences.

1. Aman is going to <u>play</u> basketball on Saturday.
2. Tara is going to —— her blog on Sunday.
3. Layla's cousins are going to —— to the USA next year.
4. Layla and her sister are going to —— next week.
5. Aman is going to —— his mother later today.
6. Tara and her brother are going to —— a cake tomorrow.

write   call   play ✓

make   go swimming

travel

Unit 3, page 59

○ **9** (WRITING) **Match the questions and answers.**

a) Match the questions with the answers. There are more answers than you need.

1. <u>What are you going to do next year?</u>
2. Where are you going to live?
3. Why are you going to do that job?
4. When are you going to start?
5. Are you going to come home often?

a. Because I like working with people.
b. In September next year.
c. <u>I'm going to train as a hotel manager.</u>
d. Yes, I am. My family is important to me!
e. She's going to train as a chef.
f. I'm going to live in another city.

Schau dir die Fragen genau an. Gibt es ein Fragewort oder kann man mit Ja oder Nein auf die Frage antworten?

Unit 4, page 73

3 Who is it? → M Peer correction, p.125

2,13

1 Josh is at school in Toronto. It's break. He and his friends Emma and Alex are talking about how they use social media.

Josh: My parents say I spend too much time online. I often get updates about Ontario hockey teams on my app. I sometimes watch TV series on my phone too. But my mum and dad watch TV every day. It's not fair!

Alex: I know what you mean. I put some photos online yesterday and my mom got angry. But what's the problem with a few selfies? I'm very careful. I never share information with people who aren't my friends.

Emma: I posted selfies a lot but now I think they're boring. I made a video at the weekend.

Alex: A video? How did you do it?

Emma: I had a film with some birds which were very beautiful. I made it in Banff National Park last summer. I used a song which I really like. I uploaded the video to a music website yesterday.

Josh: Wow! I'd like to do that!

Alex: Yes, it sounds cool.

25 Emma: It isn't difficult. There is free software which is very good. But you have to be careful with songs. They have copyright on them.

Alex: Do you have many followers on the music website?

30 Emma: No, I don't. But I said thanks to a girl who commented on my video. She's from Vancouver. She liked it a lot.

Alex: Videos sound like a lot of work to me! I like watching tutorials – you know, videos

35 that show you how to do something. I used one when I repaired my bike yesterday. The tutorial was great. I think a lot of TV series are too long. They have too many episodes. I often just chat with friends. Or I share funny photos

40 and videos with them on my phone. Oh, it's time to go. What's our next lesson?

Josh: Er, sorry?

Alex: Hey, you don't need your phone now, Josh! Let's go!

a) Put in the names. **Josh** **Alex** **Emma**

1. Alex only shares information with friends.
2. —— gets updates about hockey.
3. —— used a tutorial about bikes yesterday.
4. —— made a video about a trip.
5. —— would like to make a video.
6. —— thinks selfies are boring.
7. —— spends too much time online (maybe!).

Die unterstrichenen Sätze im Text helfen dir, die Lösungen zu finden.

_____ Unit 4, page 73

○ **4** **Work with the words from the text.**

a) Put in the right words.

commented · episodes · chat · tutorial ✔ · uploaded · share

1. A <u>tutorial</u> shows you how to do something.
2. Emma u——— a video to a website yesterday.
3. A girl c——— on the video.
4. People often s——— funny photos and videos.
5. Alex uses his phone to c——— with friends.
6. TV series often have a lot of e——— .

_____ Unit 4, page 74

○ **8** (SPEAKING) **What are the people and things?** → **M** Bus stop, p.122

a) Look at the photos and the sentences with a partner. Put in <u>who</u> or <u>which</u>.

1 A Canadian is a person <u>who</u> comes from Canada.

2 A moose is an animal ——— lives in the wilderness.

3 Toronto is a city ——— is near the US border.

4 A chef is a person ——— works at a restaurant.

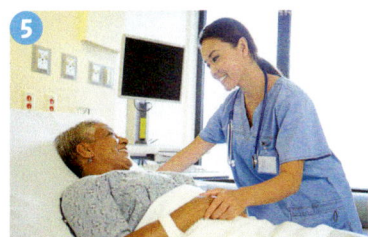

5 A nurse is someone ——— works at a hospital.

6 Nunavut is a place ——— is in the north of Canada.

people → who
things and animals → which

Unit 4, page 75

○ **9** (WRITING) **Write about photos from a trip to Bavaria.**

a) Complete the sentences for these photos from a social media site. Use <u>who</u> or <u>which</u>.

1. This is the bus <u>which</u> took us to the youth hostel.

This is the bus —— took us to the youth hostel.

This is the guide —— showed us the sights.

This is a photo —— I took on the second day.

This is a shop —— sells cool T-shirts.

This is a Canadian girl —— we met.

This is a castle —— is very old.

Vergiss nicht! Für Dinge und Tiere verwendest du „which". Für Personen verwendest du „who"!

Unit 4, page 77

○ **3** **What's the word?**

a) What is it? Choose the right answers.

1. A <u>salary</u> • scenery is the money that someone gets for a job.
2. A PE • **CV** has more information about a person who wants a job.
3. An **interview** • internship is a job for a few weeks or months.
4. When you **apply** • answer, you write and say that you want a job.
5. A **receptionist** • reservation is a person who answers phone calls and helps at a hotel.
6. A travel report • **travel agent's** is a shop which sells flights and holidays.

Unit 4, page 77

○ **4** (WRITING) **Work with a letter of application.**

a) Copy the letter of application. Complete the words.

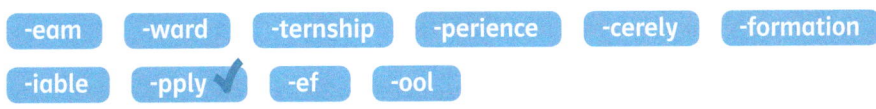

-eam　　-ward　　-ternship　　-perience　　-cerely　　-formation

-iable　　-pply ✓　　-ef　　-ool

E-MAIL

Dear Mrs Walker,

I would like to apply (1) for the job as a chef at Monte Carlo Restaurant.

I finished sch—— (2) one and a half years ago and did an in—— (3) at a café. Then I trained as a ch—— (4) at a restaurant. I got a lot of ex—— (5) there.

I am a rel—— (6) person and I like working in a t—— (7).

You will find more in—— (8) in my CV.

I look for—— (9) to hearing from you.

Yours sin—— (10),

Martin Henderson

Unit 4, page 79

○ **8** (SPEAKING) **Work with a partner. Make comparisons.**

a) Compare the jobs. Choose the right answers.

1 　　**2** 　　**3**

	Helen, hairdresser	Lisa, assistant	Marc, receptionist
journey to work (long)	15 minutes	45 minutes	15 minutes
team (large)	6 people	6 people	8 people
salary (high)	+	++	++

1. Helen's journey to work is **as long as** · **not as long** as Marc's.
2. Lisa's team is **as large as** · **not as large** as Marc's.
3. Helen's salary is **as high as** · **not as high as** Lisa's.
4. Lisa's team is **as large as** · **not as large** as Helen's.
5. Marc's journey to work is **as long as** · **not as long** as Lisa's.
6. Lisa's salary is **as high as** · **not as high as** Marc's.

Grammar

G1

Mit **G** sind die Grammatikkapitel gekennzeichnet und der Reihe nach durchnummeriert. Eine Übersicht über alle Themen findest du auf der nächsten Seite.

Beim Lupen-Symbol findest du Besonderheiten und Tipps.

(TEST YOURSELF)

Am Ende eines jeden Grammatikkapitels kannst du ausprobieren, ob du alles verstanden hast.
Die Lösungen dazu findest du auf S.119.

R = Revision (Wiederholung)

	Englisch	Deutsch	Beispiel	Seite
G1	present perfect – for and since	Perfekt – for und since	We have lived in Munich for 15 years.	106
G2	**R:** simple past	einfache Vergangenheit	I was lucky last Saturday. • I won two tickets for a concert in Munich.	107
G3	adverbs	Adverbien	I always drive carefully.	108
G4	**R:** simple present	einfache Gegenwart	How much does the ticket cost? • It costs € 5.	109
G5	reflexive pronouns – myself, yourself, …	Reflexivpronomen	We enjoyed ourselves very much. • I hurt myself yesterday.	110

G6	**R:** word order
	– SVO
	– word order with
	  – place
	  – time
	  – adverbs of manner
		Satzstellung
		– SVO
		– Angaben
		  – des Ortes
		  – der Zeit
		  – der Art und Weise
			We booked two flights on the internet last weekend. • They have planned their trip carefully. • The plane landed safely at 7:00 p.m.	111

G7	simple present (future meaning)	einfache Gegenwart für Zukünftiges	My train leaves at 12:30 p.m. and arrives at 3:00 p.m. tomorrow.	112
G8	expressions of quantity – much, many – (a) few, (a) little	Mengenangaben	I have many friends but only a little money.	113
G9	**R:** going to-future – statements – negatives – questions – short answers	Zukunft mit going to – Aussagen – verneinte Sätze – Fragen – Kurzantworten	Are you going to work in another country? • No, I'm not. • I'm going to stay in Germany.	114
G10	**R:** adjectives: comparative and superlative forms	Adjektive: 1. und 2. Steigerung	Swimming is easier than canoeing. • Rock climbing is the most exciting activity.	115
G11	passive voice – simple present – simple past	Passiv – einfache Gegenwart – einfache Vergangenheit	A lot of T-shirts are made in India. • I was born in Hof.	116
G12	defining relative clauses	Relativsätze mit who, which, that	Mr Hunt is an actor who is very funny.	117
G13	adjectives – comparative forms with (not) as … as	Adjektive – Vergleiche mit (not) as … as	Sarah is as confident as her sister.	118

Unit 1

G1 Das Perfekt mit for und since

The present perfect with for and since

Wenn eine Handlung in der Vergangenheit beginnt und in der Gegenwart zu einem Ergebnis führt, verwendest du das **present perfect**:
have/haven't oder **has/hasn't** (bei he, she, it) +
3. Form des Verbs (past participle).
Bei den meisten Verben hängst du für die 3. Form ein **-ed** an das Verb, z.B. help – help**ed**

Einige Verben haben unregelmäßige
3. Formen, z.B. be – **been**; write – **written**

Signalwörter	
already	schon
just	gerade
not ... yet	noch nicht
never	noch nie
ever (in Fragen)	jemals (in Fragen)
since	seit (Zeitpunkt)
for	seit (Zeitspanne)

Eine Liste der unregelmäßigen Verben findest du auf S. 120–121.

I **have** just **talked** to Dave.	Ich **habe gerade** mit Dave gesprochen.
She **has** already **worked** as a doctor.	Sie **hat** schon als Ärztin **gearbeitet**.
We **haven't been** to Thailand yet.	Wir **sind** noch **nicht** in Thailand **gewesen**.

Have you ever **been** homesick?	Yes, I **have**.	No, I **haven't**.
Has your friend ever **played** baseball?	Yes, she **has**.	No, she **hasn't**.

Present perfect mit for (seit) und since (seit):
since verwendest du vor einem **Zeitpunkt**, z.B. **since** 5:00 p.m., **since** July, **since** I was young etc.
for verwendest du vor einer **Zeitspanne**, z.B. **for** one hour, **for** two years, **for** a long time etc.

I haven't seen Zoe **since** Monday.	Ich habe Zoe **seit** Montag nicht gesehen.
I haven't seen Zoe **for** a week.	Ich habe Zoe **seit** einer Woche nicht gesehen.

(TEST YOURSELF) **Put the verbs in the present perfect. Choose for or since.**

1. I —— (live) in Cuba **since • for** 2010.
2. Lia —— (not see) Tom **since • for** a year.
3. My parents —— (work) **since • for** I was five.
4. Mum —— (be) in NYC **since • for** a week.
5. —— you —— (talk) to Mia **since • for** yesterday?
6. How long —— you —— (play) basketball? **Since • For** 2015.

G2 R: Die einfache Vergangenheit

Revision: The simple past

Do you remember?

Um über Dinge zu sprechen, die in der Vergangenheit passiert und vorbei sind, verwendest du das **simple past**.

Das **simple past** bildest du so:
Hänge die Endung **-ed** an das Verb.
Achte auf unregelmäßige Verben, z.B.
do → **did**; get → **got**; go → **went**.

Signalwörter	
yesterday	gestern
last month	letzten Monat
a week ago	vor einer Woche
in 2010	2010

Eine Liste der unregelmäßigen Verben findest du auf S. 120–121.

Tom help**ed** his parents last week.	Letzte Woche hat Tom seinen Eltern geholfen.
He **took** the bus to school yesterday.	Er hat gestern den Bus zur Schule genommen.

Um zu sagen, was nicht passiert ist, setzt du **didn't** (= did not) vor das Verb.

I **didn't watch** the match yesterday.	Ich habe das Spiel gestern nicht angeschaut.
Tom's parents **didn't like** Sunderland.	Toms Eltern hat Sunderland nicht gefallen.

Aussagen und Verneinungen mit **be** bildest du so:

I **was** in Berlin. I **wasn't** at home.	Ich war in Berlin. Ich war nicht zu Hause.
José **wasn't** here. He **was** at work.	José war nicht hier. Er war bei der Arbeit.
The students **were** at the club yesterday.	Die Schüler waren gestern im Klub.
They **weren't** at the workshop.	Sie waren nicht im Workshop.

Und so kannst du im **simple past** Fragen stellen und beantworten:

Did you **have** a nice weekend?	Yes, I **did.**	No, I **didn't.**
When **did** you **visit** your aunt?	I **visited** her last month.	
Were you at home?	Yes, I **was.**	No, I **wasn't.**
Was Sarah in New York?	Yes, she **was.**	No, she **wasn't.**
Were your parents at the match?	Yes, they **were.**	No, they **weren't.**

(TEST YOURSELF) **Put the verbs in the simple past.**

1. Malee —— (arrive) here a week ago.
2. I —— (not go) to New York last year.
3. —— you —— (have) a nice day?
4. What —— you —— (do) yesterday?
5. José —— (not be) at home last Friday.
6. —— (be) you in the USA in 2017?

G3 Adverbien

Adverbs

I'm a careful bat. I stopped quickly when I saw the red light.

Ich bin eine vorsichtige Fledermaus. Ich habe schnell angehalten, als ich die rote Ampel sah.

Ein **Adjektiv** beschreibt, wie etwas ist. Es beschreibt eine Person oder eine Sache.

New York is a **fantastic city.**	New York ist eine **fantastische Stadt.**
Ann is **happy.**	Ann ist **glücklich.**

Ein **Adverb** beschreibt, wie jemand etwas tut oder wie etwas geschieht.
Man erkennt Adverbien durch ein angehängtes **-ly.**

People like to **walk quickly.**	Die Leute **gehen** gerne **schnell.**
Speak slowly, please.	**Sprich** bitte **langsam.**

 Achtung Schreibweise: happy – happ**ily,** easy – eas**ily,** angry – angr**ily,**
careful – careful**ly,** fantastic – fantasti**cally**

They **live** together **happily.**	Sie **leben glücklich** zusammen.

Es gibt auch unregelmäßige Adverbien. Aus **good** wird **well.**
Manche Adverbien, wie z.B. **hard** und **fast,** verändern sich nicht. Vergleiche:

Your **English is good.**	(Adjektiv)	Dein **Englisch ist gut.**
You **can speak** English **well.**	(Adverb)	Du **kannst gut** Englisch **sprechen.**
Life in New York **is** very **fast.**	(Adjektiv)	Das **Leben** in New York **ist** sehr **schnell.**
People there **walk** so **fast.**	(Adverb)	Die Leute dort **gehen** so **schnell.**
That **was** a **hard day.**	(Adjektiv)	Das **war** ein **harter Tag.**
We **work hard** every day.	(Adverb)	Wir **arbeiten** jeden Tag **hart.**

(TEST YOURSELF) **Choose the correct word.**

1. I don't like to walk —— (quick/quickly).
2. Central Park is a —— (quiet/quietly) place.
3. You can —— (easy/easily) see the sights on foot.
4. I am always —— (careful/carefully).
5. My friend can cook very —— (good/well).
6. The Italian restaurant has very —— (good/well) food.

G4 R: Die einfache Gegenwart

Revision: The simple present

Do you remember?

Du kennst schon das **simple present**. Du benutzt es, um einen Zustand zu beschreiben oder um zu sagen, dass etwas gewohnheitsmäßig, regelmäßig oder häufig geschieht.

He she, it, das **s** muss mit!

Signalwörter
every Monday, ...
always
usually
often
sometimes
never

So bildest du das **simple present** mit <u>Vollverben</u>, z.B.:

Aussagen	I **live** in Munich.	Ich **lebe** in München.
	He never **works** on Saturdays.	Er **arbeitet** samstags nie.
	We often **eat** fish and rice.	Wir **essen** oft Fisch und Reis.
Verneinte Aussagen	I **don't live** in the country.	Ich **wohne nicht** auf dem Land.
	She **doesn't have** time.	Sie **hat keine** Zeit.
	Some people **don't like** milk.	Einige Menschen **mögen keine** Milch.
Fragen	**Do** you **like** your town?	**Magst** du deine Stadt?
	Does he **sleep** enough?	**Schläft** er genug?
	Where **do** you **live**?	Wo **wohnst** du?
	How much **does** it **cost**?	Wie viel **kostet** es?

So bildest du das **simple present** mit <u>be</u>, z.B.:

Aussagen	The castle **is** near here.	Die Burg **ist** hier in der Nähe.
	My friends **are** in a sports club.	Meine Freunde **sind** in einem Sportverein.
Verneinte Aussagen	I'**m not** from Bavaria.	Ich **bin nicht** aus Bayern.
	The campsite **isn't** cheap.	Der Campingplatz **ist nicht** billig.
	They'**re not/aren't** at school.	Sie **sind nicht** in der Schule.
Fragen	**Are** you happy?	**Bist** du / **Seid** ihr glücklich?
	Where **is** my bag?	Wo **ist** meine Tasche?

(TEST YOURSELF) **Put the verbs in the simple present.**

1. We never —— (go) on holiday by plane.
2. Sam always —— (book) his trips very early.
3. The campsite —— (be) near a farm.
4. —— (be) there any brochures about the city?
5. My best friend —— (not eat) fish.
6. —— you —— (like) rock climbing?
7. What —— visitors usually —— (ask) at the campsite?

Unit 2

G5 Reflexivpronomen

Reflexive pronouns

I have hurt myself.

Ich habe mir wehgetan.

Im Englischen werden Reflexivpronomen mit **-self** oder **-selves** gebildet. Sie beziehen sich zurück auf die Person oder das Tier. Im Deutschen werden sie meist mit „mir" oder „mich", „dir" oder „dich", „sich" usw. übersetzt.

I'll give **myself** two days to learn it.	Ich gebe **mir** zwei Tage, um es zu lernen.
Can **you** see **yourself** in the window?	Kannst **du dich** im Fenster sehen?
He taught **himself** to play the trumpet.	**Er** hat **sich** das Trompetespielen beigebracht.
She asked **herself** why it happened.	**Sie** hat **sich** gefragt, warum es passiert ist.
The cat has hurt **itself**.	**Die Katze** hat **sich** verletzt.
We are enjoying **ourselves** very much.	**Wir** haben viel Spaß.
Introduce **yourselves**, please.	Bitte stellt **euch vor**!
They hurt **themselves** at the match.	**Sie** haben **sich** beim Spiel verletzt.

I	hurt	myself.	He	hurt	himself.	We	hurt	ourselves.
You	hurt	yourself.	She	hurt	herself.	You	hurt	yourselves.
			It	hurt	itself.	They	hurt	themselves.

(TEST YOURSELF) **Put in a right reflexive pronoun.**

1. I asked —— where my bag was.
2. We enjoyed —— at the cinema last night.
3. The woman hurt —— in the accident.
4. Did you teach —— to play the trumpet?
5. Lia and Joe saw —— in the video.
6. Tom introduced —— at the party.

G6 R: Satzstellung mit Angaben des Ortes, der Zeit und der Art und Weise

Revision: Word order with words of place, time and manner

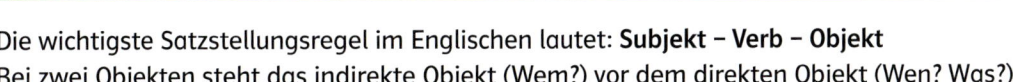

Do you remember?

Die wichtigste Satzstellungsregel im Englischen lautet: **Subjekt – Verb – Objekt**
Bei zwei Objekten steht das indirekte Objekt (Wem?) vor dem direkten Objekt (Wen? Was?).

Subjekt	Verb	Indirektes Objekt (Wem?)	Direktes Objekt (Wen? Was?)	
I	booked		two flights.	*Ich habe zwei Flüge gebucht.*
Chris	showed	me	the beach.	*Chris hat mir den Strand gezeigt.*

Eine weitere Satzstellungsregel lautet: **Ort vor Zeit** (place before time).

Subjekt	Verb	Objekt	Ort	Zeit	
She	left	her phone	in the café	yesterday.	*Sie hat gestern ihr Handy im Café liegen lassen.*

The plane landed   **in Los Angeles**   **at 10:30 p.m.**

Ortsangabe   Zeitangabe

Eine **genaue** Angabe steht immer **vor einer ungenauen** Angabe:
Ort: Jane got <u>to the airport</u> in Anchorage.   **Zeit:** She arrived <u>at 3:00 p.m.</u> on Monday.

Zeitangaben können auch am Satzanfang stehen. Vergleiche:
I'll fly to Anchorage **next week.**   **Next week** I'll fly to Anchorage.

Adverbien der Art und Weise können **am Ende** des Satzes, **aber** auch **vor** einer **Orts-** oder einer **Zeitangabe** stehen. Das gilt auch für **Fragen.**

You should go to gate 4 **quickly.**	Sie sollten **schnell** zum Gate 4 **gehen.**
You can book flights **easily** on the internet.	Du kannst Flüge **einfach** im Internet buchen.
She arrived **happily** at the airport yesterday.	Sie ist gestern **glücklich** am Flughafen angekommen.
Did you sleep **well?**	Hast du **gut** geschlafen?

(TEST YOURSELF) **Put the words in the right order.**

1. last August • They • in Chicago • had • very bad weather
2. on • another flight • you • We • can book
3. to Los Angeles • departs • at 2:30 p.m. • from gate B6 • The next flight
4. safely • landed • The plane • in LA • in the evening
5. Jane • back • quickly • the money • can get
6. the taxi driver • Did • carefully • to the airport • drive • ?

G7 Die einfache Gegenwart für Zukünftiges

The simple present (future meaning)

Du kennst schon das **simple present**. Du benutzt es, wenn du sagen möchtest, dass etwas gewohnheitsmäßig, regelmäßig oder häufig geschieht. Vergleiche G4.

He, she, it, das **s** muss mit!

Das **simple present** kannst du auch verwenden, wenn du über feste Termine **in der Zukunft** sprechen willst, z. B. über genaue Zeitangaben aus **Fahrplänen**, **Programmen**, **Stundenplänen** usw.

Our plane **arrives** at 9:00 a.m. tomorrow.	Unser Flugzeug **kommt** morgen um 9 Uhr **an**.
Your flight **departs** at 10:15 a.m. next Monday.	Ihr Flug **geht** nächsten Montag um 10:15 Uhr.
The film **starts** at the club house at 6:00 p.m.	Der Film **beginnt** um 18 Uhr im Klubhaus.
We **don't have** English on Friday.	Wir **haben** am Freitag kein Englisch.
The next train **doesn't stop** in Ulm.	Der nächste Zug **hat keinen Aufenthalt** in Ulm.
Do you **have** PE tomorrow?	**Hast** du morgen Sport(unterricht)?
Does the bus **go** to the airport?	**Fährt** der Bus zum Flughafen?
What time **does** your plane **land** in LA next Saturday?	Wann **landet** dein Flugzeug nächsten Samstag in LA?
When **does** the next train **leave**?	Wann **geht** der nächste Zug?

(TEST YOURSELF) **Put the verbs in the simple present.**

1. Your bus —— (depart) at 11:00 a.m. tomorrow.
2. My train to Munich —— (not stop) in Ulm.
3. Our boarding time —— (be) 6:30 a.m.
4. When —— your plane —— (land) in Frankfurt?
5. We —— (not have) Maths next Monday.
6. There —— (not be) any English lessons next week.
7. The football match —— (start) at 3:00 p.m. on Saturday.
8. When —— the first bus —— (leave) tomorrow?

Unit 3

G8 Mengenangaben: much, many, (a) few, (a) little

Expressions of quantity

Du kennst schon die Mengenangaben **much** und **many**.

Many (viele) verwendest du bei **zählbaren Nomen** in der Mehrzahl, z. B. boys, ideas, trees etc.

Many Americans travel a lot.	**Viele Amerikaner** reisen viel.

Much (viel) verwendest du bei **nicht zählbaren Nomen**, z. B. time, water, rain, money etc.

I don't have **much time**.	Ich habe nicht **viel Zeit**.
We had so **much rain** last summer.	Wir hatten so **viel Regen** letzten Sommer.

Wenn du nur von **einigen**, **ein paar** oder von **ein wenig**, **ein bisschen** sprechen möchtest, benutzt du **a few** oder **a little**.

a few – zählbare Nomen im Plural einige, ein paar
a little – nicht zählbare Nomen im Singular ein wenig, ein bisschen, etwas

I met **a few friends**.	Ich habe **ein paar Freunde** getroffen.
The dog needs **a little water**.	Der Hund braucht **ein bisschen Wasser**.
How many people were at the party?	**Wie viele Leute** waren auf der Party?
– Only **a few**.	– Nur **ein paar**.
How much money do you have?	**Wie viel Geld** hast du?
– Only **a little**.	– Nur **ein bisschen**.

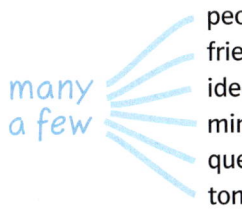

Das **a** kann man auch weglassen: **few** – sehr wenige   **little** – sehr wenig

I bought **few cards**.	Ich habe **sehr wenige Karten** gekauft.
There's **little cake** left.	Es ist **sehr wenig Kuchen** übrig.

(TEST YOURSELF) **Put in much or many (▲), or a few or a little (★).**

1. I don't eat —— sweets. (▲)
2. Do you need —— help? (★)
3. There were so —— people at the club. (▲)
4. Sorry, my bus was —— minutes late. (★)
5. I don't have —— time to cook. (▲)
6. There was only —— snow this winter. (★)

G9 R: Die Zukunft mit going to

Revision: The going to-future

Do you remember?

Mit dem **going to-future** sagst du, was du in der Zukunft vorhast, planst, beabsichtigst zu tun.

Aussagen im **going to-future** bildest du so: **am/are/is + going to + Verb**

I **am (I'm) going to train** as a nurse.	Ich **werde** eine Ausbildung zur Krankenschwester **machen**.
You **are (You're) going to work** in a café.	Du **wirst** in einem Café **arbeiten**.
Tara **is (She's) going to leave** Jamaica soon.	Tara **verlässt** Jamaika bald.
We **are (We're) going to live** in Toronto.	Wir **werden** in Toronto **leben**.
They **are (They're) going to start** their own snack bar.	Sie **werden** ihre eigene Imbissstube **eröffnen**.

So bildest du verneinte Sätze im **going to-future**:

I **am (I'm) not going to leave** Jamaica.	Ich **werde** Jamaika **nicht verlassen**.
She **is (She's) not going to work** as a vet.	Sie **wird nicht** als Tierärztin **arbeiten**.
They **are (They're) not going to stay** here.	Sie **werden nicht** hier **bleiben**.

Fragen im going to-future bildest du, indem du **am, are** oder **is an den Satzanfang** stellst. **Fragewörter** stehen noch davor am Satzanfang.

Are you **going to work** in a hotel?	**Wirst** du in einem Hotel **arbeiten**?
Yes, I am. / No, I'm not.	Ja. / Nein.
Is Nick **going to leave** Germany?	**Plant** Nick Deutschland **zu verlassen**?
Yes, he is. / No, he isn't.	Ja. / Nein.
Where are they **going to live**?	Wo **werden** sie **leben**?
When are you **going to come back**?	Wann **wirst** du **zurückkommen**?

 Aufgepasst bei Sätzen und Fragen mit dem Verb **go**!

I'm **going to go** to the USA.	Ich **werde** in die USA **gehen**.
I'm **going** to the cinema.	Ich **gehe gerade** ins Kino.

(TEST YOURSELF) **Put the verbs in the going to-future. Give short answers to questions 5. and 6. (☺ = Yes. ☹ = No.).**

1. I —— (fly) to Jamaica soon.
2. Layla and I —— (train) in the USA.
3. They —— (not visit) the museum.
4. Luke and Tim —— (not sleep) in a tent.
5. —— you —— (help) in your aunt's salon? (☹)
6. —— Tom —— (play) football on Saturday? (☺)
7. Where —— you —— (stay) in Munich?
8. What —— you —— (do) next weekend?

G10 R: Adjektive: 1. und 2. Steigerung

Revision: Adjectives: comparative and superlative forms

Do you remember?

Ein **Adjektiv** beschreibt eine **Person** oder eine **Sache**, z. B.:

You can meet really **nice people** at the camp. There are a lot of **exciting** activities.

Um Personen oder Dinge miteinander zu vergleichen, brauchst du die Steigerungsformen.

Adjektive mit einer Silbe steigerst du mit **-er/-est**.
Zweisilbige Adjektive, die auf **-y** enden, steigerst du auch mit **-er/-est**.
Alle anderen Adjektive mit zwei oder mehr Silben steigerst du mit **more** und **most**.

long, long**er**, the long**est**	lang, länger, am längsten
easy, eas**ier**, the eas**iest**	leicht, leichter, am leichtesten
expensive, **more** expensive, the **most** expensive	teuer, teurer, am teuersten

Achtung Schreibweise: big, big**ger**, the big**gest**   groß, größer, am größten
                                   nice, nic**er**, the nic**est**   schön, schöner, am schönsten

Unregelmäßige Steigerungsformen: good, **better**, the **best** und: bad, **worse**, the **worst**

Fmily's plans are the **best**.	Emilys Pläne sind **am besten**.
Horse riding is **worse than** rock climbing.	Reiten ist **schlimmer als** Klettern.

Und so kannst du ausdrücken, dass etwas weniger oder am wenigsten ist:

exciting, **less** exciting, the **least** exciting	aufregend, **weniger** aufregend, **am wenigsten** aufregend

So vergleichst du **Personen** und **Dinge** miteinander:

Max is **younger than** the rest of the team.	Max ist **jünger als** der Rest des Teams.
Rafting is **more exciting than** canoeing.	Rafting ist **aufregender als** Kanufahren.
Cycling is **less exciting than** rock climbing.	Radfahren ist **weniger aufregend als /** **nicht so aufregend wie** Klettern.
Swimming is the **most boring** thing.	Schwimmen ist die **langweiligste** Sache.

(TEST YOURSELF) **Compare the things. In some sentences (♦) two solutions are possible.**

1. Amy's bag is —— (nice) than Vicky's. (♦)
2. Our team is not —— (bad) than their team.
3. My suitcase is —— (heavy) than yours. (♦)
4. Our activities are —— (exciting) than yours. (♦)
5. The activities this year are the —— (good) ever.
6. Rafting is the —— (interesting) activity. (♦)

Unit 4

G11 Das Passiv

The passive voice (simple present and simple past)

This smartphone was made for bats. It's great!

Dieses Smartphone wurde für Fledermäuse gemacht. Es ist klasse!

Mit dem **Passiv** kannst du über eine Handlung Auskunft geben, ohne zu sagen, wer die Handlung ausführt. Im Vordergrund steht die Handlung. Passivsätze gibt es wie Aktivsätze in allen Zeiten!

Eine Liste der unregelmäßigen Verben findest du auf Seite 120–121.

So bildest du das **Passiv** im **simple present:**
am/are/is + 3. **Form** des Verbs (past participle)

This website **is used** very often.	Diese Website **wird** oft **benutzt.**
Some videos **are used** at school.	Einige Videos **werden** in der Schule **benutzt.**
English **is spoken** in a lot of countries.	In vielen Ländern **wird** Englisch **gesprochen.**

So bildest du das **Passiv** im **simple past: was/were + 3. Form** des Verbs (past participle)

Our school **was built** 20 years ago.	Unsere Schule **wurde** vor 20 Jahren **gebaut.**
A lot of photos **were taken.**	Viele Fotos **wurden gemacht.**
I **was born** in Canada.	Ich **wurde** in Kanada **geboren.**

Willst du in einem Passivsatz sagen, **wer** die Handlung ausführt, ergänzt du ihn oder sie mit **by.**

The tutorial **was made by** people who know a lot.	Das Tutorial **wurde von** Leuten **erstellt,** die viel Ahnung haben.
My video **was commented on by** a girl from Vancouver.	Mein Video **wurde von** einem Mädchen aus Vancouver **kommentiert.**

(TEST YOURSELF) **Use the passive voice, simple present or simple past.**

1. A lot of selfies —— (post) every day.
2. This programme —— (sell) on the internet.
3. The end of the series —— (show) last night.
4. Tutorials —— (use) by a lot of people.
5. The company's website —— (close) yesterday.
6. Tablets —— (use) in nearly all lessons.

G12 Relativsätze mit who, which, that

Defining relative clauses

Here are the things which I need for my breakfast.

Hier sind die Sachen, die ich für mein Frühstück brauche.

Wenn du eine **Person** oder eine **Sache** genauer beschreiben willst, verwendest du die Relativpronomen **who** oder **which**.

who → *Personen*

I never share private information with **people who** aren't my friends.
A chef is **someone who** cooks food.
Emma has good **software which** is free.
A tutorial is **a video which** gives you advice.

which → *Dinge*

Ich teile nie private Informationen mit **Leuten**, **die** nicht meine Freunde sind.
Ein Koch ist **jemand**, **der** Essen kocht.
Emma hat gute **Software**, **die** umsonst ist.
Ein Tutorial ist **ein Video**, **das** dir Rat gibt.

Fragen mit Relativpronomen bildest du so:

Is this **the boy who** helped you?
Do you know **the people who** want to sell the computer?

Ist das **der Junge**, **der** dir geholfen hat?
Kennst du **die Leute**, **die** den Computer verkaufen wollen?

Statt **who** oder **which** kannst du auch einfach **that** benutzen:

I know a lot of English songs **which/that** are difficult to understand.

The Inuit are a group of people **who/that** have lived in Canada for over 14,000 years.

(TEST YOURSELF) **Choose who or which.**

1. I'll show you the shop —— (who/which) sells the best food.
2. Hockey is a sport —— (who/which) is popular in Canada.
3. We know a lot of teens —— (who/which) post selfies every day.
4. A nurse is a person —— (who/which) works in a hospital.
5. Where is the book —— (who/which) I gave you?
6. My best friend is someone —— (who/which) laughs a lot.

G13 Adjektive: Vergleiche mit (not) as … as

Adjectives: comparative forms with (not) as … as

Ein **Adjektiv** beschreibt eine **Person** oder eine **Sache**, z. B.: Emma is a **clever** girl.

Toronto is an **amazing** city.

Um Personen oder Dinge miteinander zu vergleichen, brauchst du Adjektive und die Steigerungsformen für Adjektive, siehe auch G10.

Gleiches

vergleichst du mit

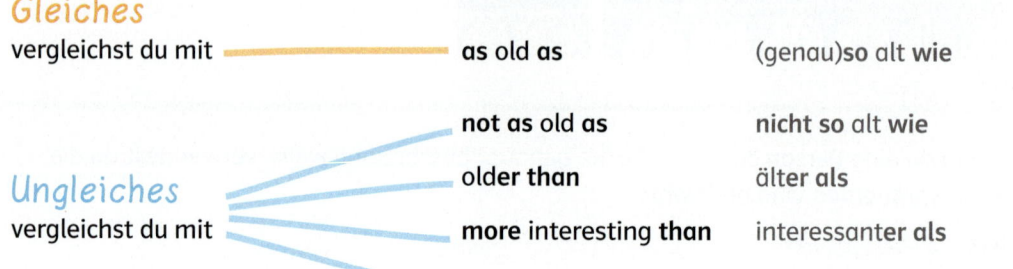

as old **as**	(genau)**so** alt **wie**

Ungleiches

vergleichst du mit

not as old **as**	**nicht so** alt **wie**
old**er than**	älter **als**
more interesting **than**	interessanter **als**
less interesting **than**	**weniger** interessant **als**, **nicht so** interessant **wie**

Derek is **as** old **as** Robin.	Derek ist **so** alt **wie** Robin.
Sarah is **as** reliable **as** her sister.	Sarah ist **so** zuverlässig **wie** ihre Schwester.
Jack is **not as** big **as** Marc.	Jack ist **nicht so** groß **wie** Marc.
He is **not as** confident **as** Marc.	Er ist **nicht so** selbstbewusst **wie** Marc.
He is **younger than** the rest of the team.	Er ist **jünger als** der Rest des Teams.
And he is **more reliable than** Marc.	Und er ist **zuverlässiger als** Marc.
Marc's job is **less dangerous than** Joe's job.	Marcs Job ist **weniger gefährlich als** Joes.

(TEST YOURSELF) **Make comparisons. In some sentences (♦) two solutions are possible.**

1. Sarah's salary is —— (high) as Emma's.
2. Derek's train ticket was not —— (expensive) as Lisa's.
3. My team is not —— (big) as your team.
4. You are —— (confident) than Jack. (♦)

5. My computer skills are —— (bad) than yours. (♦)
6. Sue's team skills are not —— (good) as Julia's.
7. Tara is —— (reliable) than Jack. (♦)
8. My friend has a —— (long) journey to work than I have. (♦)

Lösungen

G1
1. have / 've lived; since
2. has not / hasn't seen; for
3. have worked; since
4. has been; for
5. Have … talked; since
6. have … played; Since

G2
1. arrived
2. did not / didn't go
3. Did … have
4. did … do
5. was not / wasn't
6. Were

G3
1. quickly
2. quiet
3. easily
4. careful
5. well
6. good

G4
1. go
2. books
3. is
4. Are
5. does not / doesn't eat
6. Do … like
7. do … ask

G5
1. myself
2. ourselves
3. herself
4. yourself / yourselves
5. themselves
6. himself

G6
1. They had very bad weather in Chicago last August.
2. We can book you on another flight.
3. The next flight to Los Angeles departs from gate B6 at 2:30 p.m.
4. The plane landed safely in LA in the evening.
5. Jane can get the money back quickly.
6. Did the taxi driver drive carefully to the airport? / Did the taxi driver drive to the airport carefully?

G7
1. departs
2. does not / doesn't stop
3. is
4. does … land
5. do not / don't have
6. are not / aren't

7. starts
8. does … leave

G8
1. many
2. a little
3. many
4. a few
5. much
6. a little

G9
1. am / 'm going to fly
2. are going to train
3. are not / aren't going to visit
4. are not / aren't going to sleep
5. Are … going to help; No, I'm not.
6. Is … going to play; Yes, he is.
7. are … going to stay
8. are … going to do

G10
1. nicer / less nice
2. worse
3. heavier / less heavy
4. more / less exciting
5. best
6. most / least interesting

G11
1. are posted
2. is sold
3. was shown
4. are used
5. was closed
6. are used

G12
1. which (that)
2. which (that)
3. who (that)
4. who (that)
5. which (that)
6. who (that)

G13
1. as high
2. as expensive
3. as big
4. more / less confident
5. worse / less bad
6. as good
7. more / less reliable
8. longer / less long

List of irregular verbs

Hier findest du alle unregelmäßigen Verben, die im Buch vorkommen. Die Liste enthält jeweils alle drei Formen, auch wenn sie noch nicht alle in den Units vorgekommen sind.

infinitive	simple past	past participle	German
to be [biː]	was, were [wɒz, wɜː]	been [biːn]	sein
to become [bɪˈkʌm]	became [bɪˈkeɪm]	become [bɪˈkʌm]	werden
to bring [brɪŋ]	brought [brɔːt]	brought [brɔːt]	bringen; mitbringen
to build [bɪld]	built [bɪlt]	built [bɪlt]	bauen
to buy [baɪ]	bought [bɔːt]	bought [bɔːt]	kaufen
to catch [kætʃ]	caught [kɔːt]	caught [kɔːt]	fangen; nehmen
to choose [tʃuːz]	chose [tʃəʊz]	chosen [ˈtʃəʊzn]	wählen; auswählen
to come [kʌm]	came [keɪm]	come [kʌm]	kommen
to cost [kɒst]	cost [kɒst]	cost [kɒst]	kosten
to do [duː]	did [dɪd]	done [dʌn]	machen; tun
to drink [drɪŋk]	drank [dræŋk]	drunk [drʌŋk]	trinken
to drive [draɪv]	drove [drəʊv]	driven [ˈdrɪvn]	fahren; treiben
to eat [iːt]	ate [eɪt]	eaten [ˈiːtn]	essen
to fall [fɔːl]	fell [fel]	fallen [ˈfɔːln]	fallen
to feed [fiːd]	fed [fed]	fed [fed]	füttern
to feel [fiːl]	felt [felt]	felt [felt]	fühlen; sich fühlen; sich anfühlen
to fight [faɪt]	fought [fɔːt]	fought [fɔːt]	kämpfen; streiten; sich streiten
to find [faɪnd]	found [faʊnd]	found [faʊnd]	finden
to fly [flaɪ]	flew [fluː]	flown [fləʊn]	fliegen
to forget [fəˈget]	forgot [fəˈgɒt]	forgotten [fəˈgɒtn]	vergessen
to get [get]	got [gɒt]	got [gɒt]	bekommen; werden; kommen; holen; bringen
to give [gɪv]	gave [geɪv]	given [ˈgɪvn]	geben; schenken
to go [gəʊ]	went [went]	gone [gɒn]	gehen; fahren
to have [hæv]	had [hæd]	had [hæd]	haben; besitzen
to hear [hɪə]	heard [hɜːd]	heard [hɜːd]	hören
to hit [hɪt]	hit [hɪt]	hit [hɪt]	schlagen; treffen
to hold [həʊld]	held [held]	held [held]	halten; festhalten
to hurt [hɜːt]	hurt [hɜːt]	hurt [hɜːt]	verletzen; wehtun
to keep [kiːp]	kept [kept]	kept [kept]	halten; behalten
to know [nəʊ]	knew [njuː]	known [nəʊn]	kennen; wissen
to leave [liːv]	left [left]	left [left]	lassen; verlassen; abfahren; weggehen; vergessen; hinterlassen
to lose [luːz]	lost [lɒst]	lost [lɒst]	verlieren
to make [meɪk]	made [meɪd]	made [meɪd]	machen; tun; bilden
to mean [miːn]	meant [ment]	meant [ment]	bedeuten; meinen
to meet [miːt]	met [met]	met [met]	treffen; sich treffen
to put [pʊt]	put [pʊt]	put [pʊt]	setzen; legen; stellen

infinitive	simple past	past participle	German
to read [riːd]	read [red]	read [red]	lesen; vorlesen
to ride [raɪd]	rode [rəʊd]	ridden ['rɪdn]	fahren; reiten
to ring [rɪŋ]	rang [ræŋ]	rung [rʌŋ]	klingeln
to run [rʌn]	ran [ræn]	run [rʌn]	laufen; rennen
to say [seɪ]	said [sed]	said [sed]	sagen; sprechen; nennen; nachsprechen
to see [siː]	saw [sɔː]	seen [siːn]	sehen
to sell [sel]	sold [səʊld]	sold [səʊld]	verkaufen
to send [send]	sent [sent]	sent [sent]	schicken; senden
to shake [ʃeɪk]	shook [ʃʊk]	shaken ['ʃeɪkn]	beben; zittern; schütteln
to shoot [ʃuːt]	shot [ʃɒt]	shot [ʃɒt]	schießen; erschießen
to show [ʃəʊ]	showed [ʃəʊd]	shown [ʃəʊn]	zeigen
to sing [sɪŋ]	sang [sæŋ]	sung [sʌŋ]	singen
to sit [sɪt]	sat [sæt]	sat [sæt]	setzen; hinsetzen; sich setzen; sitzen
to sleep [sliːp]	slept [slept]	slept [slept]	schlafen
to speak [spiːk]	spoke [spəʊk]	spoken ['spəʊkn]	sprechen
to spend [spend]	spent [spent]	spent [spent]	verbringen; ausgeben
to stand [stænd]	stood [stʊd]	stood [stʊd]	stehen; ertragen; ausstehen
to swim [swɪm]	swam [swæm]	swum [swʌm]	schwimmen
to swing [swɪŋ]	swung [swʌŋ]	swung [swʌŋ]	schwingen; schwenken
to take [teɪk]	took [tʊk]	taken ['teɪkn]	nehmen; bringen; hinbringen; dauern; brauchen
to teach [tiːtʃ]	taught [tɔːt]	taught [tɔːt]	lehren; beibringen; unterrichten
to tell [tel]	told [təʊld]	told [təʊld]	erzählen; sagen
to think [θɪŋk]	thought [θɔːt]	thought [θɔːt]	denken; glauben
to throw [θrəʊ]	threw [θruː]	thrown [θrəʊn]	werfen
to understand [ˌʌndə'stænd]	understood [ˌʌndə'stʊd]	understood [ˌʌndə'stʊd]	verstehen
to wake up [ˌweɪk'ʌp]	woke up [ˌwəʊk'ʌp]	woken up [ˌwəʊkn'ʌp]	aufwachen; erwachen; aufwecken
to wear [weə]	wore [wɔː]	worn [wɔːn]	anhaben; tragen
to win [wɪn]	won [wʌn]	won [wʌn]	gewinnen
to write [raɪt]	wrote [rəʊt]	written ['rɪtn]	schreiben

1-minute-presentation

Step 1

Nimm ein Blatt Papier im DIN-A4-Format quer und falte es so, dass das untere Drittel nach hinten wegknickt.

Step 2

Schreibe den Vortragstext auf die oberen zwei Drittel.

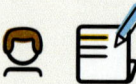

Step 3

Streiche nun die wichtigsten Stichpunkte im Text an. Notiere sie noch einmal auf dem unteren Drittel. Das ist dein Spickzettel.

Step 4

In deiner Präsentation verwendest du nur den Spickzettel. Wenn du steckenbleibst, darfst du ihn umknicken und kurz auf den Text oben schauen.

Bus stop

(Lerntempoduett)

Step 1

Bearbeite die Aufgabe zunächst allein. Schreibe deine Lösungen auf.

Step 2

Wenn du fertig bist, gehe zum „bus stop". Entweder wartet dort schon jemand oder du wartest dort auf die nächste Person. Vergleicht und korrigiert eure Ergebnisse zu zweit.

Step 3

Gehe danach wieder zu deinem Platz zurück. Bearbeite die nächste Aufgabe.

Double circle
(Kugellager)

Step 1
Teilt euch in zwei Gruppen A und B auf.
Gruppe A bildet den inneren Kreis. Gruppe B bildet den
äußeren Kreis. Steht dabei so, dass ihr euch anseht.

Step 2
Wenn ein Signal ertönt, sprecht ihr mit der Person, die
euch gegenübersteht.

Step 3
Beim nächsten Signal rückt der innere Kreis zwei Plätze
weiter nach rechts. Wiederholt den Vorgang.

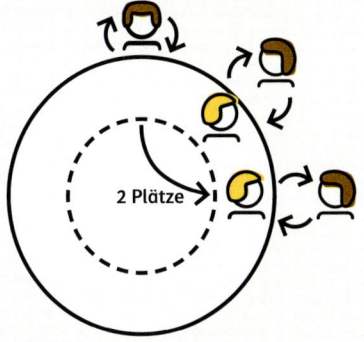

Dramatic reading
(Szenisches Lesen)

Step 1
Verteilt die Rollen innerhalb eurer Gruppe.

Step 2
Lies dir deinen Text lautlos oder ganz leise immer wieder
vor, bis du ihn gut kennst.

Step 3
Übt euren Text in der Gruppe mit der Methode „Read
and look up" (Seite 126).

Step 4
Überlegt euch, wie ihr euch in der Rolle fühlt und wie ihr
euch bewegen würdet. Tragt euren Text so frei wie
möglich vor.

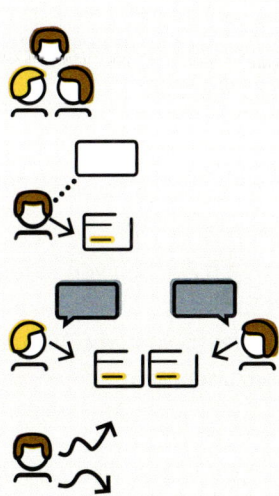

Gallery walk
(Galerierundgang)

Step 1

Hängt nach eurer Gruppenarbeit eure Produkte gut sichtbar im Klassenzimmer auf.

Step 2

Ein „Experte" aus jeder Gruppe bleibt bei dem Produkt stehen und erklärt es den anderen. Der Rest der Gruppe geht im Klassenzimmer herum. Nach jedem Durchgang wechselt der Experte.

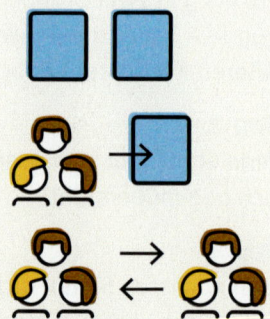

Step 3

Seht euch die Produkte der anderen an und bewertet sie.

Step 4

Wertet im Anschluss eure Ergebnisse in der Klasse aus.

Milling around
(Marktplatz)

Step 1
Bearbeite die Aufgabe zunächst allein.

Step 2
Auf ein Zeichen von eurem Lehrer oder eurer Lehrerin steht ihr auf und geht durch den Raum.
Vergesst nicht, die Aufgabe und einen Stift mitzunehmen.

Step 3
Wenn ein Signal ertönt, bleibt ihr stehen. Besprecht die Aufgabe mit der Person, die euch am nächsten steht.

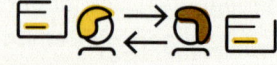

Step 4
Belm nächsten Signal trennt ihr euch und geht weiter durch den Raum. Wiederholt den Vorgang.

Peer correction
(Partnerkontrolle)

Step 1
Bearbeite die Aufgabe zunächst allein.

Step 2
Tausche deine Lösungen mit einem Partner / einer Partnerin. Kontrolliere seine oder ihre Lösungen.

Step 3
Vergleicht eure Lösungen und korrigiert sie dann gemeinsam.

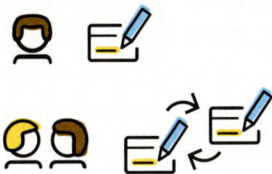

Placemat
(Platzdeckchen)

Step 1
Bildet Vierergruppen.

Step 2
Teilt ein großes Blatt Papier in fünf Bereiche ein.

Step 3
Setzt euch so hin, dass alle jeweils in eine Ecke des Blattes schreiben können.

Step 4
Jedes Gruppenmitglied denkt allein über das Thema nach und schreibt Ideen auf seinen Teil des Blattes.

Step 5
Tauscht euch über die Ideen aus. Einigt euch auf die besten Ideen und schreibt diese in die Mitte des Blattes.

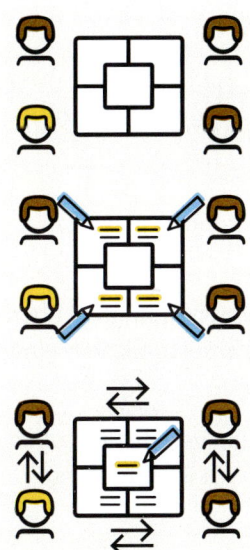

Read and look up
(Lesen und Aufschauen)

Step 1
Schaue auf deinen Text und präge dir die erste Zeile oder den ersten Satz ein. Schaue hoch und sprich deine Zeile / deinen Satz lautlos oder leise vor dich hin. Nimm dir die nächste Zeile / den nächsten Satz vor.

Step 2
Übe nun mit einem Partner/einer Partnerin. Erzähle deinen Text, Zeile für Zeile oder Satz für Satz. Dazwischen schaust du immer wieder nach unten auf deinen Text.

Step 3
Wiederhole alles, bis es gut klappt. Überlege dir, wo du stehen und wie du dich bewegen willst.

Round robin
(Blitzlicht)

Step 1
Bildet Gruppen und setzt euch in einen Kreis.

Step 2
Jedes Gruppenmitglied überlegt sich kurz einen Satz, der seine persönliche Meinung zum Thema ausdrückt.

Step 3
Wenn alle bereit sind, sagen die Gruppenmitglieder der Reihe nach ihre Meinung.

Step 4
Die anderen Gruppenmitglieder dürfen die Sätze nicht kommentieren.

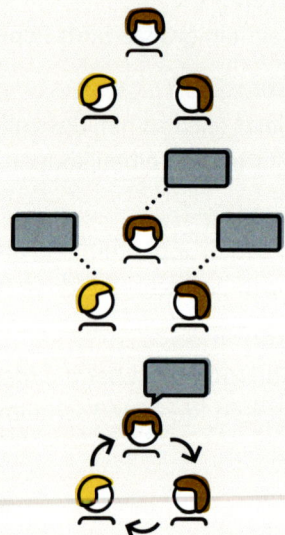

Think – pair – share

Step 1
Schreibe deine Ideen, Gedanken oder Lösungen zur Aufgabe auf.

Step 2
Tauscht euch zu zweit aus und besprecht eure Notizen.

Step 3
Präsentiert euer Ergebnis anderen Paaren oder der gesamten Klasse.

Tip top

Step 1
Sage zunächst, was dir gut gefallen hat – was „top" war.

Step 2
Sage nun, was noch nicht so gut war, und gib einen Tipp, was man noch verbessern könnte.

Writers' conference
(Schreibwerkstatt)

Step 1
Bildet Vierergruppen.

Step 2
Lest euch eure Sätze/Texte gegenseitig vor.

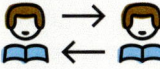

Step 3
Die Zuhörer sagen, was ihnen gefallen hat, und können Verbesserungsvorschläge machen.

Step 4
Jede Gruppe wählt den besten Text aus und liest ihn der Klasse vor.

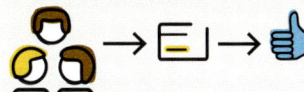

Vocabulary tips

Du kennst schon einige Tipps und Tricks zum Vokabellernen. Erinnerst du dich? Hier gibt es noch mehr Tipps.

Lerntipp: Serien und Filme im Original

Schaue dir Serien oder Filme im englischen Original an. Du wirst überrascht sein, wie viel du schon verstehst. Du kannst auch die englischen Untertitel einschalten. Durch das gleichzeitige Hören und Lesen wirst du sehr viel mehr verstehen und auch behalten.

Lerntipp: Wortfamilien

Rufe dir beim Lernen neuer Vokabeln in Erinnerung, welche Wörter derselben Wortfamilie du schon kennst. Wenn du verschiedene Wörter miteinander vernetzt, kannst du sie dir leichter merken.

Wortbildung

Es gibt verschiedene Möglichkeiten, wie Nomen gebildet werden können.

1. Aus einem Verb wird oft durch die Endung *-ing* ein Nomen der gleichen Wortfamilie.
   to build → a building
   to feel → a feeling

2. Nomen mit der Endung *-er* oder *-or* bezeichnen meistens eine Person.
   to play → a player
   to visit → a visitor

3. Sehr oft haben auch Verb und Nomen dieselbe Form:
   to answer → an answer
   to talk → a talk

4. Die Endungen *-ation*, *-ant*, *-ance*, *-ence*, *-ion* und *-ment* bei Nomen sagen etwas über einen Vorgang oder einen Zustand aus:

   to immigrate → immigrant   independent → independence
   immigrant → immigration   to correct → correction
   to avoid → avoidance   to move → movement

Die Endungen *-ful* und *-less* bei Adjektiven sagen aus, dass etwas vorhanden ist bzw. fehlt:
success → successful
home → homeless

STUDY SKILLS

Vor- und Nachsilben können dir oft Hinweise auf die Bedeutung eines Wortes geben. Das gilt für alle Wortarten, z. B. auch für Verben und Adjektive. Schaue dir auch die Seiten 66–67 an.

Diese Checkliste kann dir helfen, Fehler zu vermeiden und deine Rechtschreibung zu verbessern. Prüfe alle deine Texte damit. Du kannst auch ein „Fehlertagebuch" führen, in dem du deine eigenen häufigen Fehler aufschreibst. So bist du beim nächsten Mal sicherer.

- **Schreibung:**
  - ☐ *gh* wird meist nicht gesprochen. Vergiss es beim Schreiben nicht.
  - ☐ *k* kommt vor *t* so gut wie nie vor, z.B. activity – Aktivität, October – Oktober

- **Gleiche Aussprache, unterschiedliche Schreibung:**
  - ☐ [i:] z.B. t**ea**cher, to m**ee**t, t**ea**, Chin**e**se, peo**ple**, fi**e**ld
  - ☐ [u:] z.B. f**oo**d, fr**ui**t, to d**o**, fl**ew**, supermarket, barbec**ue**, bea**u**tiful

- **Gleiche Aussprache, unterschiedliche Schreibung und Bedeutung:**
  - ☐ [i:] z.B. to s**ee** – sehen, s**ea** – Meer
  - ☐ [u:] z.B. tw**o** – zwei, t**oo** – auch

- **Verdoppelung des Endkonsonanten:**
  - ☐ to sto**p** – sto**pp**ing, sto**pp**ed
  - ☐ to wi**n** – wi**nn**ing, wi**nn**er

- **y wird zu ie:**
  - ☐ in der 3. Person Singular: z.B. to worr**y** – he worr**ies**; aber: to bu**y** – she bu**ys**
  - ☐ im Plural: z.B. cit**y** – cit**ies**, part**y** – part**ies**; aber: bo**y** – bo**ys**
  - ☐ bei der Steigerung von Adjektiven: z.B. happ**y** – happ**ier** – (the) happ**iest**, eas**y** – eas**ier** – (the) eas**iest**

- **Ähnlich und doch anders:**
  - ☐ Wortendung *le*: z.B. tit**le** – Tit**el**; midd**le** – Mitt**el**-
  - ☐ *ph* statt *f*: z.B. **ph**one – Tele**f**on; **ph**oto – **F**oto

- **Großschreibung:**
  - ☐ Monatsnamen: z.B. January, July, December
  - ☐ Wochentage: z.B. Monday, Wednesday, Saturday
  - ☐ Eigennamen: z.B. Tom, Lisa, the Brooks, the London Eye, the Thames
  - ☐ geografische Namen: Bristol, Greenwich, Germany, Italy

- **Plural:**
  - ☐ Der Plural bekommt normalerweise ein *s*: z.B. friend – friend**s**, chair – chair**s**, film – film**s**
  - ☐ Endet ein Wort auf *s* oder *x*, wird *es* angehängt: z.B. bus – bus**es**, box – box**es**
  - ☐ Manche Wörter haben einen unregelmäßigen Plural: z.B. man – men, child – children, shelf – shelves, mouse – mice

- **Apostroph:**
  - ☐ bei Kurzformen: z.B. she is → she's; they are → they're
  - ☐ beim Genitiv-s: z.B. Sam's bike, Emma's family, the Jacksons' house, the children's games

- **Wörterbuch:**
  - ☐ Prüfe die Schreibung aller Wörter, bei denen du dir nicht ganz sicher bist, indem du sie im Wörterbuch nachschlägst.

Word bank: Interviewing a new arrival → ⊕ Find more online: 5a5g94

My home country is . . . .

Where are you from?

I'm from . . . .

get rich

finish school

be a star

learn German

live in . . .

What are your plans for the future?

help others

Interview

get a job in Germany

by train

by boat

by car

What was the journey like? We travelled . . . .

by coach

on foot

for a year

How long have you been here?

since last year

for three months

war in my country

family already here

work

Why did you come to Germany?

famine

hungry

poor

Useful phrases for an interview:

It's like . . . .

It's a kind of . . . .

It's when you . . . .

Can you say that again, please?

Let me say that again. What I mean is . . . .

I don't understand what you mean.

Do you mean . . . ?

Really?

That's interesting!

Tell me more, please.

Wow!

Word bank: **Talking about culture** → 🌐 Find more online: 5a5g94

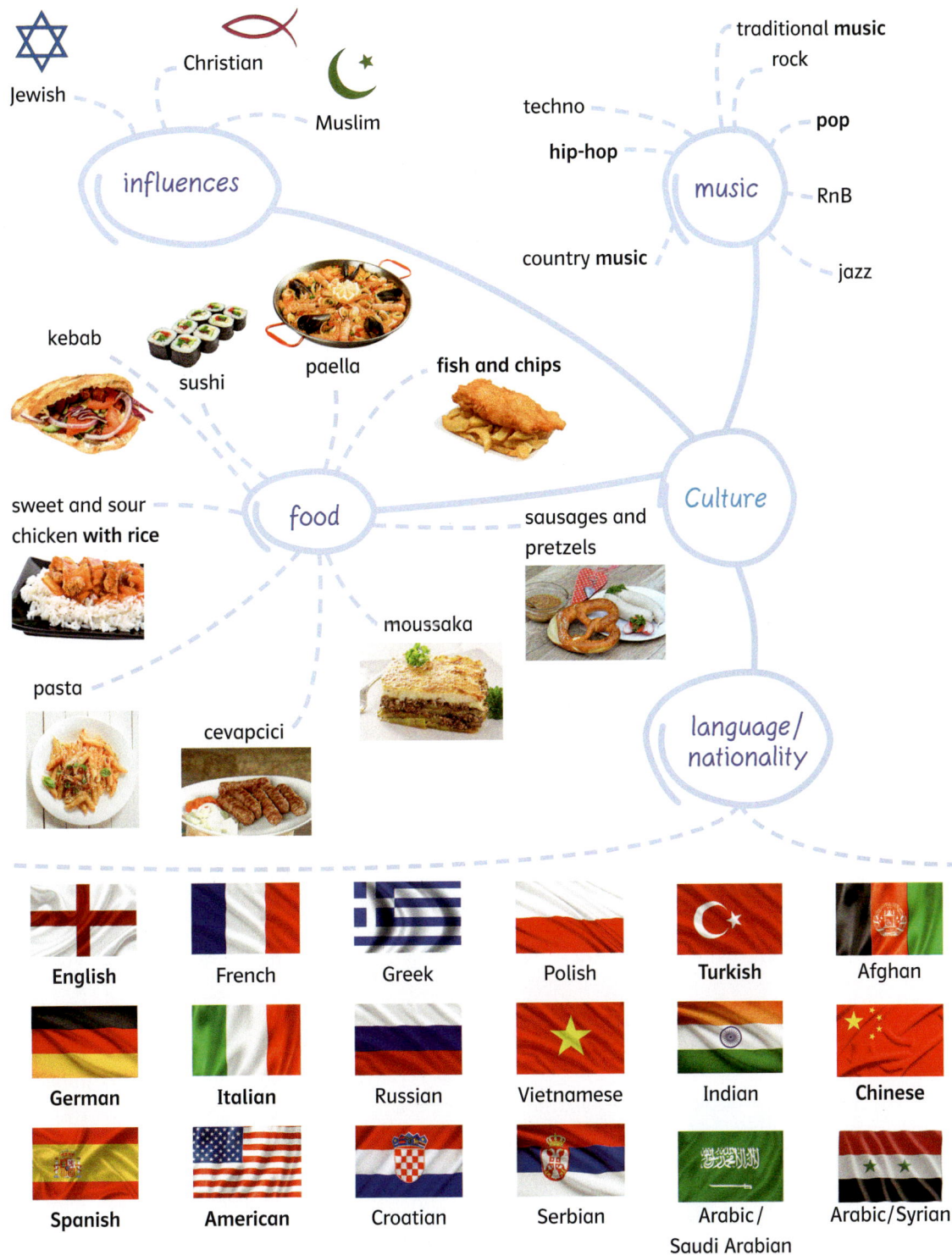

Jewish

Christian

Muslim

influences

traditional **music**

rock

techno

pop

hip-hop

music

RnB

jazz

country **music**

kebab

sushi

paella

fish and chips

sweet and sour
chicken **with rice**

food

Culture

sausages and
pretzels

moussaka

pasta

cevapcici

language/
nationality

English

French

Greek

Polish

Turkish

Afghan

German

Italian

Russian

Vietnamese

Indian

Chinese

Spanish

American

Croatian

Serbian

Arabic/
Saudi Arabian

Arabic/Syrian

Word bank: **A trip to the country** → ⊕ Find more online: 5a5g94

Activities

to go walking/hiking **to go** fishing **to go** cycling **to go rock climbing** **to go canoeing**

to go rafting **to go horse riding** **to go** windsurfing **to go swimming** **to stay on a campsite**

Places

countryside **mountains** **coast** **wood** lake

Animals

horse fox deer squirrel **rabbit**

cow buzzard owl hedgehog **sheep**

Word bank: **At the airport** → 🌐 Find more online: 5a5g94

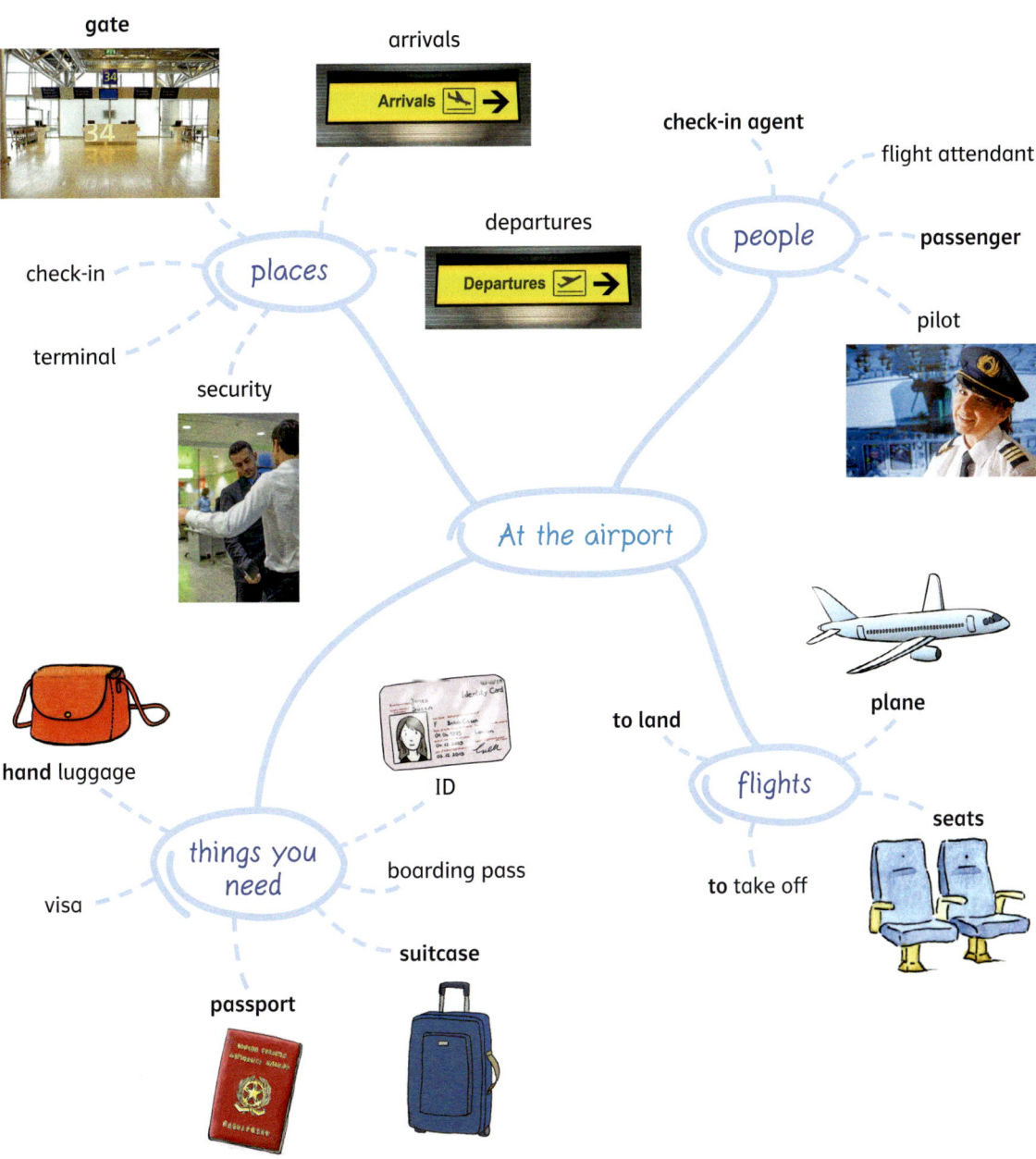

gate

arrivals

check-in agent

flight attendant

people

passenger

departures

check-in

places

pilot

terminal

security

At the airport

plane

to land

flights

hand luggage

ID

seats

things you need

boarding pass

to take off

visa

suitcase

passport

The check-in agent can say:	The passenger can say:
I'm afraid your flight is delayed. The flight departs from gate . . . . Have a good flight.	Is there anything you can do about it? What can I do about it? Which gate . . .? Thank you.

Word bank: **Ideas and suggestions** → 🌐 Find more online: 5a5g94

Agreeing with someone

I agree with you.

You're absolutely **right**.

That's true.

I think so because . . . .

Yes, that's a good idea.

That sounds good.

Disagreeing with someone

I don't agree with you.

I don't think so because . . . .

Yes, but what about . . . ?

Saying what you would like to do

I'd like to . . . . Is that OK?

I really want to . . . .

Why don't we . . . ?

Saying no

That's a great idea, but I don't have time today.

Sorry, but I'm not interested in that.

Suggesting a plan for another person:

Why don't you . . . ?
Can't you . . . ?
Maybe you should . . . .

Showing that you understand:

It's OK. I understand.
I really don't mind.
It's fine. Don't worry.
Don't you think so?
Please don't be annoyed. I just want to . . . .

Word bank: **Jobs** → 🌐 Find more online: 5a5g94

nurse

florist

hairdresser

hotel manager

chef

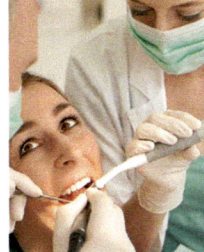
dentist's **assistant**

farmer

waiter/waitress

mechanic

flight attendant

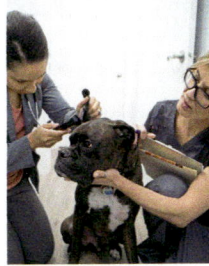
vet's assistant

carpenter

police officer

receptionist

baker

Plans for the future

I want to do an apprenticeship **and become an** electrician.
I'm applying for an internship.
A work placement **is another word for an** internship.
You can do a social placement **in a hospital.**

Maybe I can do a holiday job in the summer?
In a weekend job you work for a few hours on Saturdays and Sundays.
People can do a voluntary year. They don't earn any money but they get experience.

Word bank: Social media and technology → ⊕ Find more online: 5a5g94

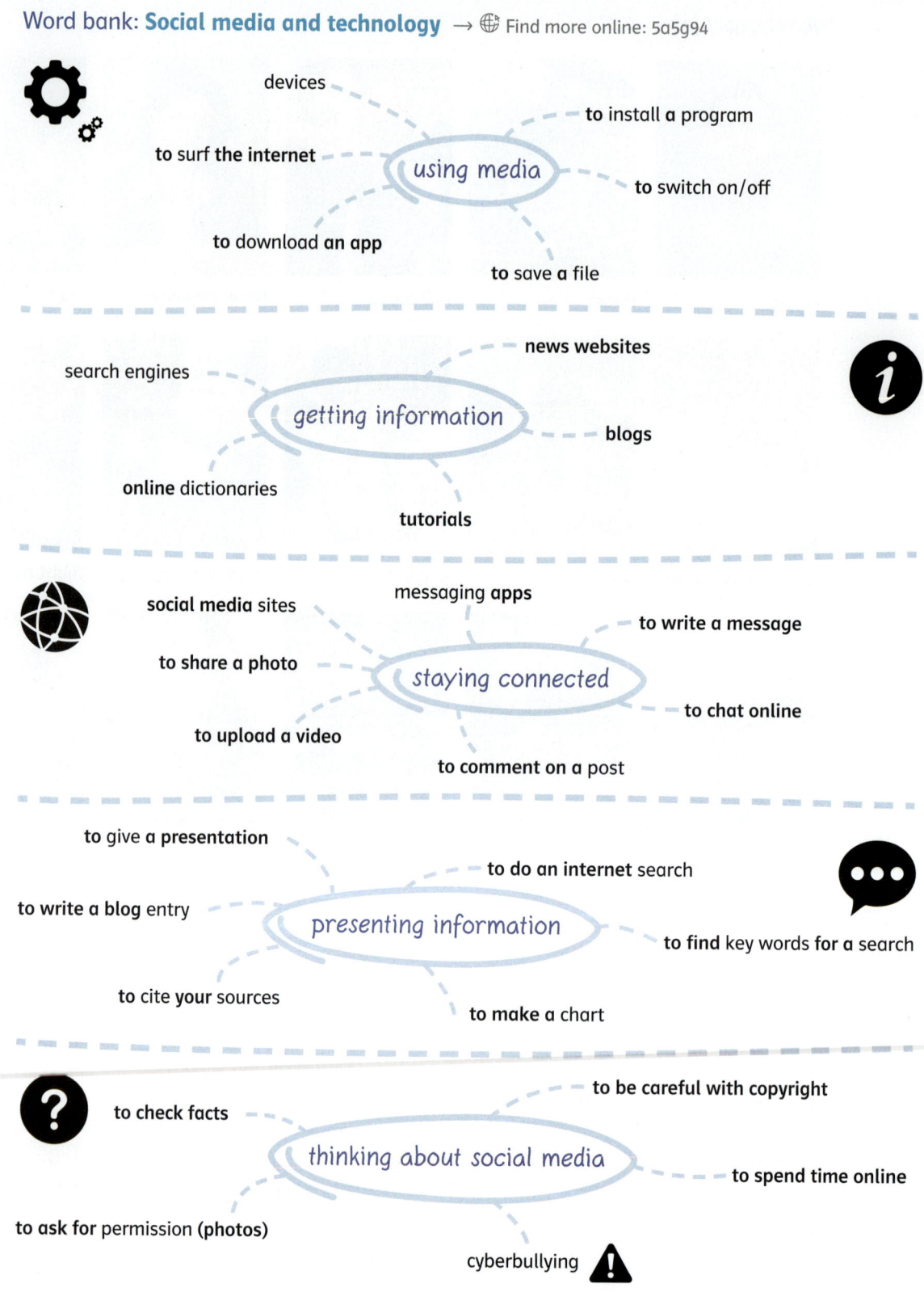

devices

to install a program

to surf the internet

using media

to switch on/off

to download an app

to save a file

---

news websites

search engines

getting information

blogs

online dictionaries

tutorials

---

social media sites

messaging apps

to write a message

to share a photo

staying connected

to chat online

to upload a video

to comment on a post

---

to give a presentation

to do an internet search

to write a blog entry

presenting information

to find key words for a search

to cite your sources

to make a chart

---

to be careful with copyright

to check facts

thinking about social media

to spend time online

to ask for permission (photos)

cyberbullying

Word bank: **Sports and activities** → 🌐 Find more online: 5a5g94

Water sports: to go . . .

Activities

swimming

surfing

windsurfing

canoeing

rafting

to ride a bike

Ball sports: to play . . .

rugby

football

netball

handball

basketball

to go rock climbing

Winter sports: to go . . .

Equipment

skiing

snowboarding

ice skating

bat

to do skateboard tricks

Athletics: to do . . .

the high jump

the long jump

running

racket

paddle

Racket sports: to play . . .

waterproofs

ball

to go jogging

tennis

badminton

squash

goggles

helmet

to go hiking

Word bank: **Job applications** → 🌐 Find more online: 5a5g94

at an old people's home

voluntary **year**   internship

social placement   *work experience*

**at an animal
rescue shelter**

summer job

Job applications

curriculum vitae (CV)

paperboy/girl

babysitter

parts of an application

part-time jobs

letter of application

waiter/waitress

certificates

to work on a market stall

Writing a letter of application	Skills and qualities
Dear Mr/Mrs . . . , I would like to apply for the job as . . . . I have . . . **years of** work experience. I have worked as . . . for the last . . . years. I believe I am well-qualified for this job. I am looking forward to hearing from you. Yours sincerely, . . .	computer/software skills fluent **in English/Spanish/** . . . hard-working communicative **flexible** efficient **reliable** **quick**

Vocabulary

Das Vocabulary enthält alle neuen Wörter und Wendungen. Sie stehen in der Reihenfolge, wie sie im Buch vorkommen.

Die Wortliste ist in drei Spalten aufgeteilt:

Links findest du das englische Wort mit der Lautschrift in Klammern. (Die Lautschrift wird ganz unten auf jeder Seite im *Dictionary* erklärt.)

In der mittleren Spalte steht die deutsche Übersetzung.

Rechts findest du Beispielsätze, Hinweise und Tipps, die dir beim Lernen helfen.

Die **fett** gedruckten Wörter musst du lernen.

Symbole und Abkürzungen:

⬳	Achtung Aussprache!	sth	something
✏	Achtung Schreibweise!	sb	somebody
↔	ist das Gegenteil von	*(sg)*	Einzahl (Singular)
→	ist verwandt mit	*(pl)*	Mehrzahl (Plural)
=	entspricht	R	ähnlich wie im Russischen
		T	ähnlich wie im Türkischen

Die *Word bank*-Seiten (S.130 bis 138) helfen dir, die *Task*-Aufgaben in den *Units* zu bearbeiten. Du findest dort nützlichen individuellen Wortschatz zum Thema der *Unit*, der dir hilft, über deine eigene Situation zu sprechen oder zu schreiben. Diese Wörter findest du auch im *Dictionary*.

Wenn du ein Wort nicht weißt und im Wörterbuch nachschlagen willst, schau auf den *Dictionary*-Seiten ab S.156 nach. Oder bei den *Instructions* auf S.198.

Zoom in – The USA

p. 8	**quiz** [kwɪz]	Quiz; Ratespiel	What are the clues for the **quiz**?
p. 9	**independence** [ˌɪndɪˈpendəns]	Unabhängigkeit	They celebrated 100 years of **independence**.
	flag [flæg]	Flagge; Fahne	
	dollar ($) [ˈdɒlə]	Dollar *(amer. Währungseinheit)*	R доллар T dolar

Unit 1 Welcome to New York!

Intro

p. 10	**borough** ['bʌrə]	Stadtteil; Bezirk	NYC has five **boroughs**.
	immigrant ['ɪmɪgrənt]	Einwanderer; Einwanderin; Immigrant; Immigrantin	A lot of **immigrants** went to America.
	statue ['stætʃuː]	Statue	The **Statue** of Liberty is in NYC.
	island ['aɪlənd]	Insel	
	France [frɑːns]	Frankreich	R Франция T Fransa
p. 11	**New Yorker** [ˌnjuː ˈjɔːkə]	New Yorker; New Yorkerin	**New Yorkers** live in New York City.
	messenger ['mesɪndʒə]	Kurier; Kurierin; Bote; Botin	Many young people work as bike **messengers**.
	lake [leɪk]	See	
	multicultural [ˌmʌltiˈkʌltʃrl]	multikulturell	New York is a very **multicultural** city.
	Italy ['ɪtli]	Italien	
	Italian [ɪˈtæliən]	italienisch; Italienisch; Italiener; Italienerin	**Italian** → Italy
	population (no pl) [ˌpɒpjəˈleɪʃn]	Bevölkerung; Einwohner; Einwohnerzahl	There is a large Chinese **population** in NYC.

Topic 1

p. 12	**interviewer** ['ɪntəvjuːə]	Interviewer; Interviewerin; Befrager; Befragerin	The **interviewer** asked me ten questions.
	magazine [ˌmægəˈziːn]	Zeitschrift	I like **magazines**.
	Cuba ['kjuːbə]	Kuba	R Куба T Küba
	for [fɔː]	seit	I have lived here **for** 13 years.
	home country [ˌhəʊm ˈkʌntri]	Heimat; Heimatland	My **home country** is Germany.
	decision [dɪˈsɪʒn]	Entscheidung	**decision** → to decide
	poor [pɔː]	arm	My family was very **poor** in Cuba.
	opportunity [ˌɒpəˈtjuːnəti]	Chance; Möglichkeit; Gelegenheit	There were better **opportunities** in the USA.
	arrival [əˈraɪvl]	Ankömmling	**arrival** → to arrive
	to be homesick [biː ˈhəʊmsɪk]	Heimweh haben	I **was homesick** for Cuba.
	to get used to (sth) [ˌget ˈjuːst tə]	sich gewöhnen an (etw.)	I **got used to** life in the USA.

had [hæd]	past participle von *to have* (haben, essen)	I have **had** = ich hatte/ich habe gehabt
since [sɪns]	seit; seitdem	I have lived here **since** March.
successful [sək'sesfl]	erfolgreich	José is a **successful** baseball player.
career [kə'rɪə]	Laufbahn; Karriere; Beruf	I've had a successful **career**.
citizen ['sɪtɪzn]	Staatsbürger; Staatsbürgerin; Staatsangehöriger; Staatsangehörige	José is now an American **citizen**.
plan [plæn]	Plan	What are your **plans** for today?
Good luck! [ˌgʊd 'lʌk]	Alles Gute!; Viel Glück!	**Good luck!** – Thank you.
future ['fjuːtʃə]	Zukunft	past – today – **future**

Das kenne ich schon

going to a new country

immigrant ['ɪmɪgrənt]	Einwanderer; Einwanderin; Immigrant; Immigrantin	successful [sək'sesfl]	erfolgreich
decision [dɪ'sɪʒn]	Entscheidung	career [kə'rɪə]	Laufbahn; Karriere; Beruf
home country [ˌhəʊm 'kʌntri]	Heimat; Heimatland	citizen ['sɪtɪzn]	Staatsbürger; Staatsbürgerin; Staatsangehöriger; Staatsangehörige
opportunity [ˌɒpə'tjuːnəti]	Chance; Möglichkeit; Gelegenheit	to be a long way away [biː ə 'lɒŋ ˌweɪ ə'weɪ]	weit weg sein
to be homesick [biː 'həʊmsɪk]	Heimweh haben	different ['dɪfrnt]	verschieden; unterschiedlich; anders
future ['fjuːtʃə]	Zukunft	culture ['kʌltʃə]	Kultur
to get used to (sth) [ˌget 'juːst tə]	sich gewöhnen an (etw.)	country ['kʌntri]	Land; ländliche Gegend
arrival [ə'raɪvl]	Ankömmling	to miss [mɪs]	vermissen
		to move [muːv]	umziehen
		to leave [liːv]	verlassen; weggehen

Topic 2

p. 16	**nationality** [ˌnæʃn'æləti]	Nationalität; Staatsangehörigkeit	People of all **nationalities** live here.
	sign [saɪn]	Schild; Zeichen; Anzeichen	⌀ Achtung Schreibweise! si**g**n
	to be born [biː 'bɔːn]	geboren werden	I **was born** in Germany.
	parade [pə'reɪd]	Parade; Umzug; Prozession	Ⓡ парад
	apartment *(AE)* [ə'pɑːtmənt]	Wohnung; Apartment	AE: **apartment** BE: flat
	to walk [wɔːk]	laufen; gehen; zu Fuß gehen	*walk*
	quick [kwɪk]	schnell	Please be **quick**! I don't want to wait.

slow [sləʊ]	langsam	slow ↔ fast
Turkish [ˈtɜːkɪʃ]	türkisch; Türkisch; aus der Türkei	**Turkish** → Turkey
Japanese [ˌdʒæpnˈiːz]	japanisch; Japanisch; aus Japan; Japaner; Japanerin	I don't like **Japanese** food.
Spanish [ˈspænɪʃ]	spanisch; Spanisch; aus Spanien	**Spanish** food is my favourite food.
safe [seɪf]	sicher; ungefährlich; in Sicherheit; unversehrt	**safe** ↔ dangerous
at night [ət ˈnaɪt]	nachts	I can't sleep well **at night**.
zoo [zuː]	Zoo; Tierpark	⬯ Achtung Aussprache!

Das kenne ich schon

city words

apartment *(AE)* [əˈpɑːtmənt]	Wohnung; Apartment	traffic [ˈtræfɪk]	Verkehr
building [ˈbɪldɪŋ]	Gebäude; Bauwerk	capital (city) [ˈkæpɪtl (ˌsɪti)]	Hauptstadt
borough [ˈbʌrə]	Stadtteil; Bezirk	city centre [ˌsɪti ˈsentə]	Stadtzentrum; Stadtmitte
multicultural [ˌmʌltiˈkʌltʃrl]	multikulturell	noisy [ˈnɔɪzi]	laut
population *(no pl)* [ˌpɒpjəˈleɪʃn]	Bevölkerung; Einwohner; Einwohnerzahl	park [pɑːk]	Park
		tower [ˈtaʊə]	Turm
statue [ˈstætʃuː]	Statue	zoo [zuː]	Zoo; Tierpark
store *(AE)* [stɔː]	Laden; Geschäft		

Text

p. 20	**witness** [ˈwɪtnəs]	Zeuge; Zeugin	He saw it, he was a **witness**.
	to **get** [get]	*hier:* holen; bringen	Can you **get** my phone for me, please?
	package [ˈpækɪdʒ]	Paket	T paket
	to **deliver** [dɪˈlɪvə]	liefern; ausliefern	Ally uses her bike to **deliver** things.
	van [væn]	Lieferwagen; Transporter	
	to **knock sb off sth** [ˌnɒk … ˈɒf]	jmdn. von etw. stoßen	A van **knocked Ally off her bike**.
	to **get out** [ˌget ˈaʊt]	aussteigen; herauskommen	The man **got out** of the van.
	scratch [skrætʃ]	Kratzer	There were **scratches** on the van.
	to **signal** [ˈsɪgnl]	*hier:* blinken	You turned right and didn't **signal**.
	police [pəˈliːs]	Polizei	R полиция T polis
	knew [njuː]	simple past von *to know* (wissen, kennen)	I **knew** = ich wusste/ich habe gewusst
p. 21	**wrecked** [rekt]	demoliert; zerstört; zertrümmert	✐ Achtung Schreibweise! wreck**ed**
	driver [ˈdraɪvə]	Fahrer; Fahrerin	Don't talk to the **driver**!

to **get in** [ˌget ˈɪn]	einsteigen	**to get in** ↔ to get out
to **drive** [draɪv], **drove** [drəʊv], **driven** [ˈdrɪvn]	fahren; treiben	**to drive** → driver
to **drive off** [ˌdraɪv ˈɒf]	wegfahren	The van **drove off** very fast.
lady [ˈleɪdi]	Frau; Dame	**lady** = woman („lady" ist förmlicher)
to **lie** [laɪ]	lügen	The man **lied** to the police officer.
to **prove** [pruːv]	beweisen	It is hard to **prove** he lied.
truth [truːθ]	Wahrheit	Tell the **truth** about the accident.

Film

elephant [ˈelɪfənt]	Elefant	**in here** [ɪn ˈhɪə]	hierin

Internet research skills

p. 26	**whale** [weɪl]	Wal	
	whale-watching [ˈweɪlˌwɒtʃɪŋ]	Walbeobachtungs-	We went on a **whale-watching** tour.
	to **find out** [ˌfaɪnd ˈaʊt]	herausfinden	**Find out** when the film starts, please.
	kayaking [ˈkaɪækɪŋ]	Kajakfahren	**Kayaking** is one of my hobbies.
	kayak [ˈkaɪæk]	Kajak	It was great to see the beach from a **kayak**.
	class [klɑːs]	Unterricht; Unterrichtsstunde; Kurs	**class** → classroom
	guide [gaɪd]	Führer; Führerin	Take a class with one of our **guides**.

Unit 2 One country – different states

Intro

p. 30	**plane** [pleɪn]	Flugzeug	
	boat [bəʊt]	Boot; Schiff	
	wild [waɪld]	wild	⬭ Achtung Aussprache!
p. 31	**surfing** [ˈsɜːfɪŋ]	Surfen; Wellenreiten; Surf-	
	landmark [ˈlænmɑːk]	Wahrzeichen	The Golden Gate Bridge is a **landmark**.
	hill [hɪl]	Berg; Hügel	
	cable car [ˈkeɪbl ˌkɑː]	seilgezogene Straßenbahn; Seilbahn	
	earthquake [ˈɜːθkweɪk]	Erdbeben	There are **earthquakes** on the west coast.

another [ə'nʌðə]	noch ein; ein anderer; andere	There's **another** problem at the airport.
to complain [kəm'pleɪn]	sich beschweren; sich beklagen	Stop **complaining** and think positive.
suitcase ['suːtkeɪs]	Koffer	
employee [ɪm'plɔɪiː]	Mitarbeiter; Mitarbeiterin; Arbeitnehmer; Arbeitnehmerin; Angestellter; Angestellte	Over 500 **employees** work here.
to get lost [ˌget 'lɒst]	verloren gehen; sich verirren	I hope the suitcase didn't **get lost**.
passenger ['pæsndʒə]	Passagier; Passagierin	The **passengers** slept on the flight.

Das kenne ich schon

air travel

airport ['eəpɔːt]	Flughafen	ticket ['tɪkɪt]	Ticket
flight [flaɪt]	Flug	boarding card ['bɔːdɪŋ ˌkaːd]	Bordkarte
plane [pleɪn]	Flugzeug		
check-in agent [ˌtʃekɪn 'eɪdʒnt]	Check-in-Mitarbeiter; Check-in-Mitarbeiterin	delayed [dɪ'leɪd]	verspätet
		to fly [flaɪ]	fliegen
gate [geɪt]	Gate; Flugsteig	to land [lænd]	landen
boarding time ['bɔːdɪŋ ˌtaɪm]	Einsteigezeit	to depart [dɪ'paːt]	abfliegen
		to arrive [ə'raɪv]	ankommen
suitcase ['suːtkeɪs]	Koffer	to leave [liːv]	abfliegen; gehen
passenger ['pæsndʒə]	Passagier; Passagierin	Have a good flight! [ˌhæv ə gʊd 'flaɪt]	Guten Flug!
journey ['dʒɜːni]	Reise		
passport ['paːspɔːt]	Pass; Reisepass		

Text

p. 40	**to shake** [ʃeɪk], **shook** [ʃʊk], **shaken** ['ʃeɪkn]	beben; zittern; schütteln	Last night the earth **shook** in San Francisco.
	in [ɪn]	bei; an	**In** an earthquake, the earth shakes.
	to happen ['hæpn]	vorkommen; sich ereignen	Storms often **happen** in the autumn.
	more often [mɔːr 'ɒfn]	häufiger; öfter	Earthquakes happen **more often** than we think.
	to cause [kɔːz]	verursachen; auslösen	The driver **caused** the accident.
	damage ['dæmɪdʒ]	Schäden; Schaden; Beschädigung	The earthquake caused a lot of **damage**.
	a year [ə 'jɪə]	pro Jahr; im Jahr	There are two earthquakes **a year**.
	crust [krʌst]	Kruste; Rinde	Look at the picture of the earth's **crust**.
	plate [pleɪt]	Teller; *hier:* (Kontinental-)Platte	The earth's crust has many different **plates**.
	to move [muːv]	(sich) bewegen; ziehen	I didn't **move** when the music stopped.
p. 41	**to destroy** [dɪ'strɔɪ]	zerstören	Earthquakes can **destroy** buildings.

tsunami [tsʊˈnɑːmi]	Tsunami *(durch Seebeben ausgelöste Flutwelle)*	Earthquakes can cause **tsunamis**.
to **design** [dɪˈzaɪn]	konstruieren; entwerfen; gestalten; entwickeln	Engineers **design** buildings which are safer.
during [ˈdʒʊərɪŋ]	bei; während	**During** an earthquake, it is best to be outside.
Richter scale *(no pl)* [ˈrɪktə ˌskeɪl]	Richterskala	The **Richter scale** shows how strong an earthquake is.
area [ˈeəriə]	Gebiet; Gegend; Areal	California is an earthquake **area**.
first-aid [ˌfɜːstˈeɪd]	Erste-Hilfe-	
item [ˈaɪtəm]	Ding; Artikel; Gegenstand	There is one **item** on the shopping list.
blanket [ˈblæŋkɪt]	Decke; Bettdecke; Wolldecke	
can [kæn]	Dose	
strong [strɒŋ]	*hier:* stabil	You should sit under a **strong** table.

Film

burger bar [ˈbɜːgə ˌbɑː]	Burger-Restaurant	

Dictionary skills

p. 48

sense of smell [ˌsens əv ˈsmel]	Geruchssinn	Bears have a good **sense of smell**.
sense [sens]	Sinn; Bedeutung	People and animals have five **senses**.
smell [smel]	Geruch; Duft	What's that **smell**?
to **keep away** [ˌkiːp əˈweɪ]	fernhalten	Visitors must **keep** food **away** from bears.
Alaskan [əˈlæskən]	alaskisch; Alaska-	**Alaskan** people are from Alaska.
husky [ˈhʌski]	Husky *(Schlittenhunderasse)*	**Huskies** are a kind of dog.
ranger *(AE)* [ˈreɪndʒə]	Ranger; Rangerin	Tony is a **ranger** in a national park.
to **train** [treɪn]	trainieren; eine Ausbildung machen; ausbilden	They **train** the huskies slowly.
sled [sled]	Schlitten	
to **transport** [trænˈspɔːt]	transportieren; befördern	Huskies help rangers **transport** things.
supplies *(pl)* [səˈplaɪz]	Vorräte	The **supplies** on a boat are the food.

Das kenne ich schon

phrases with -ing

can't stand + -ing [ˌkɑːnt ˈstænd …ɪŋ]	etw. nicht ausstehen können; etw. nicht ertragen	to look forward to + -ing [ˌlʊk ˈfɔːwəd tə …ɪŋ]	sich freuen auf
		to like + -ing [ˌlaɪk ˈ…ɪŋ]	mögen; gernhaben
to be good at + -ing [bi ˈgʊd ət …ɪŋ]	gut sein in; gut sein bei	to hate + -ing [ˌheɪt ˈ…ɪŋ]	hassen, nicht mögen

Unit 3 Southern life

p. 50	southern ['sʌðən]	südlich; Süd-; *hier:* Südstaaten-	**Southern** life is the best.

Intro

p. 51	The Caribbean [ðə ˌkærɪ'biːən]	die Karibik	The weather is good in **the Caribbean**.
p. 50	to **get on sth** [ˌget 'ɒn]	in etw. steigen; in etw. einsteigen	We **got on the boat** and went on a tour.
	steamboat ['stiːmbəʊt]	Dampfer; Dampfschiff	
	proud (of) [praʊd (əv)]	stolz (auf)	People in the American South are **proud**.
	African American [ˌæfrɪkən ə'merɪkən]	Afroamerikaner; Afroamerikanerin	There are lots of **African Americans** in the South.
p. 51	to **enjoy** [ɪn'dʒɔɪ]	genießen; Gefallen finden an	Zum Vergleich: I **enjoyed** my holidays. *(genießen)* I like football. *(mögen)*
	climate ['klaɪmət]	Klima	There is a warm **climate** in the Caribbean.
	Barbados [baː'beɪdɒs]	Barbados *(Inselstaat in der Karibik)*	Ⓡ Барбадос Ⓣ Barbados
	tourist industry ['tʊərɪst ˌɪndəstri]	Tourismus	There are jobs in the **tourist industry**.

Topic 1

p. 52	Thanksgiving [ˌθæŋks'gɪvɪŋ]	Erntedankfest	**Thanksgiving** is the 4th Thursday in November.
	holiday *(AE)* ['hɒlədeɪ]	Feiertag	Thanksgiving is a **holiday** for the Americans.
	son [sʌn]	Sohn	**son** ↔ daughter
	to **be able to (do sth)** [bi: 'eɪbl tə]	(etw. tun) können; (zu etw.) fähig sein *(Ersatzform für can)*	I can find my own way now. I **was able to** find my own way yesterday.
	a few [ə 'fjuː]	ein paar; einige; wenige	We left after **a few** hours.
	Take a seat. [ˌteɪk ə 'siːt]	Setz dich.; Setzen Sie sich.; Nimm Platz.; Nehmen Sie Platz.	Welcome. **Take a seat**.
	turkey ['tɜːki]	Truthahn; Pute	
	meat [miːt]	Fleisch	
	annoyed [ə'nɔɪd]	verärgert	Please don't be **annoyed**.
	I don't mind. [aɪ ˌdəʊnt 'maɪnd]	Es macht nichts.	I'm sorry. – No problem. **I don't mind**.
	corn [kɔːn]	Mais; Korn; Getreide	
	potato *(sg)* [pə'teɪtəʊ], potatoes *(pl)* [pə'teɪtəʊz]	Kartoffel	
	thankful ['θæŋkfl]	dankbar	**thankful** → Thank you.

happy ['hæpi]	froh; fröhlich	**happy** ↔ sad
to **be allowed to (do sth)** [bi: ə'laʊd tə]	(etw. tun) dürfen	We **were allowed to** talk in class.

=== Das kenne ich schon ===

food and drink

meal [mi:l]	Mahlzeit; Essen		chips (pl) [tʃips]	Pommes frites
meat [mi:t]	Fleisch		rice [raɪs]	Reis
turkey ['tɜ:ki]	Truthahn; Pute		fruit [fru:t]	Obst; Frucht
chicken ['tʃɪkɪn]	Hähnchen; Huhn		strawberry ['strɔ:bri]	Erdbeere
burger ['bɜ:gə]	Hamburger		plum [plʌm]	Pflaume
hot dog ['hɒt ˌdɒg]	Hotdog		apple ['æpl]	Apfel
fish (sg), fish (pl) [fɪʃ]	Fisch		banana [bə'nɑ:nə]	Banane
vegetable (veg) ['vedʒtəbl (vedʒ)]	Gemüse		pizza ['pi:tsə]	Pizza
salad ['sæləd]	Salat		sandwich ['sænwɪdʒ]	Sandwich; belegtes Brot
corn [kɔ:n]	Mais; Korn; Getreide		butter ['bʌtə]	Butter
potato (sg) [pə'teɪtəʊ], potatoes (pl) [pə'teɪtəʊz]	Kartoffel		drink [drɪŋk]	Getränk
			tea [ti:]	Tee

Topic 2

p. 56	**Caribbean** [ˌkærɪ'bi:ən]	Karibe; Karibin; karibisch	**Caribbean** → the Caribbean
	gun [gʌn]	Pistole; Schusswaffe; Waffe	He had a **gun** in his hand.
	nurse [nɜ:s]	Krankenpfleger; Krankenschwester	
	hotel [hə'tel]	Hotel	
	to **disagree** [ˌdɪsə'gri:]	anderer Meinung sein; nicht einverstanden sein	to **disagree** ↔ to agree
	violence (no pl) ['vaɪələns]	Gewalt	There's a lot of **violence on** the streets.
	drug [drʌg]	Droge	Don't take **drugs**.
	to **rely (on)** [rɪ'laɪ (ɒn)]	sich verlassen (auf); vertrauen (auf)	I can **rely on** my family.
	forever [fə'revə]	für immer; ewig	I want to live here **forever**.
	comment ['kɒment]	Kommentar	Send us your **comments**, please.
	to **avoid** [ə'vɔɪd]	aus dem Weg gehen; vermeiden; meiden; ausweichen	We can't **avoid** the violence.
	vet [vet]	Tierarzt; Tierärztin	A **vet** is a doctor for animals.
	assistant [ə'sɪstnt]	Helfer; Helferin; Assistent; Assistentin; Mitarbeiter; Mitarbeiterin	A vet's **assistant** helps the vet.

to [tuː]	für	My family is very important **to** me.
hairdresser ['heə,dresə]	Friseur; Friseurin	I go to my **hairdresser** every six weeks.
hairdressing salon ['heədresɪŋ ,sælɒn]	Friseursalon	Hairdressers work in **hairdressing salons.**
manager ['mænɪdʒə]	Manager; Managerin; Geschäftsführer; Geschäftsführerin	R̲ менеджер

Das kenne ich schon

phrasal verbs

to ask about ['ɑːsk ə,baʊt]	fragen nach; sich erkundigen nach		**to get out** [,get ˈaʊt]	aussteigen; herauskommen
to drive off [,draɪv ˈɒf]	wegfahren		**to get up** [,get ˈʌp]	aufstehen
to fall off [,fɔːl ˈɒf]	von etw. stürzen; herunterfallen; hinunterfallen		**to sit down** [,sɪt ˈdaʊn]	sich setzen; sich hinsetzen
			to take out [,teɪk ˈaʊt]	hinausbringen
to find out [,faɪnd ˈaʊt]	herausfinden		**to talk to** ['tɔːk tə]	reden mit; sprechen mit
to get in [,get ˈɪn]	einsteigen			

Text

p. 60	**century** ['senʃri]	Jahrhundert	a **century** = 100 years
	to hear about [,hɪər əˈbaʊt]	erfahren von; hören von	I was sad when I **heard about** the accident.
	to keep sb prisoner [,kiːp ˈprɪznə]	jmdn. gefangen halten	His father **kept him prisoner**.
	to escape [ɪˈskeɪp]	entkommen; fliehen; entfliehen; flüchten	We **escaped** the fire.
	dead [ded]	tot	Huck wants people to think he's **dead**.
	so that [səʊ ˈðæt]	damit; sodass	I saved money **so that** I could buy a phone.
	canoe [kəˈnuː]	Kanu	
	sky [skaɪ]	Himmel	
	probably ['prɒbəbli]	wahrscheinlich	They **probably** thought I was dead.
	boom [buːm]	Donner; Boom	Suddenly I heard a loud **boom**.
	smoke [sməʊk]	Rauch	
	to shoot [ʃuːt], **shot** [ʃɒt], **shot** [ʃɒt]	schießen; erschießen	They **shot** cannon balls into the river.
	body ['bɒdi]	Leiche; Körper	There was a man's **body** on the beach.
	to go fishing [,gəʊ ˈfɪʃɪŋ]	angeln gehen; fischen gehen	We **went fishing** at Denali.
	Miss [mɪs]	Frau *(Anrede)*	**Miss** Watson wasn't nice to Jim.
	slave [sleɪv]	Sklave; Sklavin	The man was Miss Watson's **slave**.

p. 61	**ghost** [gəʊst]	Geist; Gespenst	I don't believe in **ghosts**.
	after ['ɑːftə]	nachdem	**After** I finished my homework, I watched TV.
	anyone ['eniwʌn]	irgendjemand; irgendeiner	Has **anyone** seen my mother?
	slave trader ['sleɪv ˌtreɪdə]	Sklavenhändler; Menschenhändler	A **slave trader** came from New Orleans.
	swam [swæm]	simple past von *to swim* (schwimmen)	I **swam** = ich schwamm/ich bin geschwommen
	to **explore** [ɪk'splɔː]	erkunden; erforschen	Let's **explore** the island together.
	cave [keɪv]	Höhle	

Das kenne ich schon

conjunctions

so that [səʊ 'ðæt]	damit; sodass	**because** [bɪ'kɒz]	weil; da
after ['ɑːftə]	nachdem	**so** [səʊ]	also; deshalb
while [waɪl]	während	**if** [ɪf]	wenn; falls; ob
before [bɪ'fɔː]	bevor; vorher; zuvor	**when** [wen]	als; wenn

Film

trouble ['trʌbl]	Ärger	**football** *(AE)* ['fʊtbɔːl]	American Football; Football
pecan ['piːkæn]	Pekannuss		
pie [paɪ]	Kuchen; Pastete	**volunteer** [ˌvɒlən'tɪə]	ehrenamtlich

Vocabulary skills

p. 66	**hurricane** ['hʌrɪkən]	Hurrikan; Orkan; Wirbelsturm	There are **hurricanes** in the autumn.
	interview ['ɪntəvjuː]	Interview; Gespräch; Befragung	Mark did an **interview** on the radio.
	movement ['muːvmənt]	Bewegung	**movement** → to move
	impossible [ɪm'pɒsəbl]	unmöglich	I think it's **impossible** to win.
	given ['gɪvn]	past participle von *to give* (geben, schenken)	I have **given** = ich gab/ich habe gegeben
	to **rebuild** [ˌriː'bɪld]	wiederaufbauen	**to rebuild** → to build

Das kenne ich schon

climate

climate ['klaɪmət]	Klima	**dry** [draɪ]	trocken
hurricane ['hʌrɪkən]	Hurrikan; Orkan; Wirbelsturm	**hot** [hɒt]	heiß
		cold [kəʊld]	kalt
wind [wɪnd]	Wind		
cold [kəʊld]	Kälte		

Unit 4 Working in Canada

Intro

p. 70	**ice hockey** [ˈaɪs ˌhɒki]	Eishockey	
	second [ˈseknd]	zweit-	Canada is the **second** largest country in the world.
	border [ˈbɔːdə]	Grenze	There are more jobs near the US **border**.
p. 71	**wilderness** [ˈwɪldənəs]	Wildnis	A lot of Alaska is **wilderness**.
	moose (sg) [muːs], **moose** (pl) [muːs]	Elch	
	both [bəʊθ]	beide	We are **both** happy.
	colony [ˈkɒləni]	Kolonie	R колония T koloni
	French [frenʃ]	französisch; Französisch; aus Frankreich	**French** → France
	language [ˈlæŋgwɪdʒ]	Sprache	You can hear different **languages** in Queens.
	Canadian [kəˈneɪdiən]	Kanadier; Kanadierin; kanadisch; aus Kanada	**Canadian** → Canada
	Inuit [ˈɪnuɪt]	Inuit (Ureinwohner Kanadas)	The **Inuit** people have lived in Canada for a long time.
	group [gruːp]	Gruppe	A **group** of us went rock climbing.

Topic 1

p. 72	**fair** [feə]	fair; gerecht	I can't go to the party. It's not **fair**!
	update [ˈʌpdeɪt]	aktuelle Information; Update; Aktualisierung	Josh gets **updates** about hockey teams.
	app [æp]	App	I have lots of **apps** on my phone.
	TV [ˌtiːˈviː]	Fernseh-; Fernsehen	What do you think about the **TV** programme?
	series (no pl) [ˈsɪəriːz]	Serie	I never watch TV **series** on my phone.
	to **mean** [miːn], **meant** [ment], **meant** [ment]	meinen; bedeuten	I know what you **mean**
	selfie [ˈselfi]	Selfie	I take **selfies** with my friends.
	software [ˈsɒftweə]	Software	There is lots of good **software**.
	copyright [ˈkɒpiraɪt]	Copyright; Urheberrecht	Most songs have **copyright** on them.
	follower [ˈfɒləʊə]	Follower; Followerin; Anhänger; Anhängerin	I have 30 **followers** on the music website.

to **comment (on)** ['kɒment (ɒn)]	kommentieren	Three people **commented on** my video.
tutorial [tjuːˈtɔːriəl]	Tutorial; Anleitung	**Tutorials** show you how to do something.
to **repair** [rɪˈpeə]	reparieren	I **repaired** my bike yesterday.
episode [ˈepɪsəʊd]	Folge; Episode	⇔ Achtung Aussprache!

Topic 2

p. 76	**application** [ˌæplɪˈkeɪʃn]	Bewerbung	I sent my **application** for the job yesterday.
receptionist [rɪˈsepʃnɪst]	Empfangschef; Empfangsdame	I'd like to work as a hotel **receptionist**.
guest [gest]	Gast	We have **guests** for the weekend.
to **look for** [ˈlʊk fə]	suchen (nach)	Help me **look for** my phone, please.
experience [ɪkˈspɪəriəns]	Erfahrung; Erlebnis	It was a fantastic **experience**.
customer service [ˌkʌstəmə ˈsɜːvɪs]	Kundenbetreuung; Kunden-dienst; Kundenservice	I have good skills in **customer services**.
skill [skɪl]	Kenntnis; Fertigkeit; Fähigkeit; Geschick	Companies want to know about your **skills**.
to **offer** [ˈɒfə]	bieten; anbieten	The job **offers** great opportunities.
salary [ˈsælri]	Gehalt	The hotel offers a good **salary**.
training [ˈtreɪnɪŋ]	Ausbildung; Training	**training** → to train
CV (curriculum vitae) [ˌsiːˈviː (kəˌrɪkjələmˈviːtaɪ)]	Lebenslauf	I have to send my **CV** to the hotel.
letter of application [ˌletər əv ˌæplɪˈkeɪʃn]	Bewerbungsschreiben	Send a **letter of application** and your CV.
letter [ˈletə]	Schreiben; Brief; Buchstabe	Thank you for your **letter**.
Dear ..., [dɪə]	Sehr geehrte(r) ...,	So kannst du im Englischen Briefe und E-Mails anfangen: **Dear ...,**
to **apply (for)** [əˈplaɪ (fə)]	sich bewerben (für/um)	**to apply** → application
internship [ˈɪntɜːnʃɪp]	Praktikum; Berufspraktikum	She did an **internship** here last year.
travel agent's [ˈtrævlˌeɪdʒnts]	Reisebüro	I booked my holiday at the **travel agent's**.
confident [ˈkɒnfɪdnt]	selbstsicher; selbstbewusst; sicher	He is very **confident**.
reliable [rɪˈlaɪəbl]	verlässlich; zuverlässig; vertrau-enswürdig	She's very **reliable**. She's never late.
Yours sincerely, [jɔːz sɪnˈsɪəli]	Mit freundlichen Grüßen	So kannst du im Englischen Briefe und E-Mails abschließen: **Yours sincerely, ...**

Text

p. 80	**railway station** ['reɪlweɪ ˌsteɪʃn]	Bahnhof	
	railway ['reɪlweɪ]	Eisenbahn; Bahn	
	flexible ['fleksɪbl]	flexibel	✎ Achtung Schreibweise! flexib**le**
	working hours *(pl)* ['wɜːkɪŋ ˌaʊəz]	Arbeitszeit	My **working hours** are 9:00 to 5:00.
	hours *(pl)* ['aʊəz]	Zeiten	You have to work different **hours**.
	secondary school leaving certificate ['sekndri skuːl ˌliːvɪŋ səˈtɪfɪkət]	mittlerer Schulabschluss; Real-schulabschluss	You need a **secondary school leaving certificate** for the job.
	friendly ['frendli]	freundlich; sympathisch	**friendly** → friend
	travel agent ['trævl ˌeɪdʒnt]	Reisebürokaufmann; Reisebüro-kauffrau	There is an ad here for a **travel agent**. Look!
	to **plan** [plæn]	planen	to **plan** → plan
	to **make reservations** [ˌmeɪk rezəˈveɪʃnz]	reservieren	You will **make reservations** and book tours.
	qualification [ˌkwɒlɪfɪˈkeɪʃn]	Ausbildung; Qualifikation; Ab-schluss; Schulabschluss	What kind of **qualification** do you have?
	tourism ['tʊərɪzm]	Tourismus	ⓡ туризм ⓣ turizm
	efficient [ɪˈfɪʃnt]	effizient; leistungsfähig	She can organize **efficiently**.
p. 81	**address** [əˈdres]	Adresse	✎ Achtung Schreibweise! a**dd**ress
	date of birth [ˌdeɪt əv ˈbɜːθ]	Geburtsdatum	**date of birth** = date you were born
	education [ˌedʒʊˈkeɪʃn]	Ausbildung; Erziehung; Bildung	My **education** was at the local school.
	secondary school ['sekndri ˌskuːl]	weiterführende Schule; Mittel-schule	You go to **secondary school** after primary school.
	primary school ['praɪmri ˌskuːl]	Grundschule	You go to **primary school** first.
	Russian ['rʌʃn]	Russisch; russisch; aus Russland; Russe; Russin	**Russian** → Russia
	interest ['ɪntrəst]	Interesse	My **interests** are cooking and sport.
	reference ['refrns]	Referenz; Arbeitszeugnis; Emp-fehlung	👄 Achtung Aussprache!
	available [əˈveɪləbl]	erhältlich; verfügbar	My references are **available** if you ask.
	request [rɪˈkwest]	Anfrage	I made a **request** for a quiet room.

Das kenne ich schon

travel words

tourism ['tʊərɪzm]	Tourismus		to transport [træn'spɔːt]	transportieren; befördern
travel agent ['trævl̩ˌeɪdʒnt]	Reisebürokaufmann; Reisebürokauffrau		railway station ['reɪlweɪˌsteɪʃn]	Bahnhof
travel agent's ['trævl̩ˌeɪdʒnts]	Reisebüro		to get on sth [ˌget ˈɒn]	in etw. steigen; in etw. einsteigen
guide [gaɪd]	Führer; Führerin		to get off [ˌget ˈɒf]	aussteigen
bed and breakfast (B & B) [ˌbed ən 'brekfəst]	Frühstückspension		cable car ['keɪbl̩ ˌkɑː]	seilgezogene Straßenbahn; Seilbahn
hotel [hə'tel]	Hotel		to drive off [ˌdraɪv ˈɒf]	wegfahren
to travel ['trævl̩]	reisen		driver ['draɪvə]	Fahrer; Fahrerin

Das kenne ich schon

words for talking about jobs

education [ˌedʒʊ'keɪʃn]	Ausbildung; Erziehung; Bildung		to train [treɪn]	eine Ausbildung machen; ausbilden
experience [ɪk'spɪəriəns]	Erfahrung		successful [sək'sesfl̩]	erfolgreich
training ['treɪnɪŋ]	Ausbildung; Training		efficient [ɪ'fɪʃnt]	effizient; leistungsfähig
career [kə'rɪə]	Laufbahn; Karriere; Beruf		confident ['kɒnfɪdnt]	selbstsicher; selbstbewusst; sicher
working hours (pl) ['wɜːkɪŋ ˌaʊəz]	Arbeitszeit		reliable [rɪ'laɪəbl̩]	verlässlich; zuverlässig; vertrauenswürdig
salary ['sælri]	Gehalt		friendly ['frendli]	freundlich; sympathisch
to offer ['ɒfə]	bieten; anbieten			

Film

counselor ['kaʊnslə]	Betreuer; Betreuerin

Speaking skills

p. 88	topic ['tɒpɪk]	Thema	Choose a **topic** for the presentation.
	kilometre (km) [kɪ'lɒmɪtə]	Kilometer (km)	1 **kilometre** = 0.621 miles

Dictionary

Die Abkürzungen geben an, wo das Wort zum ersten Mal vorkommt.
Verwendete Abkürzungen und Zeichen:

U = Unit
* = unregelmäßige Verben

I = Band 1
II = Band 2
III = Band 3
IV U2, 32 = Band 4, Unit 2, S. 32
<IV U2, 42> = nur zum Nachschlagen, gehört nicht zum Lernwortschatz

A

a [ə] ein; eine I
  a few [ə 'fju:] ein paar; einige; wenige IV U3, 52
  a little (bit) [ə 'lɪtl (bɪt)] ein (kleines) bisschen; ein (klein) wenig II
  a lot [ə 'lɒt] viel; sehr I
  a lot of [ə 'lɒt ˌəv] viel; viele; eine Menge I
  a year [ə 'jɪə] pro Jahr; im Jahr IV U2, 40
  a/one hundred ['hʌndrəd] hundert; einhundert I
  a/one thousand ['θaʊznd] tausend; eintausend II
a.m. [ˌeɪ'em] vormittags (Uhrzeit) III
*to be able to (do sth) [bi: 'eɪbl tə] (etw. tun) können; (zu etw.) fähig sein (Ersatzform für can) IV U3, 52
about [ə'baʊt] über I; ungefähr; circa; etwa II; an III; wegen IV U2, 36
  to hang about [ˌhæŋ ˌə'baʊt] herumhängen I
  out and about [ˌaʊt ən ˌə'baʊt] unterwegs III
above [ə'bʌv] über; oberhalb II
absolutely [ˌæbsə'lu:tli] völlig; absolut <IV U3, 134>
accent ['æksnt] Akzent III
accident ['æksɪdnt] Unfall I
across [ə'krɒs] über II
to act [ækt] spielen; mitspielen III
  acting workshop ['æktɪŋ ˌwɜ:kʃɒp] Schauspielworkshop III
activity [æk'tɪvəti] Aktivität I
actor ['æktə] Schauspieler; Schauspielerin; Darsteller; Darstellerin III
to add [æd] hinzufügen <I>

address [ə'dres] Adresse IV U4, 81
adjective ['ædʒɪktɪv] Adjektiv; Eigenschaftswort <III>
adult ['ædʌlt] Erwachsener; Erwachsene <IV U1, 22>
adventure [əd'ventʃə] Abenteuer; Erlebnis III
ad(vert) (= advertisement) ['æd(vɜ:t) (əd'vɜ:tɪsmənt)] Werbung; Anzeige III
adverb ['ædvɜ:b] Adverb <IV U1, 38>
  adverb of manner [ˌædvɜ:b ˌəv 'mænə] Adverb der Art und Weise <IV U2, 105>
advice [əd'vaɪs] Rat; Ratschlag III
Afghan ['æfgæn] Afghanisch; afghanisch; aus Afghanistan <IV U1, 131>
I'm afraid [aɪm ə'freɪd] leider IV U2, 36
African ['æfrɪkən] afrikanisch <IV U3, 62>
  African American [ˌæfrɪkən ə'merɪkən] Afroamerikaner; Afroamerikanerin IV U3, 50
after ['ɑ:ftə] nach I; nachdem IV U3, 61
  after that [ˌɑ:ftə 'ðæt] danach I
afternoon [ˌɑ:ftə'nu:n] Nachmittag I
again [ə'gen] noch einmal; wieder I
against [ə'genst] gegen III
age [eɪdʒ] Alter; Zeitalter <IV U4, 82>
  check-in agent [ˌtʃekɪn 'eɪdʒnt] Check-in-Mitarbeiter; Check-in-Mitarbeiterin IV U2, 36
  travel agent ['trævl ˌeɪdʒnt] Reisebürokaufmann; Reisebürokauffrau IV U4, 80
  travel agent's ['trævl ˌeɪdʒnts] Reisebüro IV U4, 76
ago [ə'gəʊ] vor II

to agree (with) [ə'gri: (wɪð)] zustimmen; einer Meinung sein (mit) II
ahead [ə'hed] voraus <IV U4, 87>
air [eə] Luft III
air-conditioned ['eəkənˌdɪʃnd] klimatisiert <IV U2, 42>
airport ['eəpɔ:t] Flughafen IV U2, 32
Alaskan [ə'læskən] alaskisch; Alaska- IV U2, 48
all [ɔ:l] alle; ganz I
  all of ['ɔ:l ˌəv] ganz II
  all over [ˌɔ:l 'əʊvə] in ganz; überall II
  all around the world [ˌɔ:l əˌraʊnd ðə 'wɜ:ld] in aller Welt II
  All the best, [ˌɔ:l ðə 'best] Alles Gute II
  of all the states [əv ˌɔ:l ðə ˌsteɪts] von allen Staaten IV U2, 31
all-day ['ɔ:ldeɪ] Ganztages- III
alligator ['ælɪgeɪtə] Alligator II
*to be allowed to (do sth) [bi: ə'laʊd tə] erlaubt sein <IV U2, 42>; (etw. tun) dürfen IV U3, 52
alphabet ['ælfəbet] Alphabet <I>
alphabetical [ˌælfə'betɪkl] alphabetisch <II>
already [ɔ:l'redi] schon; bereits III
also ['ɔ:lsəʊ] auch I
always ['ɔ:lweɪz] immer I; schon immer III
amazing [ə'meɪzɪŋ] erstaunlich; unglaublich; toll II
amenity [ə'mi:nəti] Annehmlichkeit; Einrichtung <IV U2, 42>
American [ə'merɪkən] amerikanisch; Amerikanisch; aus Amerika; Amerikaner; Amerikanerin II

p pen • **b** bed • **t** ten • **d** dad • **k** cat • **g** grey • **tʃ** chair • **dʒ** job • **f** fan • **v** very • **θ** three • **ð** the

African American [ˌæfrɪkən ə'merɪkən] Afroamerikaner; Afroamerikanerin IV U3, 50

American football [ə'merɪkən 'fʊtbɔ:l] American Football II

Native American [ˌneɪtɪv ə'merɪkən] Ureinwohner Amerikas; Ureinwohnerin Amerikas; Indianer; Indianerin; indianisch III

an [æn] ein; eine I

and [ænd] und I

angry ['æŋgri] wütend; zornig; verärgert; böse II

animal ['ænɪml] Tier I

animal rescue shelter [ˌænɪml 'reskju: ˌʃeltə] Tierheim I

announcement [ə'naʊnsmənt] Durchsage; Ankündigung <II>

annoyed [ə'nɔɪd] verärgert IV U3, 52

another [ə'nʌðə] ein anderer; noch ein; andere IV U2, 36

answer ['ɑ:nsə] Antwort II

to answer ['ɑ:nsə] antworten; beantworten II

any ['eni] irgendwelche; irgendeine I

not … any more [ˌnɒt … eni 'mɔ:] nicht mehr III

not … any [ˌnɒt … eni] kein; keine III

anybody ['eniˌbɒdi] irgendjemand; jemand; jeder III

anyone ['eniwʌn] irgendjemand; irgendeiner IV U3, 61

anything ['eniθɪŋ] etwas; irgendetwas III

not … anything [nɒt … 'eniθɪŋ] nichts III

Anything else? [ˌeniθɪŋ 'els] Darf es sonst noch etwas sein? I

apartment (AE) [ə'pɑ:tmənt] Wohnung; Apartment IV U1, 16

app [æp] App IV U4, 72

apple ['æpl] Apfel I

application [ˌæplɪ'keɪʃn] Bewerbung IV U4, 76

letter of application [ˌletər əv ˌæplɪ'keɪʃn] Bewerbungsschreiben IV U4, 76

to apply (for) [ə'plaɪ (fə)] sich bewerben (für/um) IV U4, 76

apprenticeship [ə'prentɪʃɪp] Ausbildung; Lehre <IV U3, 135>

April ['eɪprl] April I

Saudi Arabian [ˌsaʊdi ə'reɪbiən] saudi-arabisch <IV U1, 131>

Arabic ['ærəbɪk] Arabisch; arabisch <IV U1, 131>

area ['eəriə] Gebiet; Gegend; Areal IV U2, 41

argument ['ɑ:gjəmənt] Auseinandersetzung; Streit II

arm [ɑ:m] Arm II

around [ə'raʊnd] um … herum II; durch; um III

to walk around [ˌwɔ:k ə'raʊnd] umherlaufen; herumlaufen <I>

to arrange [ə'reɪndʒ] anordnen; arrangieren <IV U1, 25>

arrival [ə'raɪvl] Ankömmling IV U1, 12

arrivals [ə'raɪvlz] Ankunft <IV U2, 133>

to arrive [ə'raɪv] ankommen I

Art [ɑ:t] Kunst I

artist ['ɑ:tɪst] Künstler; Künstlerin III

as [æz] wie; als II

… as well as … [əz 'wel əz] sowohl … als auch … II

as … as [əz … əz] so … wie III

to ask [ɑ:sk] fragen I

to ask about ['ɑ:sk əˌbaʊt] fragen nach; sich erkundigen nach II

to ask for ['ɑ:sk fɔ:] bitten um <III>

to ask sb to do sth ['ɑ:sk tə ˌdu:] jmdn. bitten, etw. zu tun <IV U4, 85>

to ask the way ['ɑ:sk ðə 'weɪ] nach dem Weg fragen <II>

aspect ['æspekt] Aspekt; Gesichtspunkt; Blickwinkel <IV U4, 89>

assistant [ə'sɪstnt] Verkäufer; Verkäuferin I; Helfer; Helferin; Assistent; Assistentin; Mitarbeiter; Mitarbeiterin IV U3, 56

at [æt] zu; in; an; auf; um; bei I

at home [ət 'həʊm] zu Hause; daheim I

at night [ət 'naɪt] nachts IV U1, 16

at school [ət 'sku:l] in der Schule I

at the back (of) [ət ðə 'bæk (ɒv)] hinten (in) <III>

at the doctor's [ət ðə 'dɒktəz] beim Arzt II

at the end [ət ði 'end] am Ende II

at the front (of) [ət ðə 'frʌnt (ɒv)] vorne (in) <IV U1, 24>

at the moment [ət ðə 'məʊmənt] im Moment; momentan II

at the same time [ət ðə seɪm 'taɪm] gleichzeitig; nebenher II

at the seaside [ət ðə 'si:saɪd] am Meer I

ate [eɪt] simple past von to eat II

athletics [æθ'letɪks] Leichtathletik <IV U4, 137>

attic ['ætɪk] Dachboden I

August ['ɔ:gəst] August I

aunt [ɑ:nt] Tante I

autumn ['ɔ:təm] Herbst II

available [ə'veɪləbl] erhältlich; verfügbar IV U4, 81

to avoid [ə'vɔɪd] aus dem Weg gehen; vermeiden; meiden; ausweichen IV U3, 56

away [ə'weɪ] weg; entfernt II

to be a long way away [bi: ə 'lɒŋ ˌweɪ ə'weɪ] weit weg sein II

awesome ['ɔ:səm] großartig; toll; beeindruckend III

awful ['ɔ:fl] schrecklich; furchtbar I

B

babysitter ['beɪbiˌsɪtə] Babysitter; Babysitterin <IV U4, 138>

back [bæk] zurück II

at the back (of) [ət ðə 'bæk (ɒv)] hinten (in) <III>

background ['bækgraʊnd] Hintergrund III

bacon ['beɪkn] Speck I

bad [bæd] schlecht I; schlimm II

That's too bad. [ˌðæts tu: 'bæd] Schade! II

badminton ['bædmɪntən] Badminton; Federball <IV U4, 137>

bag [bæg] Tasche; Tüte; Sack I

bagpipes (pl) ['bægpaɪps] Dudelsack III

baker ['beɪkə] Bäcker; Bäckerin <IV U3, 135>

balcony ['bælkəni] Balkon I

bald eagle [bɔ:ld 'i:gl] Weißkopfseeadler <IV U2, 47>

ball [bɔ:l] Ball I; Kugel III

banana

cannon ball ['kænən ˌbɔ:l] Kanonenkugel III

banana [bə'na:nə] Banane I

band [bænd] Band; Musikgruppe II

bar chart ['ba: ˌtʃa:t] Säulendiagramm; Balkendiagramm <IV U1, 25>

burger **bar** ['bɜ:gə ˌba:] Burger-Restaurant <IV U2, 43>

snack **bar** ['snæk ˌba:] Imbissstube; Café I

barbecue ['ba:bɪkju:] Grill; Grillfest I

to bark [ba:k] bellen II

base [beɪs] Base; Mal III

baseball ['beɪsbɔ:l] Baseball III

basic ['beɪsɪk] grundlegend <III>

basket ['ba:skɪt] Basketballkorb; Korb III

basketball ['ba:skɪtbɔ:l] Basketball II

bat [bæt] Fledermaus I; Schläger <IV U4, 137>

bathroom ['ba:θrʊm] Bad(ezimmer) II

batter ['bætə] Schlagmann; Schlagfrau III

*****to be** [bi:] sein I

to be a long way away [bi: ə 'lɒŋ ˌweɪ ə'weɪ] weit weg sein II

to be able to (do sth) [bi: 'eɪbl tə] (etw. tun) können; (zu etw.) fähig sein *(Ersatzform für can)* IV U3, 52

to be allowed to (do sth) [bi: ə'laʊd tə] erlaubt sein <IV U2, 42>; (etw. tun) dürfen IV U3, 52

to be born [bi: 'bɔ:n] geboren werden IV U1, 16

to be fed up (with) [bi: ˌfed'ʌp (wɪð)] die Nase voll haben (von) III

to be fun [bi: 'fʌn] Spaß machen; witzig sein II

to be going to do sth [bi: ˌgəʊɪŋ tə 'du:] etw. tun werden III

to be good at [bi: 'gʊd ət] gut sein in; gut sein bei I

to be homesick [bi: 'həʊmsɪk] Heimweh haben IV U1, 12

to be interested in [bi: 'ɪntrəstɪd ɪn] interessiert sein an; sich interessieren für III

to be late [bi: 'leɪt] zu spät kommen II

to be lucky [bi: 'lʌki] Glück haben II

to be scared [bi: 'skeəd] Angst haben I

to be sick [bi: 'sɪk] sich übergeben I

beach [bi:tʃ] Strand I

bear [beə] Bär II

grizzly bear ['grɪzli ˌbeə] Grizzlybär IV U2, 32

beautiful ['bju:tɪfl] schön; hübsch; wunderschön III

became [bɪ'keɪm] simple past von *to become* II

because [bɪ'kɒz] weil; da I

*****to become** [bɪ'kʌm] (zu etw.) werden II

bed [bed] Bett I

bed and breakfast (B & B) [ˌbed ən 'brekfəst] Frühstückspension III

to go to bed [ˌgəʊ tə 'bed] ins Bett gehen I

bedroom ['bedrʊm] Kinderzimmer; Schlafzimmer II

been [bi:n] past participle von *to be* III

before [bɪ'fɔ:] vor; bevor II; vorher; zuvor III

beginning [bɪ'gɪnɪŋ] Anfang; Beginn II

behind [bɪ'haɪnd] hinter I

to believe [bɪ'li:v] glauben II

bell [bel] Glocke II

below [bɪ'ləʊ] unten <IV U4, 74>

best [best] am besten; beste; am liebsten II

All the best, [ɔ:l ðə 'best] Alles Gute II

Best wishes, [ˌbest 'wɪʃɪz] Viele Grüße; Alles Gute! I

better ['betə] besser II

between [bɪ'twi:n] zwischen III

big [bɪg] groß I

big wheel [bɪg 'wi:l] Riesenrad II

bike [baɪk] Fahrrad I

to go bike riding [ˌgəʊ 'baɪk ˌraɪdɪŋ] Fahrrad fahren II

Biology [baɪ'ɒlədʒi] Biologie I

bird [bɜ:d] Vogel IV U2, 32

date of **birth** [ˌdeɪt əv 'bɜ:θ] Geburtsdatum IV U4, 81

birthday ['bɜ:θdeɪ] Geburtstag I

biscuit ['bɪskɪt] Keks III

black [blæk] schwarz I

blackboard ['blækbɔ:d] Tafel I

blanket ['blæŋkɪt] Decke; Bettdecke; Wolldecke IV U2, 41

blog [blɒg] Blog; Internettagebuch I

blue [blu:] blau I

boarding pass ['bɔ:dɪŋ ˌpa:s] Bordkarte <IV U2, 133>

boarding card ['bɔ:dɪŋ ˌka:d] Bordkarte IV U2, 36

boarding time ['bɔ:dɪŋ ˌtaɪm] Einsteigezeit IV U2, 36

boat [bəʊt] Boot; Schiff IV U2, 30

body ['bɒdi] Leiche; Körper IV U3, 60

book [bʊk] Buch; Heft I

exercise book ['eksəsaɪz ˌbʊk] Übungsheft I

to book [bʊk] buchen; reservieren III

boom [bu:m] Donner; Boom IV U3, 60

Boom! [bu:m] Bum! IV U3, 60

border ['bɔ:də] Grenze IV U4, 70

boring ['bɔ:rɪŋ] langweilig I

*****to be born** [bi: 'bɔ:n] geboren werden IV U1, 16

borough ['bʌrə] Stadtteil; Bezirk IV U1, 10

to borrow ['bɒrəʊ] (sich) ausleihen II

boss [bɒs] Boss; Chef; Chefin III

both [bəʊθ] beide IV U4, 71

a **bottle** of [ə 'bɒtl əv] eine Flasche … II

bought [bɔ:t] simple past von *to buy* I; past participle von *to buy* III

to bounce [baʊns] prellen; hüpfen III

box [bɒks] Box; Kiste; Schachtel I

telephone box ['telɪfəʊn ˌbɒks] Telefonzelle II

boy [bɔɪ] Junge; Bub I

brave [breɪv] mutig; tapfer III

bread [bred] Brot I

break [breɪk] Pause I

breakfast ['brekfəst] Frühstück I

bed and breakfast (B & B) [ˌbed ən 'brekfəst] Frühstückspension III

to have breakfast [ˌhæv 'brekfəst] frühstücken I

bridge [brɪdʒ] Brücke II

*****to bring** [brɪŋ] mitbringen; bringen II

British ['brɪtɪʃ] britisch <III>

brochure ['brəʊʃə] Broschüre; Prospekt III

brother [ˈbrʌðə] Bruder I

brought [brɔːt] simple past von *to bring* II

brown [braʊn] braun I

*to build [bɪld] bauen II

building [ˈbɪldɪŋ] Gebäude; Bauwerk II

built [bɪlt] simple past von *to build* II

burger [ˈbɜːɡə] Hamburger I

burger bar [ˈbɜːɡə ˌbɑː] Burger-Restaurant <IV U2, 43>

bus [bʌs] Bus I

on the bus [ˌɒn ðə ˈbʌs] im Bus II

busy [ˈbɪzi] beschäftigt I

a busy day [ə ˌbɪzi ˈdeɪ] ein ausgefüllter Tag II

but [bʌt] aber I

butter [ˈbʌtə] Butter I

*to buy [baɪ] kaufen I

buzzard [ˈbʌzəd] Bussard <IV U2, 132>

by [baɪ] von; an; neben III

by (train) [baɪ (treɪn)] mit (dem Zug) I

Bye. [baɪ] Tschüss. I

C

caber [ˈkeɪbə] Baumstamm III

caber toss [ˈkeɪbə ˌtɒs] Baumstammwerfen III

cable car [ˈkeɪbl ˌkɑː] seilgezogene Straßenbahn; Seilbahn IV U2, 31

café [ˈkæfeɪ] Café III

cafeteria [kæfəˈtɪəriə] Cafeteria; Mensa I

cage [keɪdʒ] Käfig II

cake [keɪk] Kuchen I

calculator [ˈkælkjəleɪtə] Taschenrechner I

phone call [ˈfəʊn ˌkɔːl] Telefonanruf; Anruf I

to call [kɔːl] anrufen; rufen; nennen III

caller [ˈkɔːlə] Anrufer; Anruferin <II>

came [keɪm] simple past von *to come* I

camp [kæmp] Camp; Lager III

*to go camping [ɡəʊ ˈkæmpɪŋ] campen gehen; zelten gehen III

campsite [ˈkæmpsaɪt] Campingplatz; Zeltplatz III

can [kæn] können I; Dose IV U2, 41

can't [kɑːnt] nicht können I

I can't wait [aɪ ˌkɑːnt ˈweɪt] ich kann es kaum erwarten III

Canadian [kəˈneɪdiən] Kanadier; Kanadierin; kanadisch; aus Kanada IV U4, 71

canal [kəˈnæl] Kanal III

cannon [ˈkænən] Kanone III

cannon ball [ˈkænən ˌbɔːl] Kanonenkugel III

canoe [kəˈnuː] Kanu IV U3, 60

canoeing [kəˈnuːɪŋ] Kanufahren I

capital (city) [ˈkæpɪtl (ˌsɪti)] Hauptstadt I

captain [ˈkæptɪn] Kapitän; Kapitänin; Mannschaftsführer; Mannschaftsführerin II

caption [ˈkæpʃn] Bildunterschrift; Untertitel <III>

car [kɑː] Auto I

car park [ˈkɑː ˌpɑːk] Parkplatz <IV U2, 42>

card [kɑːd] Karte III

boarding card [ˈbɔːdɪŋ ˌkɑːd] Bordkarte IV U2, 36

*to take care of sb [teɪk ˈkeər əv] sich um jmdn. kümmern; für jmdn. sorgen <IV U4, 82>

career [kəˈrɪə] Laufbahn; Karriere; Beruf IV U1, 12

careful [ˈkeəfl] vorsichtig; sorgfältig III

caretaker [ˈkeəteɪkə] Hausmeister; Hausmeisterin I

Caribbean [ˌkærɪˈbiːən] Karibe; Karibin; karibisch IV U3, 56

carnival [ˈkɑːnɪvl] Karneval; Fasching I

carpenter [ˈkɑːpntə] Schreiner; Schreinerin; Tischler; Tischlerin <IV U3, 135>

carpet [ˈkɑːpɪt] Teppich II

castle [ˈkɑːsl] Burg; Schloss III

cat [kæt] Katze I

*to catch [kætʃ] fangen II

*to catch (bus/train) [kætʃ (bʌs/treɪn)] nehmen (Bus/Zug); bekommen (Bus/Zug) III

caught [kɔːt] simple past von *to catch* II

to cause [kɔːz] verursachen; auslösen IV U2, 40

cave [keɪv] Höhle IV U3, 61

to celebrate [ˈseləbreɪt] feiern III

cemetery [ˈsemətri] Friedhof <IV U3, 62>

cent [sent] Cent *(Währung)* III

center *(AE)* [ˈsentə] Zentrum; Mitte; Center III

centre [ˈsentə] Zentrum; Mitte; Center III

city centre [ˌsɪti ˈsentə] Stadtzentrum; Stadtmitte II

shopping centre [ˈʃɒpɪŋ ˌsentə] Einkaufszentrum II

sports centre [ˈspɔːts ˌsentə] Sportzentrum I

century [ˈsenʃri] Jahrhundert IV U3, 60

certificate [səˈtɪfɪkət] Zeugnis; Urkunde; Zertifikat; Bescheinigung <IV U4, 138>

secondary school leaving certificate [ˈsekndri skuːl ˌliːvɪŋ səˈtɪfɪkət] mittlerer Schulabschluss; Realschulabschluss IV U4, 80

cevapcici [səˈvæpˈtʃətʃi] Cevapcici <IV U1, 131>

chain [tʃeɪn] Kette III

chair [tʃeə] Stuhl I

champion [ˈtʃæmpiən] Gewinner; Gewinnerin; Sieger; Siegerin <I>

chance [tʃɑːns] Möglichkeit; Chance; Gelegenheit III

change [tʃeɪndʒ] Wechselgeld I

to change [tʃeɪndʒ] verändern; ändern; wechseln II; umsteigen III

chant [tʃɑːnt] Sprechgesang <I>

charades [ʃəˈrɑːdz] Scharaden <II>

charity [ˈtʃærɪti] Wohltätigkeitsorganisation; Stiftung; wohltätige Zwecke; Wohltätigkeits- II

chart [tʃɑːt] Tabelle; Diagramm <I>

bar chart [ˈbɑː ˌtʃɑːt] Säulendiagramm; Balkendiagramm <IV U1, 25>

pie chart [ˈpaɪ ˌtʃɑːt] Kreisdiagramm; Tortendiagramm <IV U1, 25>

to chat [tʃæt] chatten; plaudern II

cheap [tʃiːp] günstig; billig II

to **check** [tʃek] überprüfen; kontrollieren II

check-in [ˈtʃekɪn] Check-in; Gepäckaufgabe <IV U2, 133>

check-in agent [ˌtʃekɪn ˈeɪdʒnt] Check-in-Mitarbeiter; Check-in-Mitarbeiterin IV U2, 36

checklist [ˈtʃeklɪst] Checkliste <I>

checkout [ˈtʃekaʊt] Kontrolle <I>

cheerleader [ˈtʃɪəˌliːdə] Cheerleader; Cheerleaderin III

cheerleading [ˈtʃɪəˌliːdɪŋ] Cheerleading III

cheese [tʃiːz] Käse I

chef [ʃef] Koch; Küchenchef II

chicken [ˈtʃɪkɪn] Hähnchen; Huhn I

chicken fried rice [ˈtʃɪkɪn ˌfraɪd ˈraɪs] gebratener Reis mit Hühnerfleisch II

children *(pl)* [ˈtʃɪldrn] Kinder I

chimpanzee [ˌtʃɪmpnˈziː] Schimpanse II

Chinese [tʃaɪˈniːz] chinesisch; Chinesisch; aus China; Chinese; Chinesin II

chips *(pl)* [tʃɪps] Pommes frites I

chocolate [ˈtʃɒklət] Schokolade I

*to **choose** [tʃuːz] wählen; auswählen III

chorus [ˈkɔːrəs] Refrain <I>

chose [tʃəʊz] simple past von *to choose* III

chosen [ˈtʃəʊzn] past participle von *to choose* III

Christian [ˈkrɪstʃən] christlich <IV U1, 131>

Christmas [ˈkrɪsməs] Weihnachten I
Merry Christmas! [ˌmeri ˈkrɪsməs] Frohe Weihnachten! I

church [tʃɜːtʃ] Kirche II

cinema [ˈsɪnəmə] Kino I

to **cite** [saɪt] angeben; zitieren <IV U4, 136>

citizen [ˈsɪtɪzn] Staatsbürger; Staatsbürgerin; Staatsangehöriger; Staatsangehörige IV U1, 12

city [ˈsɪti] Stadt; Großstadt I
city centre [ˌsɪti ˈsentə] Stadtzentrum; Stadtmitte II

class [klɑːs] Klasse I; Unterricht; Unterrichtsstunde; Kurs IV U1, 26

classmate [ˈklɑːsmeɪt] Klassenkamerad; Klassenkameradin; Mitschüler; Mitschülerin <IV U3, 59>

classroom [ˈklɑːsrʊm] Klassenzimmer I

to **clean** [kliːn] sauber machen; putzen II

clear [klɪə] klar; deutlich III

climate [ˈklaɪmət] Klima IV U3, 51

to **climb** [klaɪm] besteigen; klettern; erklettern; steigen II

clock [klɒk] Uhr II
o'clock [əˈklɒk] Uhr *(Zeitangabe bei vollen Stunden)* I

to **close** [kləʊz] zumachen; schließen I

closed [kləʊzd] geschlossen I

clothes *(pl only)* [kləʊðz] Kleider; Kleidung I

cloud [klaʊd] Wolke II

cloudy [ˈklaʊdi] bewölkt; wolkig II

club [klʌb] Klub; Treff; Schul-AG I

clue [kluː] Hinweis; Spur I

coach [kəʊtʃ] Bus <IV U1, 130>

coal mine [ˈkəʊl ˌmaɪn] Kohlenbergwerk; Kohlengrube III

coast [kəʊst] Küste III

coat [kəʊt] Jacke I

cola [ˈkəʊlə] Cola I

cold [kəʊld] kalt I; Erkältung; Kälte II

collar [ˈkɒlə] Halsband I

to **collect** [kəˈlekt] sammeln <I>

collection [kəˈlekʃn] Sammlung III

colony [ˈkɒləni] Kolonie IV U4, 71

color *(AE)* [ˈkʌlə] Farbe III

colour [ˈkʌlə] Farbe I

*to **come** [kʌm] kommen I

come [kʌm] past participle von *to come* <IV U1, 15>

comic [ˈkɒmɪk] Comic(heft) II

comment [ˈkɒment] Kommentar IV U3, 56

to **comment (on)** [ˈkɒment (ɒn)] kommentieren IV U4, 72

communicative [kəˈmjuːnɪkətɪv] aufgeschlossen; kommunikativ <IV U4, 138>

community [kəˈmjuːnəti] Gemeinde; Gemeinschaft <IV U3, 62>

company [ˈkʌmpəni] Unternehmen; Firma; Gesellschaft II

comparative [kəmˈpærətɪv] Komparativ <IV U3, 105>

to **compare** [kəmˈpeə] vergleichen <I>

comparison [kəmˈpærɪsn] Vergleich <IV U4, 79>

to **complain** [kəmˈpleɪn] sich beschweren; sich beklagen IV U2, 36

to **complete** [kəmˈpliːt] vervollständigen <I>

computer [kəmˈpjuːtə] Computer I

concert [ˈkɒnsət] Konzert I

conclusion [kənˈkluːʒn] Schluss; Schlussfolgerung <IV U4, 85>

confident [ˈkɒnfɪdnt] selbstsicher; selbstbewusst; sicher IV U4, 76

Congratulations! [kənˌgrætʃəˈleɪʃnz] Glückwunsch! II

staying **connected** [ˌsteɪɪŋ kəˈnektɪd] in Verbindung bleiben III

contact [ˈkɒntækt] Kontakt I

continent [ˈkɒntɪnənt] Kontinent; Erdteil II

to **cook** [kʊk] kochen II

cookie *(AE)* [ˈkʊki] Keks III

cooking [ˈkʊkɪŋ] Kochen; Koch- II

cool [kuːl] cool; super I

to **copy** [ˈkɒpi] abschreiben; kopieren <III>

copyright [ˈkɒpiraɪt] Copyright; Urheberrecht IV U4, 72

corn [kɔːn] Mais; Korn; Getreide IV U3, 52

to **correct** [kəˈrekt] verbessern; richtigstellen; korrigieren II

correct [kəˈrekt] richtig; korrekt <I>

*to **cost** [kɒst] kosten III

cost [kɒst] simple past, past participle von *to cost* III

costume [ˈkɒstjuːm] Kostüm I

could [kʊd] könnte; konnte III

counselor [ˈkaʊnslə] Betreuer; Betreuerin <IV U4, 83>

country [ˈkʌntri] Land; ländliche Gegend I; Country *(Musik)* <IV U1, 131>
home country [ˌhəʊm ˈkʌntri] Heimat; Heimatland IV U1, 12

countryside [ˈkʌntrɪsaɪd] Land; Landschaft <IV U2, 132>

of **course** [əv ˈkɔːs] natürlich; selbstverständlich II

cousin [ˈkʌzn] Cousin; Cousine II

cow [kaʊ] Kuh III

cricket [ˈkrɪkɪt] Kricket II

Croatian [krəʊˈeɪʃn] Kroatisch; kroatisch; aus Kroatien <IV U1, 131>

crown jewels *(pl)* [ˌkraʊn ˈdʒuːəlz] Kronjuwelen II

crust [krʌst] Kruste; Rinde IV U2, 40

culture [ˈkʌltʃə] Kultur III

a **cup** of [ə ˈkʌp əv] eine Tasse … II

current [ˈkʌrnt] Strömung III

customer [ˈkʌstəmə] Kunde; Kundin I
customer service [ˌkʌstəmə ˈsɜːvɪs] Kundenbetreuung; Kundendienst; Kundenservice IV U4, 76

CV (curriculum vitae) [ˌsiːˈviː (kəˌrɪkjələmˈviːtaɪ)] Lebenslauf IV U4, 76

cyberbullying [ˈsaɪbəˌbʊliɪŋ] Cyber-Mobbing <IV U4, 136>

cycling [ˈsaɪklɪŋ] Radfahren <IV U2, 132>

D

dad [dæd] Papa; Vati I

damage [ˈdæmɪdʒ] Schäden; Schaden; Beschädigung IV U2, 40

dance [daːns] Tanz III
square dance [ˈskweə ˌdaːns] Squaredance *(amerikanischer Volkstanz)* II

to **dance** [daːns] tanzen I

dancer [ˈdaːnsə] Tänzer; Tänzerin I

dancing [ˈdaːnsɪŋ] Tanz; Tanzen III

danger [ˈdeɪndʒə] Gefahr <IV U4, 87>

dangerous [ˈdeɪndʒrəs] gefährlich III

dark [daːk] dunkel I

date [deɪt] Datum; Zeitpunkt IV U4, 81
date of birth [ˌdeɪt əv ˈbɜːθ] Geburtsdatum IV U4, 81

daughter [ˈdɔːtə] Tochter I

day [deɪ] Tag I
a busy day [ə ˌbɪzi ˈdeɪ] ein ausgefüllter Tag II
lucky day [ˌlʌki ˈdeɪ] Glückstag II
one day [ˈwʌn deɪ] eines Tages I
sports day [ˈspɔːts ˌdeɪ] Sportfest II

dead [ded] tot IV U3, 60

Dear …, [dɪə] Liebe(r) …, *(Anrede in Briefen)* I
Dear …, [dɪə] Sehr geehrte(r) …, IV U4, 76

December [dɪˈsembə] Dezember I

to **decide** [dɪˈsaɪd] (sich) entscheiden; beschließen III

decision [dɪˈsɪʒn] Entscheidung IV U1, 12

deer *(sg)* [dɪə], **deer** *(pl)* [dɪə] Reh <IV U2, 132>

defining relative clause [dɪˌfaɪnɪŋ ˈrelətɪv ˌklɔːz] notwendiger Relativsatz <IV U4, 105>

delayed [dɪˈleɪd] verspätet IV U2, 36

to **deliver** [dɪˈlɪvə] liefern; ausliefern IV U1, 20

dentist [ˈdentɪst] Zahnarzt; Zahnärztin <IV U3, 135>

to **depart** [dɪˈpaːt] abfliegen; abfahren IV U2, 36

departures [dɪˈpaːtʃəz] Abflug <IV U2, 133>

to **describe** [dɪˈskraɪb] beschreiben <III>

design [dɪˈzaɪn] Design; Gestaltung; Entwurf II
DT (Design Technology) [ˌdiːˈtiː (dɪˌzaɪn tekˈnɒlədʒi)] Technik I

to **design** [dɪˈzaɪn] konstruieren; entwerfen; gestalten; entwickeln IV U2, 41

desk [desk] Schreibtisch; Tisch II

destination [ˌdestɪˈneɪʃn] Ziel; Reiseziel <IV U4, 87>

to **destroy** [dɪˈstrɔɪ] zerstören IV U2, 41

detail [ˈdiːteɪl] Detail; Einzelheit <III>

detective [dɪˈtektɪv] Detektiv; Detektivin I

device [dɪˈvaɪs] Gerät <IV U4, 136>

dialogue [ˈdaɪəlɒg] Dialog; Gespräch II

diameter [daɪˈæmɪtə] Durchmesser II

diamond [ˈdaɪəmənd] Diamant <II>

diary [ˈdaɪəri] Tagebuch I

dictionary [ˈdɪkʃnri] Wörterbuch <II>

did [dɪd] simple past von *to do* I

to **die** [daɪ] sterben III

difference [ˈdɪfrns] Unterschied <IV U1, 10>

different [ˈdɪfrnt] verschieden; unterschiedlich; anders I; andere III

difficult [ˈdɪfɪklt] schwierig; schwer; kompliziert III

dinner [ˈdɪnə] Mittagessen; Abendessen I

directions *(pl)* [dɪˈrekʃnz] Wegbeschreibung; Anweisungen <III>
giving directions [ˌgɪvɪŋ dɪˈrekʃnz] eine Wegbeschreibung geben; Anweisungen geben <II>

dirty [ˈdɜːti] dreckig; schmutzig I

to **disagree** [ˌdɪsəˈgriː] anderer Meinung sein; nicht einverstanden sein IV U3, 56

to empty the **dishwasher** [ˌemti ðə ˈdɪʃwɒʃə] die Spülmaschine ausräumen II

to load the **dishwasher** [ˌləʊd ðə ˈdɪʃwɒʃə] die Spülmaschine einräumen II

distance [ˈdɪstns] Entfernung; Distanz <IV U1, 22>

*to **do** [duː] machen; tun I
to do homework [ˌduː ˈhəʊmwɜːk] Hausaufgabe(n) machen I
to do magic [ˌduː ˈmædʒɪk] zaubern II

doctor [ˈdɒktə] Arzt; Ärztin II
at the doctor's [ət ðə ˈdɒktəz] beim Arzt II

dog [dɒg] Hund I
dog walker [ˈdɒg ˌwɔːkə] Hundeausführer; Hundeausführerin <IV U4, 82>

dollar ($) [ˈdɒlə] Dollar *(amer. Währungseinheit)* IV ZI, 9

done [dʌn] past participle von *to do* III

door [dɔː] Tür II

doorbell [ˈdɔːbel] Türklingel I

down [daʊn] hinunter; herunter III

to **download** [daʊnˈləʊd] herunterladen <IV U4, 136>

draft [draːft] Entwurf <II>

drama [ˈdraːmə] Theater-; Drama; Schauspielerei III

drank [dræŋk] simple past von *to drink* II

*to **draw** [drɔː] zeichnen <I>

dream [driːm] Traum I

s six • **z** zoo • **ʃ** she • **ʒ** usually • **h** her • **m** me • **n** no • **ŋ** sing • **iə** hear • **l** let • **r** red • **j** yes

161

dream

dress

dress [dres] Kleid I

fancy dress [ˌfænsi ˈdres] Kostüm; Verkleidung I

drink [drɪŋk] Getränk I

*to **drink** [drɪŋk] trinken II

*to **drive** [draɪv] fahren; treiben IV U1, 21

to drive off [ˌdraɪvˈɒf] wegfahren IV U1, 21

driven [ˈdrɪvn] past participle von *to drive* IV U1, 21

driver [ˈdraɪvə] Fahrer; Fahrerin IV U1, 21

drove [drəʊv] simple past von *to drive* IV U1, 21

drug [drʌg] Droge IV U3, 56

dry [draɪ] trocken II

DT (Design Technology) [ˌdiːˈtiː (dɪˌzaɪn tekˈnɒlədʒi)] Technik I

during [ˈdʒʊərɪŋ] bei; während IV U2, 41

DVD [ˌdiːviːˈdiː] DVD I

E

e.g. (= for example) [ˌiːˈdʒiː] z. B. (= zum Beispiel) <II>

each [iːtʃ] jede <I>

each one [ˌiːtʃ ˈwʌn] jedes <IV U4, 75>

each other [iːtʃ ˈʌðə] einander; sich; gegenseitig III

bald **eagle** [ˌbɔːld ˈiːgl] Weißkopfseeadler <IV U2, 47>

early [ˈɜːli] früh II

to **earn** [ɜːn] verdienen <IV U3, 135>

earth [ɜːθ] Welt; Erde III

earthquake [ˈɜːθkweɪk] Erdbeben IV U2, 31

east [iːst] Ost-; Osten III

easy [ˈiːzi] einfach; leicht I

*to **eat** [iːt] essen I

education [ˌedʒʊˈkeɪʃn] Ausbildung; Erziehung; Bildung IV U4, 81

efficient [ɪˈfɪʃnt] effizient; leistungsfähig IV U4, 80

egg [eg] Ei I

Eid [iːd] *muslimisches Fest* I

eight [eɪt] acht I

eighteen [eɪˈtiːn] achtzehn I

eighty [ˈeɪti] achtzig I

not ... **either** [nɒt ... ˈaɪðə] auch nicht III

electrician [ˌelɪkˈtrɪʃn] Elektriker; Elektrikerin <IV U3, 135>

elephant [ˈelɪfənt] Elefant <IV U1, 23>

eleven [ɪˈlevn] elf I

e-mail [ˈiːmeɪl] E-Mail II

employee [ɪmˈplɔɪiː] Mitarbeiter; Mitarbeiterin; Arbeitnehmer; Arbeitnehmerin; Angestellter; Angestellte IV U2, 36

to **empty** the dishwasher [ˌemti ðə ˈdɪʃwɒʃə] die Spülmaschine ausräumen II

end [end] Ende; Schluss II

at the end [ˌət ði ˈend] am Ende II

end-of-term [ˌend əv ˈtɜːm] Schuljahresabschluss <I>

ending [ˈendɪŋ] Ende; Schluss <III>

search **engine** [ˈsɜːtʃ ˌendʒɪn] Suchmaschine <IV U1, 27>

engineer [ˌendʒɪˈnɪə] Ingenieur; Ingenieurin; Techniker; Technikerin II

English [ˈɪŋglɪʃ] Englisch I; englisch; aus England III

the English [ðɪ ˈɪŋglɪʃ] die Engländer III

to **enjoy** [ɪnˈdʒɔɪ] genießen; Gefallen finden an IV U3, 51

to enjoy oneself [ɪnˈdʒɔɪ wʌnˌself] Spaß haben; sich amüsieren IV U2, 32

enough [ɪˈnʌf] genug; genügend III

entry [ˈentri] Eintrag; Eintritt <II>

environment [ɪnˈvaɪrnmənt] Umwelt; Umgebung II

episode [ˈepɪsəʊd] Folge; Episode IV U4, 72

equipment [ɪˈkwɪpmənt] Ausrüstung; Zubehör; Ausstattung <III>

to **escape** [ɪˈskeɪp] entkommen; fliehen; entfliehen; flüchten IV U3, 60

euro [ˈjʊərəʊ] Euro *(Währung)* III

European [ˌjʊərəˈpiːən] Europäer; Europäerin; europäisch; aus Europa III

evening [ˈiːvnɪŋ] Abend I

in the evening [ɪn ðɪ ˈiːvnɪŋ] abends I

event [ɪˈvent] Veranstaltung; Ereignis II

ever [ˈevə] schon einmal; jemals; überhaupt III

every [ˈevri] jede I; alle II

everyone [ˈevriwʌn] alle; jeder; zusammen II

everything [ˈevriθɪŋ] alles II

everywhere [ˈevriweə] überallhin; überall II

example [ɪgˈzaːmpl] Beispiel III

for example [fərˌɪgˈzaːmpl] zum Beispiel III

excited [ɪkˈsaɪtɪd] aufgeregt; begeistert II

exciting [ɪkˈsaɪtɪŋ] spannend; aufregend I

Excuse me. [ɪkˈskjuːz mi] Entschuldigung. II

exercise [ˈeksəsaɪz] Übung I

exercise book [ˈeksəsaɪz ˌbʊk] Übungsheft I

exhibition [ˌeksɪˈbɪʃn] Ausstellung III

expensive [ɪkˈspensɪv] teuer I

experience [ɪkˈspɪəriəns] Erfahrung; Erlebnis IV U4, 76

work experience [ˈwɜːk ɪkˌspɪəriəns] Berufserfahrung; Praktikum <IV U4, 138>

experiment [ɪkˈsperɪmənt] Versuch; Experiment II

to **explore** [ɪkˈsplɔː] erkunden; erforschen IV U3, 61

expression [ɪkˈspreʃn] Ausdruck; Wendung; Äußerung <IV U3, 105>

extra [ˈekstrə] zusätzlich <IV U4, 77>

eye [aɪ] Auge I

F

face [feɪs] Gesicht I

face painting [ˈfeɪs peɪntɪŋ] Schminken II

fact [fækt] Fakt; Tatsache II

factory [ˈfæktri] Fabrik; Werk III

fair [feə] Fest; Messe; Jahrmarkt II; fair; gerecht IV U4, 72

fall *(AE)* [fɔːl] Herbst III

*to **fall** [fɔːl] fallen; hinfallen I

to fall off [fɔːlˈɒf] von etw. stürzen; herunterfallen; hinunterfallen II

to fall out [fɔːlˈaʊt] herausfallen III

fallen [ˈfɔːlən] past participle von *to fall* III

family ['fæmli] Familie I
    family tree [ˌfæmli 'tri:] Familien-
    stammbaum <I>
famine ['fæmɪn] Hungersnot
    <IV U1, 130>
famous ['feɪməs] berühmt I
fan [fæn] Fan I
fancy dress [ˌfænsi 'dres] Kostüm;
    Verkleidung I
fantastic [fæn'tæstɪk] fantastisch;
    großartig II
far [fɑː] weit II
fare [feə] Fahrpreis <IV U1, 22>
farm [fɑːm] Bauernhof I
farmer ['fɑːmə] Bauer; Bäuerin; Land-
    wirt; Landwirtin I
fashion ['fæʃn] Mode IV U1, 20
fast [fɑːst] schnell II
father ['fɑːðə] Vater I
favorite (AE) ['feɪvrɪt] Lieblings- III
favourite ['feɪvrɪt] Lieblings- I
February ['februri] Februar I
fed [fed] simple past von *to feed* I
*to be **fed up (with)** [bi: ˌfed ˌʌp (wɪð)]
    die Nase voll haben (von) III
fee [fiː] Gebühr <IV U1, 22>
*to **feed** [fiːd] füttern I
feedback ['fiːdbæk] Rückmeldung;
    Feedback <I>
*to **feel** [fiːl] (sich) fühlen II; sich
    anfühlen III
feeling ['fiːlɪŋ] Gefühl <II>
fell [fel] simple past von *to fall* I
felt [felt] simple past von *to feel* II;
    past participle von *to feel* III
festival ['festɪvl] Festival; Fest III
a few [ə 'fjuː] ein paar; einige;
    wenige IV U3, 52
science fiction [ˌsaɪəns 'fɪkʃn] Science-
    Fiction I
field ['fiːld] Spielfeld; Feld; Gebiet III
    playing field ['pleɪɪŋ ˌfiːld] Sport-
    platz II
fifteen [ˌfɪf'tiːn] fünfzehn I
fifty ['fɪfti] fünfzig I
*to **fight** [faɪt] kämpfen; (sich) strei-
    ten II
figure ['fɪgə] Figur; Gestalt II
file [faɪl] Datei <IV U4, 136>
to **fill** [fɪl] füllen <II>

to **fill in** [fɪl ˌɪn] eintragen; ausfül-
    len <II>
film [fɪlm] Film I
*to **find** [faɪnd] finden; herausfinden I
    to **find out** [ˌfaɪnd ˌaʊt] herausfin-
    den IV U1, 26; erkundigen <I>
fine [faɪn] gut; in Ordnung; schön I
    I'm fine. [aɪm 'faɪn] Mir geht es
    gut. I
to **finish** ['fɪnɪʃ] fertigstellen;
    vervollständigen I; beenden;
    fertig machen; erledigen; enden;
    aufhören II
fire [faɪə] Feuer III
first ['fɜːst] erste I; zuerst; als Erstes II
    the first time [ðə fɜːst 'taɪm] das
    erste Mal I
first-aid [ˌfɜːst'eɪd] Erste-Hilfe-
    IV U2, 41
fish (sg) [fɪʃ], **fish** (pl) [fɪʃ] Fisch I
fishing ['fɪʃɪŋ] Angeln; Fischen
    <IV U2, 132>
    to **go fishing** [ˌgəʊ 'fɪʃɪŋ] angeln
    gehen; fischen gehen IV U3, 60
fit [fɪt] fit III
fitness center ['fɪtnəs ˌsentə] Fitness-
    studio; Fitnesscenter <IV U2, 42>
five [faɪv] fünf I
flag [flæg] Flagge; Fahne IV ZI, 9
flat [flæt] Wohnung I
flea [fliː] Floh I
    flea market [ˌfliː ˌmɑːkɪt] Floh-
    markt I
flew [fluː] simple past von *to fly* II
flexible ['fleksɪbl] flexibel IV U4, 80
flight [flaɪt] Flug IV U2, 32
    flight attendant ['flaɪt ˌəˌtendnt]
    Flugbegleiter; Flugbegleiterin
    <IV U2, 133>
    Have a good flight! [ˌhæv ə gʊd
    'flaɪt] Guten Flug! IV U2, 36
floor [flɔː] Stockwerk; Etage II
florist ['flɒrɪst] Florist; Floristin
    <IV U3, 135>
fluent ['fluːənt] fließend; flüssig
    <IV U4, 138>
*to **fly** [flaɪ] fliegen II
flyer ['flaɪə] Flyer; Faltblatt <III>
flying ['flaɪɪŋ] Fliegen III
follower ['fɒləʊə] Follower; Followe-
    rin; Anhänger; Anhängerin IV U4, 72

food [fuːd] Essen; Lebensmittel I
foot (sg) [fʊt], **feet** (pl) [fiːt] Fuß II
    on foot [ɒn 'fʊt] zu Fuß I
football ['fʊtbɔːl] Fußball I
    American football [əˌmerɪkən
    'fʊtbɔːl] American Football II
football (AE) ['fʊtbɔːl] American
    Football; Football <IV U3, 63>
for [fɔː] für I; seit IV U1, 12
    for example [fər ɪg'zɑːmpl] zum
    Beispiel III
    for sale [fə 'seɪl] zu verkaufen
    <IV U4, 87>
    for the 200th time [fə ðə 'tuː
    hʌndrədθ ˌtaɪm] zum 200. Mal III
foreground ['fɔːgraʊnd] Vordergrund
    III
forever [fə'revə] für immer; ewig
    IV U3, 56
*to **forget** [fə'get] vergessen II
forgot [fə'gɒt] simple past von *to
    forget* II
form [fɔːm] Form <I>
forty ['fɔːti] vierzig I
to look **forward** to (+ -ing) [ˌlʊk
    'fɔːwəd tə] sich freuen auf IV U2, 32
fought [fɔːt] simple past von *to fight*
    II
found [faʊnd] simple past von *to find*
    II; past participle von *to find* III
    lost and found notice [ˌlɒst ən
    'faʊnd ˌnəʊtɪs] Suchplakat; Aus-
    hang III
four [fɔː] vier I
fourteen [ˌfɔː'tiːn] vierzehn I
fox [fɒks] Fuchs <IV U2, 132>
free [friː] kostenlos; frei III
    free time [ˌfriː 'taɪm] Freizeit I
    free-time [ˌfriː'taɪm] Freizeit- <I>
freeze frame ['friːz ˌfreɪm] Standbild
    <II>
French [frenʃ] Französisch; franzö-
    sisch; aus Frankreich IV U4, 71
Friday ['fraɪdeɪ] Freitag I
chicken fried rice ['tʃɪkɪn ˌfraɪd 'raɪs]
    gebratener Reis mit Hühnerfleisch
    II
friend [frend] Freund; Freundin I
    to **make friends** [ˌmeɪk 'frendz]
    Freundschaft(en) schließen II

friendly ['frendli] freundlich; sympathisch IV U4, 80

frisbee ['frɪzbi] Frisbee; Frisbeescheibe I

from [frɒm] aus; von I

at the **front** (of) [ət ðə 'frʌnt (ɒv)] vorne (in) <IV U1, 24>

in **front** [ɪn 'frʌnt] vorn II

in **front** of [ɪn 'frʌnt ˌɒv] vor; davor I

fruit [fru:t] Obst; Frucht I

fun [fʌn] Spaß; Freude I; lustig; spaßig; amüsant III

to be **fun** [bi: 'fʌn] Spaß machen; witzig sein II

funeral ['fju:nrəl] Beerdigung; Begräbnis <IV U3, 62>

funny ['fʌni] merkwürdig; komisch; lustig I

future ['fju:tʃə] Zukunft IV U1, 12

G

game [geɪm] Spiel I

gap [gæp] Lücke; Spalt <II>

garden ['gɑ:dn] Garten I

gas (AE) [gæs] Benzin <IV U1, 22>

gate [geɪt] Gate; Flugsteig IV U2, 36

gave [geɪv] simple past von to give I

German ['dʒɜ:mən] Deutsch I; Deutscher; Deutsche; deutsch; aus Deutschland II

*to **get** [get] bekommen; werden; kommen I; holen; bringen IV U1, 20

to **get** into [ˌget ˈɪntə] bilden <I>

to **get** lost [ˌget 'lɒst] verloren gehen; sich verirren IV U2, 36

to **get** off [ˌget ˈɒf] aussteigen II

to **get** on sth [ˌget ˈɒn] in etw. steigen; in etw. einsteigen IV U3, 50

to **get** out [ˌget ˈaʊt] aussteigen; herauskommen IV U1, 20

to **get** up [ˌget ˈʌp] aufstehen I

to **get** used to (sth) [ˌget 'ju:st tə] sich gewöhnen an (etw.) IV U1, 12

to **get** in [ˌget ˈɪn] einsteigen IV U1, 21

ghost [gəʊst] Geist; Gespenst IV U3, 61

girl [gɜ:l] Mädchen I

*to **give** [gɪv] geben; schenken I; halten <III>

giving directions [ˌgɪvɪŋ dɪˈrekʃnz] eine Wegbeschreibung geben; Anweisungen geben <II>

given ['gɪvn] past participle von to give IV U3, 66

glove [glʌv] Handschuh II

*to **go** [gəʊ] gehen; fahren I; hinkommen <IV U4, 77>

to **go** bike riding [gəʊ 'baɪk ˌraɪdɪŋ] Fahrrad fahren II

to **go** camping [gəʊ 'kæmpɪŋ] campen gehen; zelten gehen III

to **go** fishing [gəʊ 'fɪʃɪŋ] angeln gehen; fischen gehen IV U3, 60

to **go** on [gəʊ ˈɒn] weitergehen <III>

to **go** rafting [gəʊ 'rɑ:ftɪŋ] raften gehen III

to **go** skating [gəʊ 'skeɪtɪŋ] inlineskaten gehen; Schlittschuhlaufen gehen II

to **go** surfing [gəʊ 'sɜ:fɪŋ] surfen gehen III

to **go** swimming [gəʊ 'swɪmɪŋ] schwimmen gehen I

to **go** tandem bike riding [gəʊ 'tændəm ˌbaɪk raɪdɪŋ] Tandem fahren II

to **go** to bed [gəʊ tə 'bed] ins Bett gehen I

to **go** together [gəʊ təˈgeðə] zusammenpassen <III>

goal [gəʊl] Tor; Treffer; Ziel III

goalpost ['gəʊlpəʊst] Torpfosten; Torstange III

goat [gəʊt] Ziege III

goggles (pl) ['gɒglz] Brille; Schutzbrille <IV U4, 137>

gold [gəʊld] Gold; golden; Gold- III

gone [gɒn] past participle von to go III

good [gʊd] gut I

to be **good** at [bi: 'gʊd ˌət] gut sein in; gut sein bei I

Good luck! [ˌgʊd 'lʌk] Alles Gute!; Viel Glück! IV U1, 12

Have a **good** flight! [ˌhæv ə gʊd 'flaɪt] Guten Flug! IV U2, 36

Goodbye. [gʊdˈbaɪ] Auf Wiedersehen; Servus. I

got [gɒt] simple past von to get I; past participle von to get IV U1, 12

GPS (Global Positioning System) [ˌdʒi:pi:'es] GPS (ein satellitengestütztes System zur weltweiten Positionsbestimmung) I

grade (AE) [greɪd] Klasse; Jahrgangsstufe; Note II

grammar ['græmə] Grammatik <I>

grandfather ['grænˌfɑ:ðə] Großvater II

grandma ['grænmɑ:] Oma I

grandparents (pl) ['grænˌpeərnts] Großeltern II

great [greɪt] großartig; toll I; groß; riesig III

great-great-grandad [ˌgreɪtgreɪt 'grændæd] Ururopa I

Greek [gri:k] Griechisch; griechisch; aus Griechenland <IV U1, 131>

green [gri:n] grün I

grey [greɪ] grau I

grizzly bear ['grɪzli ˌbeə] Grizzlybär IV U2, 32

group [gru:p] Gruppe IV U4, 71

to **guess** [ges] überlegen; raten; erraten I

Guess what? [ges 'wɒt] Stellt euch vor!; Stell dir vor! II

guest [gest] Gast IV U4, 76

guide [gaɪd] Führer; Führerin IV U1, 26

guinea pig ['gɪni ˌpɪg] Meerschweinchen II

gun [gʌn] Pistole; Schusswaffe; Waffe IV U3, 56

H

had [hæd] simple past von to have I; past participle von to have IV U1, 12

hairdresser ['heəˌdresə] Friseur; Friseurin IV U3, 56

hairdressing salon ['heədresɪŋ ˌsælɒn] Friseursalon IV U3, 56

half [hɑ:f] halb III

half past (seven) [ˌhɑ:f 'pɑ:st (ˌsevn)] halb (acht) II

half a million [ˌhɑ:f ə 'mɪljən] eine halbe Million III

Halloween [ˌhæləʊ'i:n] Halloween I

hammer ['hæmə] Hammer III

hammer throwing [ˈhæmə ˌθrəʊɪŋ] Hammerwerfen III

hamster [ˈhæmstə] Hamster I

hand [hænd] Hand II

handball [ˈhænbɔːl] Handball <IV U4, 137>

*to hang about [ˌhæŋ‿əˈbaʊt] herumhängen I

to happen [ˈhæpn] passieren; geschehen II; vorkommen; sich ereignen IV U2, 40

That's what happened. [ˌðæts wɒt ˈhæpnd] Das ist passiert. II

happy [ˈhæpi] glücklich I; froh; fröhlich IV U3, 52

hard [hɑːd] hart; schwer; schwierig II

hard-working [ˌhɑːdˈwɜːkɪŋ] fleißig <IV U4, 138>

hat [hæt] Mütze; Hut II

to hate [heɪt] hassen; nicht mögen I

*to have [hæv] haben; besitzen; essen; trinken I

to have (got) to [ˈhæv (gɒt) tə] müssen II

to have a party [hæv‿ə ˈpɑːti] eine Party feiern I

to have breakfast [hæv ˈbrekfəst] frühstücken I

to have got [hæv ˈgɒt] haben; besitzen II

to have to [ˈhæv tə] müssen II

Have a good flight! [ˌhæv‿ə gʊd ˈflaɪt] Guten Flug! IV U2, 36

he [hiː] er I

head [hed] Kopf II

headache [ˈhedeɪk] Kopfweh; Kopfschmerzen II

heading [ˈhedɪŋ] Überschrift <I>

healthy [ˈhelθi] gesund III

*to hear [hɪə] hören II

to hear about [ˌhɪər‿əˈbaʊt] erfahren von; hören von IV U3, 60

heard [hɜːd] simple past von to hear II; past participle von to hear IV U3, 60

hearing [ˈhɪərɪŋ] Gehör II

heaven [ˈhevn] Himmel <IV U3, 62>

heavy [ˈhevi] schwer; stark; schwierig III

hedgehog [ˈhedʒhɒg] Igel <IV U2, 132>

height [haɪt] Höhe II

held [held] simple past von to hold II

Hello. [həˈləʊ] Hallo. I

helmet [ˈhelmət] Helm I

help [help] Hilfe I

to help [help] helfen I

helper [ˈhelpə] Helfer; Helferin <IV U4, 82>

her [hɜː] ihr I; sie II

here [hɪə] hier I; hierhin; hierher III

in here [ɪn ˈhɪə] hierin <IV U1, 23>

Here you are. [ˌhɪə juˈɑː] Bitte schön. I

hers [hɜːz] ihre III

herself [həˈself] sich selbst; sich; selbst IV U2, 32

Hi. [haɪ] Hi.; Hallo. I

high [haɪ] hoch; groß II

high jump [ˈhaɪ ˌdʒʌmp] Hochsprung <IV U4, 137>

junior high school [ˌdʒuːniə ˈhaɪ skuːl] Junior Highschool (Mittelschule in den USA, in der Regel Klassenstufe 7–9) II

high-speed [ˌhaɪˈspiːd] superschnell <IV U2, 42>

hiking [ˈhaɪkɪŋ] Wandern <IV U2, 132>

hill [hɪl] Berg; Hügel IV U2, 31

him [hɪm] ihm; ihn II

himself [hɪmˈself] sich; selbst; sich selbst IV U2, 32

hip-hop [ˈhɪphɒp] Hip-Hop (Musik) <IV U1, 131>

his [hɪz] sein I; seine III

Hispanic [hɪˈspænɪk] Hispanoamerikaner; Hispanoamerikanerin; hispanisch IV U2, 31

*to hit [hɪt] schlagen; treffen III

hit [hɪt] simple past, past participle von to hit III

hobby [ˈhɒbi] Hobby II

hockey [ˈhɒki] Eishockey; Hockey IV U4, 70

ice hockey [ˈaɪs ˌhɒki] Eishockey IV U4, 70

*to hold [həʊld] halten; festhalten II

hole [həʊl] Loch I

holiday [ˈhɒlədeɪ] Ferien; Urlaub II

holiday (AE) [ˈhɒlədeɪ] Feiertag IV U3, 52

home [həʊm] Zuhause; Heim; nach Hause I

at home [ət ˈhəʊm] zu Hause; daheim I

home country [ˌhəʊm ˈkʌntri] Heimat; Heimatland IV U1, 12

*to be homesick [biː ˈhəʊmsɪk] Heimweh haben IV U1, 12

homework [ˈhəʊmwɜːk] Hausaufgabe(n) I

to do homework [ˌduː ˈhəʊmwɜːk] Hausaufgabe(n) machen I

to hoover [ˈhuːvə] staubsaugen II

to hope (for) [həʊp (fə)] hoffen (auf) II

horse [hɔːs] Pferd I

horse riding [ˈhɔːs ˌraɪdɪŋ] Reiten I

hospital [ˈhɒspɪtl] Krankenhaus II

hostel [ˈhɒstl] Herberge; Hostel II

hot [hɒt] heiß I

hot dog [ˈhɒt ˌdɒg] Hotdog II

hotel [həˈtel] Hotel IV U3, 56

hour [aʊə] Stunde II

hours (pl) [ˈaʊəz] Zeiten IV U4, 80

working hours (pl) [ˈwɜːkɪŋ ˌaʊəz] Arbeitszeit IV U4, 80

house [haʊs] Haus I

how [haʊ] wie I

How are you? [ˌhaʊ‿ˈɑː jə] Wie geht es dir? I

How can I help you? [ˌhaʊ kæn aɪ ˈhelp ju] Was kann ich für euch/ dich tun? I

How much (is/are) …? [ˌhaʊ ˈmʌtʃ (ɪz/ɑː)] Wie viel (kostet/kosten) …? I

How old are you? [haʊ‿ˈəʊld‿ə juː] Wie alt bist du? I

how to … [ˈhaʊ tə] wie man … IV U2, 32

a/one hundred [ˈhʌndrəd] hundert; einhundert I

hungry [ˈhʌŋgri] hungrig I

treasure hunt [ˈtreʒə ˌhʌnt] Schnitzeljagd; Schatzsuche II

hurling [ˈhɜːlɪŋ] Hurling (ähnliche Sportart wie Hockey) III

hurricane [ˈhʌrɪkən] Hurrikan; Orkan; Wirbelsturm IV U3, 66

*to hurt [hɜːt] verletzen; wehtun II

hurt [hɜːt] simple past von to hurt II; verletzt III

husky ['hʌski] Husky *(Schlittenhunderasse)* IV U2, 48

I

I [aɪ] ich I

I can't find … [aɪ kɑːnt 'faɪnd] ich kann … nicht finden I

I can't wait [aɪ ˌkɑːnt 'weɪt] ich kann es kaum erwarten III

I don't mind. [aɪ 'dəʊnt ˌmaɪnd] Es macht nichts. IV U3, 52

I don't know. [ˌaɪ dəʊnt 'nəʊ] Ich weiß (es) nicht! I

I wouldn't like (to) … [aɪ 'wʊdnt laɪk (tə)] ich möchte nicht …; ich würde nicht gerne … I

I'm afraid [aɪm ə'freɪd] leider IV U2, 36

I'm sorry. [aɪm 'sɒri] Es tut mir leid.; Entschuldigung. II

I'd (= I would) [aɪd] ich würde; ich hätte gern I

I'd like (to) … (= I would like to) [aɪd 'laɪk (tə)] ich möchte …; ich würde gerne … I

I'd love (to) … (= I would love to) [aɪd 'lʌv (tə)] ich würde sehr gern …; ich hätte gern … IV U2, 32

I'm fine. [aɪm 'faɪn] Mir geht es gut. I

ice cream [ˌaɪs 'kriːm] Eis; Eiscreme II

ice hockey ['aɪs ˌhɒki] Eishockey IV U4, 70

ice skating ['aɪs ˌskeɪtɪŋ] Schlittschuhlaufen <IV U4, 137>

ID [ˌaɪ'diː] Ausweis; Personalausweis <IV U2, 133>

idea [aɪ'dɪə] Idee I

if [ɪf] wenn; falls; ob IV U2, 32

to **imagine** [ɪ'mædʒɪn] sich vorstellen <II>

immigrant ['ɪmɪɡrənt] Einwanderer; Einwanderin; Immigrant; Immigrantin IV U1, 10

important [ɪm'pɔːtnt] wichtig III

impossible [ɪm'pɒsəbl] unmöglich IV U3, 66

in [ɪn] im; in; auf; am I; bei; an IV U2, 40

in front [ɪn 'frʌnt] vorn II

in here [ɪn 'hɪə] hierin <IV U1, 23>

in the middle of [ɪn ðə 'mɪdl ˌəv] mitten in II

in a park [ɪn ə 'pɑːk] im Park I

in front of [ɪn 'frʌnt ˌəv] vor; davor I

in the evening [ɪn ði ˌ'iːvnɪŋ] abends I

in the north of [ˌɪn ðə 'nɔːθ ˌəv] im Norden von III

independence [ˌɪndɪ'pendəns] Unabhängigkeit IV ZI, 9

Indian ['ɪndiən] Indisch; indisch <IV U1, 131>

indoor [ɪn'dɔː] Hallen-; Innen- III

industry ['ɪndəstri] Industrie III

tourist industry ['tʊərɪst ˌɪndəstri] Tourismus <IV U3, 51>

influence ['ɪnfluəns] Einfluss <IV U1, 131>

information [ˌɪnfə'meɪʃn] Information(en) II

piece of information [ˌpiːs əv ɪnfə'meɪʃn] Information <IV U3, 65>

inside cover [ˌɪnsaɪd 'kʌvə] Umschlaginnenseite <II>

to **install** [ɪn'stɔːl] installieren <IV U4, 136>

interest ['ɪntrəst] Interesse IV U4, 81

*to be **interested** in [biː 'ɪntrəstɪd ˌɪn] interessiert sein an; sich interessieren für III

interesting ['ɪntrəstɪŋ] interessant I

internet ['ɪntənet] Internet I

to surf the internet [sɜːf ði 'ɪntənet] im Internet surfen <III>

internship ['ɪntɜːnʃɪp] Praktikum; Berufspraktikum IV U4, 76

interview ['ɪntəvjuː] Interview; Befragung; Gespräch IV U3, 66

job interview ['dʒɒb ˌɪntəvjuː] Vorstellungsgespräch <IV U4, 78>

to **interview** ['ɪntəvjuː] befragen; interviewen <II>

interviewer ['ɪntəvjuːə] Interviewer; Interviewerin; Befrager; Befragerin IV U1, 12

into ['ɪntu] in; in … hinein II

intro ['ɪntrəʊ] Auftakt; Einführung <I>

to **introduce sb to sb** [ˌɪntrə'djuːs] jmdn. jmdm. vorstellen III

introduction [ˌɪntrə'dʌkʃn] Einleitung; Einführung <III>

Inuit ['ɪnuɪt] Inuit *(Ureinwohner Kanadas)* IV U4, 71

invitation [ˌɪnvɪ'teɪʃn] Einladung I

to **invite** [ɪn'vaɪt] einladen II

Irish ['aɪrɪʃ] irisch; Irisch; aus Irland III

is [ɪz] ist I

Is something wrong? [ɪz 'sʌmθɪŋ rɒŋ] Stimmt etwas nicht? II

island ['aɪlənd] Insel IV U1, 10

it [ɪt] es; er; sie I; ihn; ihm II

it's (= it is) [ɪts] es ist I

It's ten pounds. [ɪts ˌten 'paʊndz] Es kostet zehn Pfund. I

Italian [ɪ'tæliən] italienisch; Italienisch; Italiener; Italienerin IV U1, 11

item ['aɪtəm] Ding; Artikel; Gegenstand IV U2, 41

its [ɪts] sein; ihr I

J

January ['dʒænjuri] Januar I

Japanese [ˌdʒæpn'iːz] japanisch; Japanisch; aus Japan; Japaner; Japanerin IV U1, 16

jazz [dʒæz] Jazz *(Musik)* <IV U1, 131>

jeans *(pl)* [dʒiːnz] Jeans I

crown jewels *(pl)* [ˌkraʊn 'dʒuːəlz] Kronjuwelen II

Jewish ['dʒuːɪʃ] jüdisch <IV U1, 131>

job [dʒɒb] Job I; Aufgabe; Tätigkeit III

job ad ['dʒɒb æd] Stellenanzeige <IV U4, 76>

job interview ['dʒɒb ˌɪntəvjuː] Vorstellungsgespräch <IV U4, 78>

jogging ['dʒɒɡɪŋ] Joggen <IV U4, 137>

journey ['dʒɜːni] Fahrt; Reise III

juice [dʒuːs] Saft I

July [dʒʊ'laɪ] Juli I

high jump ['haɪ ˌdʒʌmp] Hochsprung <IV U4, 137>

long jump ['lɒŋ ˌdʒʌmp] Weitsprung II

to **jump** [dʒʌmp] springen III

June [dʒuːn] Juni I

junior high school [ˌdʒuːniə 'haɪ skuːl] Junior Highschool *(Mittelschule in den USA, in der Regel Klassenstufe 7–9)* II

just [dʒʌst] gerade (eben); soeben; einfach; nur III

just for fun [ˌdʒʌst fə 'fʌn] nur (so) zum Spaß <I>

p pen • b bed • t ten • d dad • k cat • g grey • tʃ chair • dʒ job • f fan • v very • θ three • ð the

K

kayak ['kaɪæk] Kajak IV U1, 26

kayaking ['kaɪækɪŋ] Kajakfahren IV U1, 26

kebab [kɪ'bæb] Döner <IV U1, 131>

*to keep [ki:p] halten II

    to keep away [,ki:p_ə'weɪ] fernhalten IV U2, 48

    to keep in touch [,ki:p ɪn 'tʌtʃ] in Kontakt bleiben II

    to keep sb prisoner [ki:p 'prɪznə] jmdn. gefangen halten IV U3, 60

kept [kept] simple past von to keep II; past participle von to keep IV U2, 48

key [ki:] Schlüssel III

    key word ['ki: ,wɜ:d] Stichwort; Schlüsselwort <IV U3, 65>

to kick [kɪk] schießen; treten III

kid [kɪd] Kind I

kilo (kg, kilogram) ['kɪləʊ] Kilo (kg, Kilogramm) I

kilometre (km) [kɪ'lɒmɪtə] Kilometer (km) IV U4, 88

kilt [kɪlt] Kilt; Schottenrock III

kind [kaɪnd] Art; Sorte II

king [kɪŋ] König II

newspaper kiosk ['nju:speɪpə ,ki:ɒsk] Zeitungsstand II

kitchen ['kɪtʃɪn] Küche II

knew [nju:] simple past von to know IV U1, 20

to knock sb off sth [,nɒk … 'ɒf] jmdn. von etw. stoßen IV U1, 20

*to know [nəʊ] wissen; kennen I

    I don't know. [,aɪ dəʊnt 'nəʊ] Ich weiß (es) nicht! I

L

label ['leɪbl] Beschriftung; Etikett <IV U1, 25>

to label ['leɪbl] beschriften <II>

ladder ['lædə] Leiter I

lady ['leɪdi] Frau; Dame IV U1, 21

lake [leɪk] See IV U1, 11

lamp [læmp] Lampe II

to land [lænd] landen IV U2, 36

landmark ['lænmɑ:k] Wahrzeichen IV U2, 31

language ['læŋgwɪdʒ] Grammatik <I>; Sprache IV U4, 71

lantern ['læntən] Laterne II

laptop ['læptɒp] Laptop I

large [lɑ:dʒ] groß II

to last [lɑ:st] dauern; andauern II

last [lɑ:st] letzte I

late [leɪt] (zu) spät II

    to be late [bi: 'leɪt] zu spät kommen II

later ['leɪtə] später I

to laugh [lɑ:f] lachen II

leader ['li:də] Leiter; Leiterin III

to learn [lɜ:n] lernen II

*to leave [li:v] verlassen; lassen; abfahren; weggehen II; vergessen; hinterlassen III; abfliegen; gehen IV U2, 36

leaving ['li:vɪŋ] Abschieds- II

left [left] links; simple past von to leave II; übrig; past participle von to leave III

    on the left [ɒn ðə 'left] links; auf der linken Seite II

leg [leg] Bein II

less [les] weniger III

lesson ['lesn] Schulstunde; Unterricht I

*to let [let] lassen <IV U1, 130>

    let's (= let us) [lets] lass(t) uns I

letter ['letə] Buchstabe; Brief; Schreiben IV U4, 76

    letter of application [,letər_əv_ æplɪ'keɪʃn] Bewerbungsschreiben IV U4, 76

library ['laɪbri] Bibliothek; Bücherei <IV U3, 64>

to lie [laɪ] lügen IV U1, 21

life (sg) [laɪf], lives (pl) [laɪvz] Leben II

lift [lɪft] Aufzug II

to like [laɪk] mögen; gernhaben I

    like + -ing [,laɪk '…ɪŋ] … gerne I

like [laɪk] wie I; als ob IV U2, 32

    like this [laɪk 'ðɪs] so; auf diese Weise <I>

line [laɪn] Linie III; Zeile <IV U1, 20>

    zip line ['zɪp ,laɪn] Seilrutsche III

mountain lion ['maʊntɪn ,laɪən] Puma II

list [lɪst] Liste <I>

    shopping list ['ʃɒpɪŋ ,lɪst] Einkaufszettel I

to listen (to) ['lɪsn (tə)] anhören; hören; zuhören I

listening ['lɪsnɪŋ] Hörverstehen <I>

    listening skills ['lɪsnɪŋ ,skɪlz] Fertigkeit Hören <I>

little ['lɪtl] klein I

    a little (bit) [ə 'lɪtl (bɪt)] ein (kleines) bisschen; ein (klein) wenig II

to live [lɪv] wohnen; leben I

living room ['lɪvɪŋ ,rʊm] Wohnzimmer II

to load the dishwasher [,ləʊd ðə 'dɪʃwɒʃə] die Spülmaschine einräumen II

local ['ləʊkl] örtlich; lokal; hiesig II

locked [lɒkt] abgeschlossen I

lonely ['ləʊnli] einsam III

long [lɒŋ] lang III

    to be a long way away [bi: ə 'lɒŋ ,weɪ ə'weɪ] weit weg sein II

    long jump ['lɒŋ ,dʒʌmp] Weitsprung II

longer ['lɒŋgə] länger I

to look [lʊk] schauen; aussehen; sehen; nachschauen I

    to look after [lʊk 'ɑ:ftə] aufpassen auf; hüten; sich kümmern um II

    to look at ['lʊk_ət] anschauen I

    to look for ['lʊk fə] suchen (nach) IV U4, 76

    to look forward to (+ -ing) [,lʊk 'fɔ:wəd tə] sich freuen auf IV U2, 32

*to lose [lu:z] verlieren II

lost [lɒst] simple past von to lose II; past participle von to lose III

    to get lost [get 'lɒst] verloren gehen; sich verirren IV U2, 36

    lost and found notice [,lɒst_ən 'faʊnd ,nəʊtɪs] Suchplakat; Aushang III

parking lot (AE) ['pɑ:kɪŋ ,lɒt] Parkplatz <IV U2, 42>

a lot [ə 'lɒt] viel; sehr I

a lot of [ə 'lɒt_əv] viel; viele; eine Menge I

lots of ['lɒts_əv] jede Menge; viel; viele I

loud [laʊd] laut I

Love, [lʌv] Liebe Grüße; Herzliche Grüße I

to love [lʌv] lieben; gern mögen I

I'd love (to) … (= I would love to) [aɪd 'lʌv (tə)] ich würde sehr gern …; ich hätte gern … IV U2, 32

Good luck! [ˌgʊd 'lʌk] Alles Gute!; Viel Glück! IV U1, 12

lucky ['lʌki] glücklich; Glück bringend II

to be lucky [bi: ˌ'lʌki] Glück haben II

lucky day [ˌlʌki 'deɪ] Glückstag II

luggage ['lʌgɪdʒ] Gepäck <IV U2, 133>

lunch [lʌnʃ] Mittagessen I

lunchtime ['lʌnʃtaɪm] Mittagspause; Mittagszeit I

M

made [meɪd] simple past von *to make* II; past participle von *to make* III

magazine [ˌmægə'zi:n] Zeitschrift IV U1, 12

*to do magic [ˌdu: 'mædʒɪk] zaubern II

magician [mə'dʒɪʃn] Zauberkünstler; Zauberkünstlerin II

main [meɪn] wichtigste <III>; Haupt- <IV U4, 85>

*to make [meɪk] erstellen; basteln; machen; tun I; bilden; ausmachen <II>

to make friends [ˌmeɪk 'frendz] Freundschaft(en) schließen II

to make reservations [ˌmeɪk rezə'veɪʃnz] reservieren IV U4, 80

to make sure [meɪk 'ʃɔ:] dafür sorgen; sich versichern <IV U4, 85>

mall [mɔ:l] Einkaufspassage; Einkaufszentrum II

man (sg) [mæn], men (pl) [men] Mann I

manager ['mænɪdʒə] Manager; Managerin; Geschäftsführer; Geschäftsführerin IV U3, 56

many ['meni] viele I

map [mæp] Karte; Plan II

March [ma:tʃ] März I

to march in [ˌma:tʃ 'ɪn] einmarschieren <IV U3, 62>

market ['ma:kɪt] Markt I

flea market ['fli: ˌma:kɪt] Flohmarkt I

match [mætʃ] Spiel; Match I

to match [mætʃ] zuordnen <I>

Math (AE) [mæθ] Mathe; Mathematik III

Maths [mæθs] Mathe I

May [meɪ] Mai I

maybe ['meɪbi] vielleicht II

me [mi:] ich; mich; mir I

meal [mi:l] Essen; Mahlzeit II

*to mean [mi:n] bedeuten; meinen IV U4, 72

meaning ['mi:nɪŋ] Bedeutung <III>

meant [ment] simple past, past participle von *to mean* IV U4, 72

meat [mi:t] Fleisch IV U3, 52

mechanic [mɪ'kænɪk] Mechaniker; Mechanikerin <IV U3, 135>

medal ['medl] Medaille II

media ['mi:diə] Medien <II>

social media [ˌsəʊʃl 'mi:diə] soziale Medien III

mediation [ˌmi:di'eɪʃn] Sprachmittlung <I>

mediation skills [ˌmi:di'eɪʃn ˌskɪlz] Fertigkeit Sprachmittlung <I>

*to meet [mi:t] kennenlernen; treffen I; (sich) treffen II

Merry Christmas! [ˌmeri 'krɪsməs] Frohe Weihnachten! I

mess [mes] Durcheinander; Unordnung I

message ['mesɪdʒ] Nachricht; SMS II

messaging ['mesɪdʒɪŋ] Messaging-; Chat- <IV U4, 136>

messenger ['mesɪndʒə] Kurier; Kurierin; Bote; Botin IV U1, 11

met [met] simple past von *to meet* II

metal ['metl] Metall-; metallen III

meter (AE) ['mi:tə] Meter III

metre ['mi:tə] Meter II

middle ['mɪdl] Mitte III

in the middle of [ɪn ðə 'mɪdl ˌəv] mitten in II

mild [maɪld] mild II

mile [maɪl] Meile III

million ['mɪljən] Million I

half a million [ˌha:f ə 'mɪljən] eine halbe Million III

mind map ['maɪnd ˌmæp] Wörternetz <I>

Never mind. [ˌnevə 'maɪnd] Macht nichts.; Schon gut.; Mach dir nichts draus. II

coal mine ['kəʊl ˌmaɪn] Kohlenbergwerk; Kohlengrube III

mine [maɪn] meine III

minute ['mɪnɪt] Minute I

to miss [mɪs] verpassen; vermissen II

Miss [mɪs] Frau (Anrede) IV U3, 60

model ['mɒdl] Vorlage; Muster <I>

modern ['mɒdn] modern I

mom (AE) [mɒm] Mama III

at the moment [ət ðə 'məʊmənt] im Moment; momentan II

Monday ['mʌndeɪ] Montag I

money ['mʌni] Geld I

to raise money [ˌreɪz 'mʌni] Geld sammeln; Geld aufbringen II

month [mʌnθ] Monat II

moose (sg) [mu:s], moose (pl) [mu:s] Elch IV U4, 71

more [mɔ:] mehr; weitere II

more often [mɔ:r ˌ'ɒfn] häufiger; öfter IV U2, 40

morning ['mɔ:nɪŋ] Morgen; Vormittag I

this morning [ðɪs 'mɔ:nɪŋ] heute Morgen II

most [məʊst] die meisten; die Mehrheit; am meisten III

mother ['mʌðə] Mutter I

to motivate ['məʊtɪveɪt] anspornen; motivieren III

mountain ['maʊntɪn] Berg II

mountain lion ['maʊntɪn ˌlaɪən] Puma II

mouse (sg) [maʊs], mice (pl) [maɪs] Maus I

moussaka [mu'sa:kə] Moussaka <IV U1, 131>

mouth [maʊθ] Mund II

to move [mu:v] umziehen II; (sich) bewegen; ziehen IV U2, 40

movement ['mu:vmənt] Bewegung IV U3, 66

movie (AE) ['mu:vi] Film III

Mr ['mɪstə] Herr (Anrede) I

Mrs ['mɪsɪz] Frau (Anrede) I

much [mʌtʃ] viel I

mud [mʌd] Schlamm; Matsch I

muffin ['mʌfɪn] Muffin II

multicultural [ˌmʌltiˈkʌltʃrl] multikulturell IV U1, 11

mum [mʌm] Mama; Mutti I

museum [mjuːˈziːəm] Museum II

music [ˈmjuːzɪk] Musik I

musician [mjuːˈzɪʃn] Musiker; Musike-
rin <IV U3, 62>

Muslim [ˈmʊzlɪm] Muslim; Muslimin
I; muslimisch <IV U1, 131>

must [mʌst] müssen II

my [maɪ] mein I

My name is … [maɪ ˈneɪm ɪz] Ich
heiße … I

myself [maɪˈself] mich; selbst III; mir;
mich selbst IV U2, 32

N

name [neɪm] Name I

to **name** [neɪm] benennen <I>; nennen <IV U4, 85>

narrator [nəˈreɪtə] Erzähler; Erzählerin I

nation [ˈneɪʃn] Volk; Nation; Land;
Staat III

national [ˈnæʃnl] National-; national
III

national park [ˌnæʃnl ˈpɑːk] Nationalpark III

nationality [ˌnæʃnˈæləti] Nationalität;
Staatsangehörigkeit IV U1, 16

Native American [ˌneɪtɪv əˈmerɪkən]
Ureinwohner Amerikas; Urein-
wohnerin Amerikas; Indianer;
Indianerin; indianisch III

near [nɪə] in der Nähe von I; nah II

nearly [ˈnɪəli] fast; beinahe II

neck [nek] Hals; Nacken II

to **need** [niːd] brauchen I

to need to [ˈniːd tə] müssen III

negative [ˈnegətɪv] negativ
<IV U3, 105>

neighbour [ˈneɪbə] Nachbar; Nachbarin I

netball [ˈnetbɔːl] Korbball I

never [ˈnevə] nie; niemals II

Never mind. [ˌnevə ˈmaɪnd] Macht
nichts.; Schon gut.; Mach dir nichts
draus. II

new [njuː] neu I

New Yorker [ˌnjuː ˈjɔːkə] New Yorker; New Yorkerin IV U1, 11

news [njuːz] Nachricht(en);
Neuigkeit(en) II

newspaper [ˈnjuːsˌpeɪpə] Zeitung III

newspaper kiosk [ˈnjuːspeɪpə
ˌkiːɒsk] Zeitungsstand II

next [nekst] nächste I; als Nächstes II

next to [ˈnekst tə] neben I

nice [naɪs] schön; nett I

Nice to meet you. [naɪs tə ˈmiːt juː]
Schön, dich kennenzulernen. I

night [naɪt] Nacht I

at night [ət ˈnaɪt] nachts IV U1, 16

nine [naɪn] neun I

nineteen [ˌnaɪnˈtiːn] neunzehn I

ninety [ˈnaɪnti] neunzig I

no [nəʊ] kein; keine; nein I

no one [ˈnəʊ wʌn] niemand I

nobody [ˈnəʊbədi] niemand II

noise [nɔɪz] Geräusch I

noisy [ˈnɔɪzi] laut III

north [nɔːθ] Norden; Nord- III

in the north of [ˌɪn ðə ˈnɔːθ əv] im
Norden von III

nose [nəʊz] Nase II

not [nɒt] nicht I

not … any more [ˌnɒt … eni ˈmɔː]
nicht mehr III

not … anything [ˌnɒt … ˈeniθɪŋ]
nichts III

not … either [ˌnɒt … ˈaɪðə] auch
nicht III

not … yet [ˌnɒt … ˈjet] noch nicht
III

not … any [ˌnɒt … eni] kein; keine
III

notes (pl) [nəʊts] Notizen <I>

to take notes [teɪk ˈnəʊts] sich
Notizen machen <I>

nothing [ˈnʌθɪŋ] nichts II

lost and found **notice** [ˌlɒst ən ˈfaʊnd
ˌnəʊtɪs] Suchplakat; Aushang III

November [nəˈvembə] November I

now [naʊ] jetzt; nun I

number [ˈnʌmbə] Zahl; Nummer I

nurse [nɜːs] Krankenpfleger; Krankenschwester IV U3, 56

O

o'clock [əˈklɒk] Uhr (Zeitangabe bei
vollen Stunden) I

occasionally [əˈkeɪʒnli] gelegentlich
III

October [ɒkˈtəʊbə] Oktober I

odd one out [ˌɒd wʌn ˈaʊt] das Wort,
das nicht in die Gruppe passt <I>

of [ɒv] von I; mit; vor; aus III

of course [əv ˈkɔːs] natürlich;
selbstverständlich II

of all the states [əv ˈɔːl ðə ˌsteɪts]
von allen Staaten IV U2, 31

to knock sb **off** sth [ˌnɒk … ˈɒf] jmdn.
von etw. stoßen IV U1, 20

to **offer** [ˈɒfə] bieten; anbieten
IV U4, 76

police **officer** [pəˈliːs ˌɒfɪsə] Polizeibeamter; Polizeibeamtin I

official [əˈfɪʃl] offiziell <IV U1, 27>

often [ˈɒfn] oft; häufig II

more often [mɔːr ˈɒfn] häufiger;
öfter IV U2, 40

oh [əʊ] Null (bei Uhrzeiten und Telefonnummern) III

oil [ɔɪl] Öl II

OK (okay) [əʊˈkeɪ] okay I

old [əʊld] alt I

old people's home [ˌəʊld ˈpiːplz
ˌhəʊm] Altersheim <IV U4, 138>

on [ɒn] auf; an; am I; mit II

on TV [ɒn ˌtiːˈviː] im Fernsehen III

to put on [ˌpʊt ˈɒn] anziehen II

to try on [traɪ ˈɒn] anprobieren II

on foot [ɒn ˈfʊt] zu Fuß I

on Saturdays [ɒn ˈsætədeɪz] sams-
tags I

on the bus [ɒn ðə ˈbʌs] im Bus II

on the left [ɒn ðə ˈleft] links; auf
der linken Seite II

on the right [ɒn ðə ˈraɪt] rechts; auf
der rechten Seite II

once [wʌns] einmal; einst II

once upon a time [ˌwʌns əpɒn ə
ˈtaɪm] es war einmal II

one [wʌn] eins; ein I

a/one hundred [ˈhʌndrəd] hundert;
einhundert I

a/one thousand [ˈθaʊznd] tausend;
eintausend II

each one [ˌiːtʃ ˈwʌn] jedes
<IV U4, 75>

no one [ˈnəʊ wʌn] niemand I

one day [ˈwʌn deɪ] eines Tages I

one stop [ˌwʌn ˈstɒp] einmal umsteigen <IV U1, 22>

one(s) [wʌn(z)] *Platzhalter für ein Nomen* III

one-way [ˌwʌnˈweɪ] einfach <IV U1, 22>

online [ɒnˈlaɪn] online; Online- II

only [ˈəʊnli] nur I

to open [ˈəʊpn] öffnen; aufmachen I

open [ˈəʊpn] geöffnet I

opportunity [ˌɒpəˈtjuːnəti] Chance; Möglichkeit; Gelegenheit IV U1, 12

opposite [ˈɒpəzɪt] Gegenteil <I>; gegenüber II

or [ɔː] oder I

orange [ˈɒrɪndʒ] orange; Orange I

order [ˈɔːdə] Reihenfolge <I>
  word order [ˈwɜːdˌɔːdə] Wortstellung; Satzstellung <II>

to organize [ˈɔːgnaɪz] organisieren I

other [ˈʌðə] andere II
  each other [iːtʃˈʌðə] einander; sich; gegenseitig III

others [ˈʌðəz] anderen II

our [aʊə] unser I

ours [aʊəz] unsere III

ourselves [ˌaʊəˈselvz] uns; selbst; uns selbst IV U2, 32

out and about [ˌaʊt ən əˈbaʊt] unterwegs III

out of … [ˈaʊtˌəv] aus … heraus I

outgoing trip [ˈaʊtgəʊɪŋ ˈtrɪp] Hinfahrt <IV U1, 22>

outside [ˌaʊtˈsaɪd] außerhalb; außen; draußen; im Freien II

oval [ˈəʊvl] oval; eiförmig III

over [ˈəʊvə] vorbei <II>; über; herüber; drüben III
  all over [ɔːlˈəʊvə] in ganz; überall II
  to turn over [tɜːn ˈəʊvə] umkippen; (sich) umdrehen III

owl [aʊl] Eule <IV U2, 132>

to own [əʊn] besitzen III

own [əʊn] eigene II

P

p.m. [ˌpiːˈem] nachmittags *(Uhrzeit)* III

to pack [pæk] packen; einpacken III

package [ˈpækɪdʒ] Paket IV U1, 20

paddle [ˈpædl] Paddel <IV U4, 137>

paella [paɪˈelə] Paella <IV U1, 131>

page [peɪdʒ] Seite <I>

to paint [peɪnt] bemalen; malen; streichen II

face **painting** [ˈfeɪs peɪntɪŋ] Schminken II

wall **painting** [ˈwɔːl peɪntɪŋ] Wandmalerei II

pair [peə] Paar <II>

paper [ˈpeɪpə] Papier III

paperboy [ˈpeɪpəˌbɔɪ] Zeitungsausträger <IV U4, 138>

papergirl [ˈpeɪpəˌgɜːl] Zeitungsausträgerin <IV U4, 138>

parade [pəˈreɪd] Parade; Umzug; Prozession IV U1, 16

parents *(pl)* [ˈpeərnts] Eltern I

park [pɑːk] Park I
  national park [ˌnæʃnl ˈpɑːk] Nationalpark III
  theme park [ˈθiːm ˌpɑːk] Freizeitpark II

parking lot *(AE)* [ˈpɑːkɪŋ ˌlɒt] Parkplatz <IV U2, 42>
  underground parking lot *(AE)* [ˌʌndəgraʊnd ˈpɑːkɪŋ ˌlɒt] Tiefgarage <IV U2, 42>

part [pɑːt] Teil; Rolle II
  to take part (in) [teɪk ˈpɑːt (ɪn)] mitmachen (bei); teilnehmen (an) II

partner [ˈpɑːtnə] Partner; Partnerin I

part-time [ˌpɑːtˈtaɪm] Teilzeit-; Halbtags- <IV U4, 138>

party [ˈpɑːti] Party; Feier I
  to have a party [hæv ə ˈpɑːti] eine Party feiern I

boarding **pass** [ˈbɔːdɪŋ ˌpɑːs] Bordkarte <IV U2, 133>

to pass on [ˌpɑːsˈɒn] weitergeben <IV U2, 42>

passenger [ˈpæsndʒə] Passagier; Passagierin IV U2, 36

passive voice [ˈpæsɪv ˌvɔɪs] Passiv <IV U4, 105>

passport [ˈpɑːspɔːt] Pass; Reisepass IV U2, 36

past [pɑːst] vorbei (an) I; nach *(bei Uhrzeitangaben)* II; Vergangenheit III
  half past (seven) [hɑːf ˈpɑːst (ˌsevn)] halb (acht) II

quarter to/past [ˈkwɔːtə tə/pɑːst] Viertel vor/nach II

pasta [ˈpæstə] Pasta; Nudeln <IV U1, 131>

***to pay** [peɪ] bezahlen <IV U4, 87>

PE (Physical Education) [ˌpiːˈiː (ˌfɪzɪkl edʒʊˈkeɪʃn)] Sportunterricht I

pecan [ˈpiːkæn] Pekannuss <IV U3, 63>

pen [pen] Stift; Füller I

pencil [ˈpensl] Bleistift I

penfriend [ˈpenfrend] Brieffreund; Brieffreundin III

people *(pl only)* [ˈpiːpl] Leute; Menschen I

per [pɜː] pro <IV U4, 82>

percent (%) [pəˈsent] Prozent III

present perfect [ˌpreznt ˈpɜːfɪkt] das Perfekt <III>

permission [pəˈmɪʃn] Genehmigung; Erlaubnis <IV U4, 136>

person *(sg)* [ˈpɜːsn] Mensch; Person II; **people** [ˈpiːpl] oder **persons** *(pl)* [ˈpɜːsns] Leute; Menschen I

pet [pet] Haustier I

phone [fəʊn] Telefon; Handy I
  phone call [ˈfəʊn ˌkɔːl] Telefonanruf; Anruf I

to phone [fəʊn] anrufen; telefonieren II

photo [ˈfəʊtəʊ] Foto I
  to take photos (of) [teɪk ˈfəʊtəʊz (əv)] Fotos machen; fotografieren II

phrase [freɪz] Wortverbindung; Satzteil; Satz; Redewendung <III>

picnic [ˈpɪknɪk] Picknick I

picture [ˈpɪktʃə] Bild I

picture-based [ˈpɪktʃəbeɪst] bildbezogen <III>

pie [paɪ] Kuchen; Pastete <IV U3, 63>
  pie chart [ˈpaɪ ˌtʃɑːt] Kreisdiagramm; Tortendiagramm <IV U1, 25>

a piece of [ə ˈpiːs əv] ein Stück … II
  piece of information [ˌpiːs əv ɪnfəˈmeɪʃn] Information <IV U3, 65>

pier [pɪə] Pier II

pilot [ˈpaɪlət] Pilot; Pilotin <IV U2, 133>

pink [pɪŋk] pink; rosa I

pizza [ˈpiːtsə] Pizza I

place [pleɪs] Platz; Stelle; Ort I

to take place [ˌteɪk ˈpleɪs] stattfinden <IV U3, 62>

plan [plæn] Plan IV U1, 12

to **plan** [plæn] planen IV U4, 80

plane [pleɪn] Flugzeug IV U2, 30

planner [ˈplænə] Kalender; Planer II

plant [plɑːnt] Pflanze III

plate [pleɪt] Teller; (Kontinental-)Platte IV U2, 40

play [pleɪ] Theaterstück III

to **play** [pleɪ] spielen I

player [ˈpleɪə] Spieler; Spielerin II

playground [ˈpleɪɡraʊnd] Schulhof; Pausenhof; Spielplatz I

playing field [ˈpleɪɪŋ ˌfiːld] Sportplatz II

please [pliːz] bitte I

plum [plʌm] Pflaume I

poem [ˈpəʊɪm] Gedicht III

point [pɔɪnt] Punkt III

to **point** [pɔɪnt] zeigen <I>

police [pəˈliːs] Polizei IV U1, 20

police officer [pəˈliːs ˌɒfɪsə] Polizeibeamter; Polizeibeamtin I

Polish [ˈpəʊlɪʃ] Polnisch; polnisch; aus Polen <IV U1, 131>

swimming **pool** [ˈswɪmɪŋ ˌpuːl] Schwimmbad I

poor [pɔː] arm IV U1, 12

pop [pɒp] Pop (Musik) II

popular [ˈpɒpjələ] beliebt III

population (no pl) [ˌpɒpjəˈleɪʃn] Bevölkerung; Einwohner; Einwohnerzahl IV U1, 11

positive [ˈpɒzətɪv] positiv III

post [pəʊst] Post; Beitrag <IV U4, 136>

to **post** [pəʊst] posten; online stellen III

postcard [ˈpəʊskɑːd] Postkarte I

poster [ˈpəʊstə] Poster II

pot [pɒt] Topf III

potato (sg) [pəˈteɪtəʊ], **potatoes** (pl) [pəˈteɪtəʊz] Kartoffel IV U3, 52

pound (£) [paʊnd] Pfund (brit. Währungseinheit) I

practice [ˈpræktɪs] Training; Übung I

to **practise** [ˈpræktɪs] üben; trainieren <II>

to **prepare** [prɪˈpeə] vorbereiten <IV U1, 15>

present [ˈpreznt] Geschenk I

present perfect [ˌpreznt ˈpɜːfɪkt] das Perfekt <III>

present progressive [ˌpreznt prəˈɡresɪv] Verlaufsform der Gegenwart <II>

to **present** [prɪˈzent] präsentieren <I>

presentation [ˌpreznˈteɪʃn] Präsentation; Referat; Vortrag III

presentation skills [ˌpreznˈteɪʃn ˌskɪlz] Fertigkeit Präsentieren <III>

presenter [prɪˈzentə] Präsentator; Präsentatorin <IV U3, 65>

president [ˈprezɪdnt] Präsident; Präsidentin III

pretty [ˈprɪti] hübsch II

pretzel [ˈpretsl] Brezel <IV U1, 131>

price [praɪs] Preis I

primary school [ˈpraɪmri ˌskuːl] Grundschule IV U4, 81

prisoner [ˈprɪznə] Gefangener; Gefangene IV U3, 60

to keep sb prisoner [ˌkiːp ˈprɪznə] jmdn. gefangen halten IV U3, 60

prize [praɪz] Preis; Gewinn II

probably [ˈprɒbəbli] wahrscheinlich IV U3, 60

problem [ˈprɒbləm] Problem I

procession [prəˈseʃn] Umzug; Festzug II

to **produce** [prəˈdjuːs] erzeugen; herstellen; anbauen IV U2, 31

profile [ˈprəʊfaɪl] Profil; Steckbrief III

program [ˈprəʊɡræm] Computerprogramm <IV U4, 136>

programme [ˈprəʊɡræm] Sendung; Programm III

present progressive [ˌpreznt prəˈɡresɪv] Verlaufsform der Gegenwart <II>

project [ˈprɒdʒekt] Projekt II

to **protect** [prəˈtekt] schützen III

proud (of) [praʊd (əv)] stolz (auf) IV U3, 50

to **prove** [pruːv] beweisen IV U1, 21

public transport [ˌpʌblɪk ˈtrænspɔːt] öffentliche Verkehrsmittel III

to **pull** [pʊl] ziehen I

pullover [ˈpʊləʊvə] Pullover I

to **push** [pʊʃ] schieben I

stone **put** [ˈstəʊn ˌpʊt] Steinstoßen III

*to **put** [pʊt] setzen; legen; stellen I; bringen; stecken II

to put in [ˌpʊt ˈɪn] einsetzen <I>

to put into [ˌpʊt ˈɪntə] eingeben (in) <IV U1, 27>

to put on [ˌpʊt ˈɒn] anziehen II

put [pʊt] simple past von to put I

Q

qualification [ˌkwɒlɪfɪˈkeɪʃn] Ausbildung; Qualifikation; Abschluss; Schulabschluss IV U4, 80

quantity [ˈkwɒntəti] Menge <IV U3, 105>

quarter to/past [ˈkwɔːtə tə/pɑːst] Viertel vor/nach II

queen [kwiːn] Königin II

question [ˈkwestʃən] Frage I

queue [kjuː] Warteschlange II

quick [kwɪk] schnell IV U1, 16

quiet [ˈkwaɪət] leise; ruhig; still II

quite [kwaɪt] ziemlich; ganz; völlig II

quiz [kwɪz] Rätsel <I>; Quiz; Ratespiel IV ZI, 8

R

rabbit [ˈræbɪt] Kaninchen I

raccoon [rəˈkuːn] Waschbär I

race [reɪs] Wettrennen; Rennen; Wettlauf II

sack race [ˈsæk ˌreɪs] Sackhüpfen II

racket [ˈrækɪt] Schläger <IV U4, 137>

radio [ˈreɪdiəʊ] Radio III

raffle [ˈræfl] Gewinnspiel; Tombola II

raft [rɑːft] Raft; Floß III

rafting [ˈrɑːftɪŋ] Rafting III

to go rafting [ˌɡəʊ ˈrɑːftɪŋ] raften gehen III

railway [ˈreɪlweɪ] Eisenbahn; Bahn IV U4, 80

railway station [ˈreɪlweɪ ˌsteɪʃn] Bahnhof IV U4, 80

to **rain** [reɪn] regnen I

rainbow [ˈreɪnbəʊ] Regenbogen III

rainy [ˈreɪni] regnerisch II

to **raise** money [ˌreɪz ˈmʌni] Geld sammeln; Geld aufbringen II

ran [ræn] simple past von to run II

rang [ræŋ] simple past von to ring II

ranger (AE) [ˈreɪndʒə] Ranger; Rangerin IV U2, 48

rap [ræp] Rap I

rapid ['ræpɪd] Stromschnelle III

rarely ['reəli] selten III

*__to read__ [riːd] lesen; vorlesen II

read [red] simple past von *to read* II

reading ['riːdɪŋ] Lesen <I>
  reading skills ['riːdɪŋ ˌskɪlz] Fertig-keit Lesen <I>

ready ['redi] bereit; fertig I

really ['rɪəli] wirklich; eigentlich I

*__to rebuild__ [ˌriːˈbɪld] wiederaufbauen IV U3, 66

receptionist [rɪˈsepʃnɪst] Empfangs-chef; Empfangsdame IV U4, 76

to record [rɪˈkɔːd] aufnehmen; auf-zeichnen <I>

red [red] rot I

reference ['refrns] Referenz; Arbeits-zeugnis; Empfehlung IV U4, 81

reflexive pronoun [rɪˌfleksɪv 'prəʊnaʊn] Reflexivpronomen <IV U2, 105>

reggae ['regeɪ] Reggae *(Musik)* IV U3, 51

registration [ˌredʒɪˈstreɪʃn] Überprü-fung der Anwesenheit I

reliable [rɪˈlaɪəbl] verlässlich; zuver-lässig; vertrauenswürdig IV U4, 76

to rely (on) [rɪˈlaɪ (ɒn)] sich verlassen (auf); vertrauen (auf) IV U3, 56

to remember [rɪˈmembə] sich erinnern (an); sich merken III; gedenken <IV U3, 62>

to repair [rɪˈpeə] reparieren IV U4, 72

to repeat [rɪˈpiːt] wiederholen <I>

report [rɪˈpɔːt] Bericht <II>

to report [rɪˈpɔːt] berichten <III>

request [rɪˈkwest] Anfrage IV U4, 81

animal **rescue** shelter [ˌænɪml 'reskjuː ˌʃeltə] Tierheim I

research [rɪˈsɜːtʃ] Recherche; For-schung <IV U1, 26>

reservation [ˌrezəˈveɪʃn] Reservat; Reservierung III
  to make reservations [ˌmeɪk rezəˈveɪʃnz] reservieren IV U4, 80

rest [rest] Rest II

restaurant ['restrɒnt] Restaurant II

result [rɪˈzʌlt] Ergebnis <I>

return ticket [rɪˈtɜːn ˌtɪkɪt] Hin- und Rückfahrkarte III

return trip [rɪˌtɜːn 'trɪp] Rückfahrt <IV U1, 22>

rhyme [raɪm] Reim <III>

to rhyme [raɪm] (sich) reimen <III>

rice [raɪs] Reis II
  chicken fried rice ['tʃɪkɪn ˌfraɪd 'raɪs] gebratener Reis mit Hühnerfleisch II

rich [rɪtʃ] reich <IV U1, 130>

Richter scale *(no pl)* ['rɪktə ˌskeɪl] Richterskala IV U2, 41

ride [raɪd] Fahrt; Fahrgeschäft; Ritt II

*__to ride__ [raɪd] fahren; reiten I

horse **riding** ['hɔːs ˌraɪdɪŋ] Reiten I

right [raɪt] richtig; korrekt I; rechts; rechte II
  on the right [ɒn ðə 'raɪt] rechts; auf der rechten Seite II
  You're right. [jɔː ˈraɪt] Du hast recht. I

*__to ring__ [rɪŋ] klingeln; läuten I

river ['rɪvə] Fluss I

RnB (rhythm'n'blues) [ˌɑːnˈbiː (ˌrɪðm ən 'bluːz)] RnB (Rhythm'n'Blues) *(Musik)* <IV U1, 131>

road [rəʊd] Straße I

rock climbing ['rɒk ˌklaɪmɪŋ] Klet-tern I

rock [rɒk] Rock *(Musik)* <IV U1, 131>

rocket ['rɒkɪt] Rakete III

role play ['rəʊl ˌpleɪ] Rollenspiel <I>

roller coaster ['rəʊlə ˌkəʊstə] Achter-bahn II

roof [ruːf] Dach III

room [ruːm] Zimmer; Raum I

root word [ˌruːt 'wɜːd] Grundwort; Stammwort <IV U3, 67>

round trip [ˌraʊnd 'trɪp] Hin- und Rückflug; Hin- und Rückfahrt <IV U1, 22>

rubber ['rʌbə] Radiergummi I

rubbish ['rʌbɪʃ] Müll; Abfall I

rugby ['rʌgbi] Rugby III

rule [ruːl] Regel <I>

ruler ['ruːlə] Lineal I

*__to run__ [rʌn] laufen; rennen; fahren II
  to run away [ˌrʌn əˈweɪ] weglaufen II

Russian ['rʌʃn] Russisch; russisch; aus Russland; Russe; Russin IV U4, 81

S

sack race ['sæk ˌreɪs] Sackhüpfen II

sad [sæd] traurig I

safe [seɪf] sicher; ungefährlich; in Sicherheit; unversehrt IV U1, 16

said [sed] simple past von *to say* I; past participle von *to say* III

saint [seɪnt] Heiliger; Heilige <IV U3, 62>

salad ['sæləd] Salat I

salary ['sæləri] Gehalt IV U4, 76

for **sale** [fə 'seɪl] zu verkaufen <IV U4, 87>

hairdressing **salon** ['heədresɪŋ ˌsælɒn] Friseursalon IV U3, 56

the **same** [ðə 'seɪm] der gleiche; derselbe; gleich; genauso II
  at the same time [ət ðə seɪm 'taɪm] gleichzeitig; nebenher II

sandwich ['sænwɪdʒ] Sandwich; belegtes Brot I

sang [sæŋ] simple past von *to sing* II

sat [sæt] simple past, past participle von *to sit* IV U2, 32

Saturday ['sætədeɪ] Samstag I
  on Saturdays [ɒn 'sætədeɪz] sams-tags I

Saudi Arabian [ˌsaʊdi əˈreɪbiən] saudi-arabisch <IV U1, 131>

sausage ['sɒsɪdʒ] Wurst <IV U1, 131>

to save [seɪv] retten; sparen II; spei-chern <IV U4, 136>

saw [sɔː] simple past von *to see* I

saxophone ['sæksəfəʊn] Saxofon I

*__to say__ [seɪ] nennen; sagen; nach-sprechen; sprechen I; aussprechen III

Richter scale *(no pl)* ['rɪktə ˌskeɪl] Richterskala IV U2, 41

to scan [skæn] nach Details durchsu-chen; scannen <III>

to scare [skeə] erschrecken <II>

*__to be scared__ [biː ˈskeəd] Angst haben I

scarf *(sg)* [skɑːf], **scarves** *(pl)* [skɑːvz] Schal; Tuch II

scary ['skeəri] unheimlich; gruselig; beängstigend I

scene [siːn] Szene <II>

scenery ['siːnri] Kulissen; Bühnenbild III

p pen • **b** bed • **t** ten • **d** dad • **k** cat • **g** grey • **tʃ** chair • **dʒ** job • **f** fan • **v** very • **θ** three • **ð** the

school [skuːl] Schule I
  at school [ət 'skuːl] in der Schule I
  junior high school [ˌdʒuːniə 'haɪ skuːl] Junior Highschool *(Mittelschule in den USA, in der Regel Klassenstufe 7–9)* II
  primary school ['praɪmri ˌskuːl] Grundschule IV U4, 81
  school trip [ˌskuːl 'trɪp] Klassenfahrt; Schulausflug II
  secondary school ['sekndri ˌskuːl] weiterführende Schule; Mittelschule IV U4, 81
science ['saɪəns] Naturwissenschaft; Wissenschaft III
  science fiction [ˌsaɪəns 'fɪkʃn] Science-Fiction I
to score [skɔː] erzielen III
Scottish ['skɒtɪʃ] schottisch; aus Schottland III
scratch [skrætʃ] Kratzer IV U1, 20
screenshot ['skriːnʃɒt] Bildschirmfoto <IV U4, 75>
sea [siː] Meer I
search [sɜːtʃ] Recherche; Suche <IV U1, 27>
  search engine ['sɜːtʃ ˌendʒɪn] Suchmaschine <IV U1, 27>
at the seaside [ət ðə 'siːsaɪd] am Meer I
season ['siːzn] Jahreszeit; Saison II
seat [siːt] Sitzplatz; Sitz III
  Take a seat. [ˌteɪk ə 'siːt] Setz dich.; Setzen Sie sich.; Nimm Platz.; Nehmen Sie Platz. IV U3, 52
second ['seknd] Sekunde <I>; zweite II; zweit- IV U4, 70
secondary school ['sekndri ˌskuːl] weiterführende Schule; Mittelschule IV U4, 81
secondary school leaving certificate ['sekndri skuːl ˌliːvɪŋ sə'tɪfɪkət] mittlerer Schulabschluss; Realschulabschluss IV U4, 80
second-hand [ˌsekn'hænd] gebraucht; secondhand; aus zweiter Hand I
security [sɪ'kjʊərəti] Sicherheitskontrolle <IV U2, 133>
*to see [siː] sehen I
  See you. ['siː ˌjuː] Wir sehen uns.; Bis bald.; Tschüss. II

See you soon. [ˌsiː ˌjuː 'suːn] Bis bald. I
seen [siːn] past participle von *to see* III
selfie ['selfi] Selfie IV U4, 72
*to sell [sel] verkaufen I
*to send [send] schicken; senden I
sense [sens] Sinn; Bedeutung IV U2, 48
  sense of smell [ˌsens ˌəv 'smel] Geruchssinn IV U2, 48
sent [sent] simple past von *to send* I
sentence ['sentəns] Satz <I>
September [sep'tembə] September I
Serbian ['sɜːbiən] Serbisch; serbisch; aus Serbien <IV U1, 131>
series *(no pl)* ['sɪəriːz] Serie IV U4, 72
serious ['sɪəriəs] ernst; schwer II
customer service [ˌkʌstəmə 'sɜːvɪs] Kundenbetreuung; Kundendienst; Kundenservice IV U4, 76
shuttle service ['ʃʌtl ˌsɜːvɪs] Fahrdienst <IV U2, 42>
seven ['sevn] sieben I
seventeen [ˌsevn'tiːn] siebzehn I
seventy ['sevnti] siebzig I
*to shake [ʃeɪk] beben; zittern; schütteln IV U2, 40
shaken ['ʃeɪkn] past participle von *to shake* IV U2, 40
shamrock ['ʃæmrɒk] Kleeblatt III
to share [ʃeə] teilen III
shark [ʃɑːk] Hai I
she [ʃiː] sie I
sheep *(sg)* [ʃiːp], **sheep** *(pl)* [ʃiːp] Schaf I
shelf *(sg)* [ʃelf], **shelves** *(pl)* [ʃelvz] Regal; Regalbrett II
animal rescue shelter [ˌænɪml 'reskjuːˌʃeltə] Tierheim I
ship [ʃɪp] Schiff I
shirt [ʃɜːt] Hemd; Shirt I
shoe [ʃuː] Schuh I
shook [ʃʊk] simple past von *to shake* IV U2, 40
*to shoot [ʃuːt] schießen; erschießen IV U3, 60
shop [ʃɒp] Geschäft; Laden I
  sports shop ['spɔːts ˌʃɒp] Sportgeschäft II
shopping ['ʃɒpɪŋ] Einkaufen I

shopping centre ['ʃɒpɪŋ ˌsentə] Einkaufszentrum I
shopping list ['ʃɒpɪŋ ˌlɪst] Einkaufszettel I
short [ʃɔːt] kurz II
shorts *(pl)* [ʃɔːts] Shorts; kurze Hose II
shot [ʃɒt] simple past, past participle von *to shoot* IV U3, 60
should [ʃʊd] sollte III
to shout [ʃaʊt] rufen; schreien I
show [ʃəʊ] Show; Aufführung I
*to show [ʃəʊ] zeigen II
shuttle service ['ʃʌtl ˌsɜːvɪs] Fahrdienst <IV U2, 42>
*to be sick [bi 'sɪk] sich übergeben I
side [saɪd] Seite II
sight [saɪt] Sehenswürdigkeit II
sign [saɪn] Schild; Zeichen; Anzeichen IV U1, 16
to signal ['sɪgnl] blinken IV U1, 20
silly ['sɪli] albern II
simple past [ˌsɪmpl 'pɑːst] einfache Vergangenheit <II>
simple present [ˌsɪmpl 'preznt] einfache Gegenwart; Präsens <II>
since [sɪns] seit; seitdem IV U1, 12
Yours sincerely, [ˌjɔːz sɪn'sɪəli] Mit freundlichen Grüßen IV U4, 76
*to sing [sɪŋ] singen I
singer ['sɪŋə] Sänger; Sängerin I
single ticket [ˌsɪŋgl 'tɪkɪt] einfache Fahrkarte III
sister ['sɪstə] Schwester I
*to sit [sɪt] sitzen IV U2, 32
  to sit (down) [sɪt ('daʊn)] sich setzen; sich hinsetzen I
site [saɪt] Seite *(im Internet)* <IV U4, 75>
situation [ˌsɪtjuˈeɪʃn] Situation <II>
six [sɪks] sechs I
sixteen [ˌsɪkˈstiːn] sechzehn I
sixty ['sɪksti] sechzig I
size [saɪz] Größe II
to skate [skeɪt] inlineskaten; Schlittschuh laufen II
skateboard ['skeɪtbɔːd] Skateboard I
skater ['skeɪtə] Skater; Skaterin I
*to go skating [ˌgəʊ 'skeɪtɪŋ] inlineskaten gehen; Schlittschuhlaufen gehen II

ice **skating** [ˈaɪs ˌskeɪtɪŋ] Schlittschuhlaufen <IV U4, 137>

skiing [ˈskiːɪŋ] Skifahren <IV U4, 137>

skill [skɪl] Fertigkeit; Geschick; Kenntnis; Fähigkeit IV U4, 76

to **skim** [skɪm] überfliegen <III>

skirt [skɜːt] Rock III

sky [skaɪ] Himmel IV U3, 60

slave [sleɪv] Sklave; Sklavin IV U3, 60
slave trader [ˈsleɪv ˌtreɪdə] Skla-
venhändler; Menschenhändler
IV U3, 61

slavery [ˈsleɪvri] Sklaverei <IV U3, 62>

sled [sled] Schlitten IV U2, 48

*to **sleep** [sliːp] schlafen II

slept [slept] simple past von *to sleep*
II

slow [sləʊ] langsam IV U1, 16

small [smɔːl] klein I

smell [smel] Geruch; Duft IV U2, 48
sense of **smell** [ˌsens ʌv ˈsmel]
Geruchssinn IV U2, 48

smoke [sməʊk] Rauch IV U3, 60

smurf [smɜːf] Schlumpf I

snack bar [ˈsnæk ˌbɑː] Imbissstube;
Café I

snow [snəʊ] Schnee II

snowboard [ˈsnəʊbɔːd] Snowboard I

snowboarding [ˈsnəʊbɔːdɪŋ] Snow-
boarden <IV U4, 137>

snowy [ˈsnəʊi] schneereich; verschneit II

so [səʊ] also; deshalb I; so; dermaßen II
so that [səʊ ˈðæt] damit; sodass
IV U3, 60

soccer (AE) [ˈsɒkə] Fußball II

social placement [ˌsəʊʃl ˈpleɪsmənt]
Sozialpraktikum <IV U3, 135>

social media [ˌsəʊʃl ˈmiːdiə] soziale
Medien III

software [ˈsɒfweə] Software IV U4, 72

sold [səʊld] simple past von *to sell* II

some [sʌm] etwas; einige; ein paar I

somebody [ˈsʌmbədi] jemand I

someone [ˈsʌmwʌn] jemand; irgendjemand III

something [ˈsʌmθɪŋ] etwas I

sometimes [ˈsʌmtaɪmz] manchmal I

son [sʌn] Sohn IV U3, 52

song [sɒŋ] Lied I

soon [suːn] bald II
See you soon. [ˌsi: ju: ˈsuːn] Bis
bald. I

Sorry. [ˈsɒri] Tut mir leid.; Entschuldi-
gung. I
I'm sorry. [aɪm ˈsɒri] Es tut mir leid.;
Entschuldigung. II

to **sort** [sɔːt] sortieren <IV U3, 54>

sound [saʊnd] Laut; Geräusch; Ton
<I>

to **sound** [saʊnd] klingen III

sweet and **sour** [ˌswiːt ən ˈsaʊə] süß-
sauer <IV U1, 131>

source [sɔːs] Quelle <IV U4, 136>

south [saʊθ] Süd-; Süden III

southern [ˈsʌðən] südlich; Süd-; Süd-
staaten- IV U3, 50

souvenir [ˌsuːvnˈɪə] Souvenir; Andenken II

space [speɪs] Raumfahrt; Weltraum
III

Spanish [ˈspænɪʃ] spanisch; Spanisch;
aus Spanien IV U1, 16

*to **speak** [spiːk] sprechen I

speaking [ˈspiːkɪŋ] Sprechen <I>
speaking skills [ˈspiːkɪŋ ˌskɪlz]
Fertigkeit Sprechen <I>

special [ˈspeʃl] besonders; speziell I

spelling [ˈspelɪŋ] Rechtschreibung I

*to **spend** [spend] verbringen (*Zeit*);
ausgeben (*Geld*) II

spent [spent] simple past von *to
spend* II

spoke [spəʊk] simple past von *to
speak* <IV U3, 65>

sport [spɔːt] Sport III

sports (pl only) [spɔːts] Sportarten I
sports centre [ˈspɔːts ˌsentə] Sportzentrum I
sports day [ˈspɔːts ˌdeɪ] Sportfest II
sports shop [ˈspɔːts ˌʃɒp] Sportgeschäft II

spring [sprɪŋ] Frühling II

to **spy** [spaɪ] sehen I

square dance [ˈskweə ˌdɑːns] Squaredance (*amerikanischer Volkstanz*) II

squash [skwɒʃ] Squash <IV U4, 137>

squirrel [ˈskwɪrl] Eichhörnchen
<IV U2, 132>

stadium [ˈsteɪdiəm] Stadion I

stage [steɪdʒ] Bühne II

stall [stɔːl] Stand; Bude I

*to **stand** [stænd] stehen II
can't stand + -ing [ˌkɑːnt ˈstænd
…ɪŋ] etw. nicht ausstehen können;
etw. nicht ertragen III
to stand for [ˈstænd fə] stehen für
III

star [stɑː] Star I; Stern <IV U2, 46>

start [stɑːt] Anfang; Beginn; Start <I>

to **start** [stɑːt] anfangen; beginnen;
starten I

state [steɪt] Bundesstaat; Staat III
of all the states [əvˌɔːl ðə ˌsteɪts]
von allen Staaten IV U2, 31

statement [ˈsteɪtmənt] Aussage
<IV U2, 33>

station [ˈsteɪʃn] Station; Bahnhof;
Haltestelle III
railway station [ˈreɪlweɪ ˌsteɪʃn]
Bahnhof IV U4, 80
train station [ˈtreɪn ˌsteɪʃn] Bahnhof
<III>

statue [ˈstætʃuː] Statue IV U1, 10

to **stay** [steɪ] bleiben; übernachten I
staying connected [ˌsteɪɪŋ
kəˈnektɪd] in Verbindung bleiben III

steamboat [ˈstiːmbəʊt] Dampfer;
Dampfschiff IV U3, 50

step [step] Schritt; Stufe II

stick [stɪk] Schläger; Stock III

still [stɪl] noch; immer noch II

stone [stəʊn] Stein III
stone put [ˈstəʊn ˌpʊt] Steinstoßen
III

stood [stʊd] simple past von *to stand*
II

stop [stɒp] Haltestelle; Halt II
one stop [ˌwʌn ˈstɒp] einmal
umsteigen <IV U1, 22>

to **stop** [stɒp] beenden; aufhören;
anhalten II

store (AE) [stɔː] Laden; Geschäft III

storm [stɔːm] Sturm I

story [ˈstɔːri] Geschichte I

straight on [streɪtˈɒn] geradeaus II

strawberry [ˈstrɔːbri] Erdbeere I

street [striːt] Straße I

stripe [straɪp] Streifen <IV U2, 46>

strong [strɒŋ] stark III; stabil IV U2, 41

*to be **stuck** [bi: ˈstʌk] feststecken;
stecken bleiben I

student ['stju:dnt] Schüler; Schülerin I

study skills [ˌstʌdi 'skɪlz] Fertigkeit Lern- und Arbeitstechniken <I>

subject ['sʌbdʒɪkt] Schulfach I; Betreff III

subtotal ['sʌbˌtəʊtl] Zwischensumme <IV U1, 22>

successful [sək'sesfl] erfolgreich IV U1, 12

suddenly ['sʌdnli] plötzlich; auf einmal I

to suggest [sə'dʒest] vorschlagen <IV U3, 134>

suggestion [sə'dʒestʃn] Vorschlag; Anregung <IV U3, 134>

suitcase ['su:tkeɪs] Koffer IV U2, 36

summer ['sʌmə] Sommer II

sun [sʌn] Sonne II

Sunday ['sʌndeɪ] Sonntag I

sunny ['sʌni] sonnig II

superlative [su:'pɜ:lətɪv] Superlativ <IV U3, 105>

supermarket ['su:pəˌmɑ:kɪt] Supermarkt I

supplies (pl) [sə'plaɪz] Vorräte IV U2, 48

sure [ʃɔ:] sicher II

to make sure [meɪk 'ʃɔ:] dafür sorgen; sich versichern <IV U4, 85>

to surf the internet [ˌsɜ:f ði 'ɪntənet] im Internet surfen <III>

surfing ['sɜ:fɪŋ] Surfen; Wellenreiten; Surf- IV U2, 31

to go surfing [ˌgəʊ 'sɜ:fɪŋ] surfen gehen III

surprise [sə'praɪz] Überraschung III

surprised [sə'praɪzd] überrascht II

survey ['sɜ:veɪ] Umfrage <III>

sushi ['su:ʃi] Sushi <IV U1, 131>

swam [swæm] simple past von to swim IV U3, 61

sweet [swi:t] Süßigkeit; Bonbon I

sweet and sour [ˌswi:t ən 'saʊə] süß-sauer <IV U1, 131>

*to swim [swɪm] schwimmen I

*to go swimming [ˌgəʊ 'swɪmɪŋ] schwimmen gehen I

swimming pool ['swɪmɪŋ ˌpu:l] Schwimmbad I

*to swing [swɪŋ] schwingen; schwenken III

to switch off [ˌswɪtʃ 'ɒf] ausschalten <IV U4, 136>

to switch on [ˌswɪtʃ 'ɒn] einschalten <IV U4, 136>

sword [sɔ:d] Schwert III

swung [swʌŋ] simple past, past participle von to swing III

symbol ['sɪmbl] Symbol III

Syrian ['sɪriən] syrisch; aus Syrien <IV U1, 131>

T

table ['teɪbl] Tisch; Tabelle <I>

tail [teɪl] Schwanz I

*to take [teɪk] mitnehmen; nehmen I; hinbringen II; dauern; brauchen III

to take care of sb [ˌteɪk 'keər ˌəv] sich um jmdn. kümmern; für jmdn. sorgen <IV U4, 82>

to take notes [teɪk 'nəʊts] sich Notizen machen <I>

to take off [teɪk 'ɒf] starten; abheben <IV U2, 133>

to take out [ˌteɪk 'aʊt] hinausbringen II

to take part (in) [ˌteɪk 'pɑ:t (ɪn)] mitmachen (bei); teilnehmen (an) II

to take photos (of) [teɪk 'fəʊtəʊz (əv)] Fotos machen; fotografieren II

to take place [teɪk 'pleɪs] stattfinden <IV U3, 62>

to take the dog for a walk [teɪk ðə dɒg fɔ:r ə 'wɔ:k] den Hund ausführen I

to take turns [teɪk 'tɜ:nz] sich abwechseln <I>

Take a seat. [ˌteɪk ə 'si:t] Setz dich.; Setzen Sie sich.; Nimm Platz.; Nehmen Sie Platz. IV U3, 52

taken ['teɪkn] past participle von to take III

talent ['tælənt] Talent; Begabung I

talk [tɔ:k] Vortrag; Gespräch; Unterhaltung <III>

to talk (to) [tɔ:k (tə)] reden (mit); sprechen (mit) I

tall [tɔ:l] hoch; groß II

tandem ['tændəm] Tandem II

task [tɑ:sk] Aufgabe; Auftrag <I>

taught [tɔ:t] simple past, past participle von to teach IV U2, 32

tax [tæks] Steuer <IV U1, 22>

tea [ti:] Tee; Abendessen I

*to teach [ti:tʃ] lehren; beibringen; unterrichten IV U2, 32

teacher ['ti:tʃə] Lehrer; Lehrerin I

team [ti:m] Mannschaft; Team; Gruppe I

techno ['teknəʊ] Techno (Musik) <IV U1, 131>

technology [tek'nɒlədʒi] Technik; Technologie III

DT (Design Technology) [ˌdi:'ti: (dɪˌzaɪn tek'nɒlədʒi)] Technik I

teddy ['tedi] Teddybär I

teen [ti:n] Jugend-; Teenager; Teenagerin; Jugendlicher; Jugendliche II

teenager ['ti:nˌeɪdʒə] Teenager; Jugendlicher; Jugendliche <IV U1, 16>

telephone box ['telɪfəʊn ˌbɒks] Telefonzelle II

television ['telɪvɪʒn] Fernsehen; Fernseher III

*to tell [tel] erzählen; sagen I

to tell sb to do sth ['tel tə ˌdu:] jmdm. etw. auftragen III

ten [ten] zehn I

tennis ['tenɪs] Tennis I

tent [tent] Zelt II

terminal ['tɜ:mɪnl] Terminal <IV U2, 133>

to test [test] testen; prüfen II

text [tekst] Text <I>

than [ðæn] als II

Thank you. ['θæŋk ju] Danke. I

thankful ['θæŋkfl] dankbar IV U3, 52

Thanks. [θæŋks] Danke. I

Thanksgiving [ˌθæŋks'gɪvɪŋ] Erntedankfest IV U3, 52

that [ðæt] das; dieses; jene I; dass II; der; die III

after that [ˌɑ:ftə 'ðæt] danach I

so that [səʊ 'ðæt] damit; sodass IV U3, 60

that's why ['ðæts waɪ] deshalb; deswegen II

That's too bad. [ˌðæts tu: 'bæd] Schade! II

the [ðə] die; der; das I

the

theater *(AE)* [ˈθɪətə] Theater III

theatre [ˈθɪətə] Theater III

their [ðeə] ihr I

theirs [ðeəz] ihre III

them [ðem] sie *(Pl.)* I; ihnen II

theme [θiːm] Thema; Motto <I>
  theme park [ˈθiːm ˌpaːk] Freizeit-park II

themselves [ðəmˈselvz] sich; selbst; sie selbst III; sich selbst IV U2, 32

then [ðen] dann; danach I

there [ðeə] da; dort; dorthin; dahin I
  there are [ðeərˈaː] da sind; es gibt I
  there's (= there is) [ðeəz] da ist; dort ist; es gibt I

these [ðiːz] diese II

they [ðeɪ] sie *(Pl.)* I

thing [θɪŋ] Sache; Ding I

*to **think** [θɪŋk] denken; glauben II; überlegen <IV U2, 40>
  to think about [ˌθɪŋk əˈbaʊt] nachdenken über; sich überlegen; denken an III
  to think of [ˈθɪŋk ɒv] denken an/über; sich einfallen lassen; sich ausdenken III

third [θɜːd] dritte II

thirteen [θɜːˈtiːn] dreizehn I

thirty [ˈθɜːti] dreißig I

this [ðɪs] das; dies I
  this morning [ðɪs ˈmɔːnɪŋ] heute Morgen II
  like this [laɪk ˈðɪs] so; auf diese Weise <I>

those [ðəʊz] jene II

thought [θɔːt] simple past von *to think* II; past participle von *to think* III

a/one **thousand** [ˈθaʊznd] tausend; eintausend II

three [θriː] drei I

threw [θruː] simple past von *to throw* II

through [θruː] durch III

*to **throw** [θrəʊ] werfen II

Thursday [ˈθɜːzdeɪ] Donnerstag I

ticket [ˈtɪkɪt] Ticket; Eintrittskarte; Fahrschein II
  return ticket [rɪˈtɜːn ˌtɪkɪt] Hin- und Rückfahrkarte III

single ticket [ˌsɪŋgl ˈtɪkɪt] einfache Fahrkarte III

to **tidy** [ˈtaɪdi] aufräumen; in Ordnung bringen II

tidy [ˈtaɪdi] ordentlich <II>

time [taɪm] Zeit; Uhrzeit; Mal I
  at the same time [ət ðə seɪm ˈtaɪm] gleichzeitig; nebenher II
  boarding time [ˈbɔːdɪŋ ˌtaɪm] Ein-steigezeit IV U2, 36
  free time [ˌfriː ˈtaɪm] Freizeit I
  for the 200th time [fə ðə ˈtuː hʌndrədθ ˌtaɪm] zum 200. Mal III
  the first time [ðə fɜːst ˈtaɪm] das erste Mal I

timetable [ˈtaɪmˌteɪbl] Stundenplan I; Fahrplan III

tip [tɪp] Tipp; Ratschlag <I>

tired [ˈtaɪəd] müde I

title [ˈtaɪtl] Titel; Überschrift <I>

to [tuː] zu; nach; in I; um zu; an II; auf; bei; bis III; für IV U3, 56
  quarter to/past [ˈkwɔːtə tə/paːst] Viertel vor/nach II

today [təˈdeɪ] heute I

together [təˈgeðə] zusammen I
  to go together [ˌgəʊ təˈgeðə] zusammenpassen <III>

told [təʊld] simple past von *to tell* I; past participle von *to tell* III

tomato *(sg)* [təˈmɑːtəʊ], **tomatoes** *(pl)* [təˈmɑːtəʊz] Tomate I

tomorrow [təˈmɒrəʊ] morgen II

too [tuː] auch; zu I

took [tʊk] simple past von *to take* II

tooth *(sg)* [tuːθ], **teeth** *(pl)* [tiːθ] Zahn II

top [tɒp] Spitze; oberer Teil; oberes Ende II

topic [ˈtɒpɪk] Thema IV U4, 88

topic-based [ˈtɒpɪkbeɪst] themenbe-zogen <IV U4, 88>

torch [tɔːtʃ] Taschenlampe I

caber **toss** [ˈkeɪbə ˌtɒs] Baumstamm-werfen III

total [ˈtəʊtl] Gesamt-; gesamt; Gesamtsumme <IV U1, 22>

*to keep in **touch** [ˌkiːp ɪn ˈtʌtʃ] in Kontakt bleiben II

tour [tʊə] Tour; Führung; Reise III

tourism [ˈtʊərɪzm] Tourismus IV U4, 80

tourist [ˈtʊərɪst] Tourist; Touristin II
  tourist industry [ˈtʊərɪstˌɪndəstri] Tourismus <IV U3, 51>

tower [ˈtaʊə] Turm II

town [taʊn] Stadt I
  twin town [ˌtwɪn ˈtaʊn] Partner-stadt III

townhouse [ˈtaʊnhaʊs] Reihenhaus III

slave **trader** [ˈsleɪv ˌtreɪdə] Skla-venhändler; Menschenhändler IV U3, 61

tradition [trəˈdɪʃn] Tradition III

traditional [trəˈdɪʃnl] traditionell <IV U1, 131>

traffic [ˈtræfɪk] Verkehr III

train [treɪn] Zug I
  train station [ˈtreɪn ˌsteɪʃn] Bahnhof <III>

to **train** [treɪn] trainieren; eine Ausbil-dung machen; ausbilden IV U2, 48

trainer [ˈtreɪnə] Turnschuh II

training [ˈtreɪnɪŋ] Ausbildung; Trai-ning IV U4, 76

tram [træm] Straßenbahn I

transport [ˈtrænspɔːt] Verkehr; Transport II
  public transport [ˌpʌblɪk ˈtrænspɔːt] öffentliche Verkehrsmittel III

to **transport** [trænˈspɔːt] transportie-ren; befördern IV U2, 48

travel agent [ˈtrævlˌeɪdʒnt] Reisebü-rokaufmann; Reisebürokauffrau IV U4, 80

travel agent's [ˈtrævlˌeɪdʒnts] Reise-büro IV U4, 76

to **travel** [ˈtrævl] fahren; reisen II

treasure hunt [ˈtreʒə ˌhʌnt] Schnitzel-jagd; Schatzsuche II

tree [triː] Baum I

trick [trɪk] Kunststück; Trick I; Streich II

trip [trɪp] Ausflug; Fahrt; Reise I
  outgoing trip [ˌaʊtgəʊɪŋ ˈtrɪp] Hinfahrt <IV U1, 22>
  return trip [rɪˈtɜːn ˈtrɪp] Rückfahrt <IV U1, 22>
  round trip [ˌraʊnd ˈtrɪp] Hin- und Rückflug; Hin- und Rückfahrt <IV U1, 22>

school trip [ˌskuːl ˈtrɪp] Klassenfahrt; Schulausflug II

trouble [ˈtrʌbl] Ärger <IV U3, 63>

true [truː] richtig; wahr <IV U2, 33>

trumpet [ˈtrʌmpɪt] Trompete II

truth [truːθ] Wahrheit IV U1, 21

to **try** [traɪ] versuchen; probieren;
ausprobieren III

to **try on** [traɪ ˈɒn] anprobieren II

T-shirt [ˈtiːʃɜːt] T-Shirt II

tsunami [tsʊˈnaːmi] Tsunami *(durch
Seebeben ausgelöste Flutwelle)*
IV U2, 41

Tuesday [ˈtjuːzdeɪ] Dienstag I

turkey [ˈtɜːki] Truthahn; Pute IV U3, 52

Turkish [ˈtɜːkɪʃ] türkisch; Türkisch; aus
der Türkei IV U1, 16

to **turn** [tɜːn] abbiegen II

to **turn over** [ˌtɜːn ˈəʊvə] umkippen;
(sich) umdrehen III

Turn the music down. [ˌtɜːn ðə
mjuːzɪk ˈdaʊn] Mach die Musik
leiser. I

*to take **turns** [teɪk ˈtɜːnz] sich
abwechseln <I>

tutorial [tjuːˈtɔːriəl] Tutorial; Anleitung IV U4, 72

TV [ˌtiːˈviː] Fernseher I; Fernseh-;
Fernsehen IV U4, 72

on **TV** [ɒn ˌtiːˈviː] im Fernsehen III

to watch **TV** [ˌwɒtʃ tiːˈviː] fernsehen I

twelve [twelv] zwölf I

twenty [ˈtwenti] zwanzig I

twenty-one [ˌtwentiˈwʌn] einundzwanzig I

twin town [ˌtwɪn ˈtaʊn] Partnerstadt
III

two [tuː] zwei I

type [taɪp] Sorte; Art; Typ <III>

typical [ˈtɪpɪkl] typisch; charakteris-
tisch <I>

U

uncle [ˈʌŋkl] Onkel I

under [ˈʌndə] unter I

underground [ˈʌndəgraʊnd] U-Bahn I

underground parking lot *(AE)*
[ˌʌndəgraʊnd ˈpaːkɪŋ ˌlɒt] Tiefgarage <IV U2, 42>

underlined [ˌʌndəˈlaɪnd] unterstri-
chen <III>

*to **understand** [ˌʌndəˈstænd] verstehen II

understood [ˌʌndəˈstʊd] simple past
von *to understand* II

unhappy [ʌnˈhæpi] unglücklich;
traurig II

uniform [ˈjuːnɪfɔːm] Uniform I

unit [ˈjuːnɪt] Lektion; Kapitel <I>

until [ʌnˈtɪl] bis III

up [ʌp] hinauf; oben; hoch II

update [ˈʌpdeɪt] aktuelle Information;
Update; Aktualisierung IV U4, 72

to **upload** [ʌpˈləʊd] hochladen II

US [ˌjuːˈes] US-amerikanisch III

us [ʌs] uns; wir II

use [juːs] Benutzung <IV U2, 42>

to **use** [juːz] benutzen; verwenden;
nehmen; nutzen III

to get **used** to (sth) [get ˈjuːst tə]
sich gewöhnen an (etw.) IV U1, 12

useful [ˈjuːsfl] nützlich; hilfreich;
brauchbar III

usually [ˈjuːʒli] normalerweise;
gewöhnlich II

V

vacation *(AE)* [vəˈkeɪʃn] Urlaub; Ferien
III

valley [ˈvæli] Tal III

van [væn] Lieferwagen; Transporter
IV U1, 20

vegetable (veg) [ˈvedʒtəbl (vedʒ)]
Gemüse IV U2, 31

vegetarian [ˌvedʒɪˈteəriən] Vegetarier;
Vegetarierin I

verb [vɜːb] Verb <II>

very [ˈveri] sehr I

vet [vet] Tierarzt; Tierärztin IV U3, 56

video [ˈvɪdiəʊ] Video III

Vietnamese [ˌvjetnəˈmiːz] Vietnamesisch; vietnamesisch; aus Vietnam
<IV U1, 131>

viewing [ˈvjuːɪŋ] Hör-/Sehverstehen
<I>

viewing skills [ˈvjuːɪŋ ˌskɪlz] Fertigkeit Hör-/Sehverstehen <I>

village [ˈvɪlɪdʒ] Dorf I

violence *(no pl)* [ˈvaɪələns] Gewalt
IV U3, 56

visa [ˈviːzə] Visum <IV U2, 133>

visit [ˈvɪzɪt] Besuch III

to **visit** [ˈvɪzɪt] besuchen I

visitor [ˈvɪzɪtə] Besucher; Besucherin
II

vocabulary [vəˈkæbjəlri] Vokabular;
Wortschatz <IV U3, 66>

voluntary [ˈvɒləntri] freiwillig
<IV U3, 135>

volunteer [ˌvɒlənˈtɪə] ehrenamtlich
<IV U3, 63>

W

to **wait** (for) [weɪt (fə)] warten (auf) II

waiter [ˈweɪtə] Kellner; Bedienung
<IV U3, 135>

waitress [ˈweɪtrəs] Kellnerin; Bedienung <IV U3, 135>

*to **wake up** [weɪk ˈʌp] aufwachen;
erwachen; aufwecken III

walk [wɔːk] Wanderung; Spaziergang I

to **walk** [wɔːk] laufen; gehen; zu Fuß
gehen IV U1, 16

to **walk around** [ˌwɔːk əˈraʊnd]
umherlaufen; herumlaufen <I>

dog **walker** [ˈdɒg ˌwɔːkə] Hundeausführer; Hundeausführerin
<IV U4, 82>

walking [ˈwɔːkɪŋ] Wandern
<IV U2, 132>

wall [wɔːl] Wand; Mauer II

wall painting [ˈwɔːl ˌpeɪntɪŋ] Wandmalerei II

to **want** (to) [wɒnt (tə)] wollen;
mögen I

war [wɔː] Krieg <IV U1, 130>

wardrobe [ˈwɔːdrəʊb] Kleiderschrank
II

warm [wɔːm] warm II

warm-up [ˈwɔːmʌp] Aufwärmtraining; Aufwärmen II

was [wɒz] simple past von *to be* I

wash [wɒʃ] Wäsche II

to **wash** [wɒʃ] (sich) waschen; spülen
II

to **watch** [wɒtʃ] anschauen; ansehen
I; zuschauen; zusehen; beobachten II

to **watch TV** [ˌwɒtʃ tiːˈviː] fernsehen I

watch

water ['wɔːtə] Wasser I

waterproofs ['wɔːtəpruːfs] Regenbe-
kleidung <IV U4, 137>

wave [weɪv] Welle III

wax [wæks] Wachs II

way [weɪ] Weg I; Art und Weise III

to ask the way [ɑːsk ðə 'weɪ] nach
dem Weg fragen <II>

to be a long way away [bi ə 'lɒŋ
ˌweɪ ə'weɪ] weit weg sein II

we [wiː] wir I

***to wear** [weə] tragen; anhaben I

weather ['weðə] Wetter; Witterung II

website ['websaɪt] Website; Internetseite III

Wednesday ['wenzdeɪ] Mittwoch I

week [wiːk] Woche I

weekday ['wiːkdeɪ] Werktag
<IV U4, 82>

weekend ['wiːkend] Wochenende I

welcome (to) ['welkəm (tə)] willkommen (bei/in) I

You're welcome. [jɔː 'welkəm] Gern
geschehen. <IV U1, 15>

well [wel] gut II

Well, … [wel] Na ja, …; Also … II

… as well as … [əz 'wel ̩əz]
sowohl … als auch … II

Well done! [ˌwel 'dʌn] Gut
gemacht! II

well-qualified [ˌwel'kwɒlɪfaɪd] geeig-
net <IV U4, 138>

Welsh [welʃ] Walisisch; walisisch; aus
Wales III

went [went] simple past von *to go* I

were [wɜː] simple past von *to be* I

west [west] Westen; West- III

wet [wet] nass I

whale [weɪl] Wal IV U1, 26

whale-watching ['weɪlˌwɒtʃɪŋ] Walbe-
obachtungs- IV U1, 26

what [wɒt] was; welche I

What about …? [ˌwɒt ̩ə'baʊt] Und
…?; Was ist mit …? II

What colour is …? [ˌwɒt 'kʌlər ̩ɪz]
Welche Farbe hat …? I

What time is it? [ˌwɒt 'taɪm ̩ɪz ̩ɪt]
Wie viel Uhr ist es?; Wie spät ist
es? I

What's the weather like? [ˌwɒts ðə
'weðə laɪk] Wie ist das Wetter? II

What's your name? [ˌwɒts jə 'neɪm]
Wie heißt du? I

wheel [wiːl] Rad II

big wheel [ˌbɪg 'wiːl] Riesenrad II

wheelchair ['wiːltʃeə] Rollstuhl I

when [wen] wann I; wenn; als II

where [weə] wo; wohin; woher I

Where are you from? [ˌweər ̩ə ju
'frɒm] Woher kommst du? I

which [wɪtʃ] welche; was II; das; der;
die III

while [waɪl] während IV U2, 32

white [waɪt] weiß I

who [huː] wer I; die; der; das III

whose [huːz] wessen <III>

why [waɪ] warum I

that's why ['ðæts waɪ] deshalb;
deswegen II

wild [waɪld] wild IV U2, 30

wilderness ['wɪldənəs] Wildnis
IV U4, 71

will [wɪl] werden II

***to win** [wɪn] siegen; gewinnen I

wind [wɪnd] Wind I

window ['wɪndəʊ] Fenster I

windsurfing ['wɪnsɜːfɪŋ] Windsurfen
<IV U2, 132>

windy ['wɪndi] windig II

winner ['wɪnə] Sieger; Siegerin;
Gewinner; Gewinnerin I

winter ['wɪntə] Winter I

Best wishes, [ˌbest 'wɪʃɪz] Viele Grüße;
Alles Gute! I

with [wɪð] mit I; bei II

without [wɪ'ðaʊt] ohne II

witness ['wɪtnəs] Zeuge; Zeugin
IV U1, 20

wizard ['wɪzəd] Zauberer II

woke up [ˌwəʊk ̩'ʌp] simple past von
to wake up III

woken up [ˌwəʊkn ̩'ʌp] past participle
von *to wake up* III

wolf *(sg)* [wʊlf], **wolves** *(pl)* [wʊlvz]
Wolf II

woman *(sg)* ['wʊmən], **women** *(pl)*
['wɪmɪn] Frau I

won [wʌn] simple past von *to win* II;
past participle von *to win* III

won't (= will not) [wəʊnt] nicht
werden II

wood [wʊd] Holz I; Wald IV U2, 32

woof [wʊf] wau I

wool [wʊl] Wolle I

word [wɜːd] Wort II

key word ['kiː ̩wɜːd] Stichwort;
Schlüsselwort <IV U3, 65>

root word [ˌruːt 'wɜːd] Grundwort;
Stammwort <IV U3, 67>

word order ['wɜːd ̩ɔːdə] Wortstellung; Satzstellung <II>

wore [wɔː] simple past von *to wear* I

work [wɜːk] Arbeit II

work experience ['wɜːk ̩ɪkˌspɪəriəns]
Berufserfahrung; Praktikum
<IV U4, 138>

work placement ['wɜːk ̩pleɪsmənt]
Praktikum <IV U3, 135>

to work [wɜːk] arbeiten I

worker ['wɜːkə] Arbeiter; Arbeiterin;
Angestellter; Angestellte IV U2, 31

working hours *(pl)* ['wɜːkɪŋ ̩aʊəz]
Arbeitszeit IV U4, 80

workshop ['wɜːkʃɒp] Workshop;
Seminar III

acting workshop ['æktɪŋ ̩wɜːkʃɒp]
Schauspielworkshop III

world [wɜːld] Welt I

all around the world [ɔːl ̩əˌraʊnd ðə
'wɜːld] in aller Welt II

worried ['wʌrid] beunruhigt; besorgt
II

to worry ['wʌri] sich Sorgen machen I

Don't worry. [dəʊnt 'wʌri] Mach dir
keine Sorgen. I

worse [wɜːs] schlechter; schlimmer II

worst [wɜːst] schlimmste; schlechteste II

would [wʊd] würde(n) <IV U2, 36>

I wouldn't like (to) … [aɪ 'wʊdnt
laɪk (tə)] ich möchte nicht …; ich
würde nicht gerne … I

I'd (= I would) [aɪd] ich würde; ich
hätte gern I

I'd love (to) … (= I would love to)
[aɪd 'lʌv (tə)] ich würde sehr gern
…; ich hätte gern … IV U2, 32

Would you like (to) …? [ˌwʊd jə
'laɪk (tə)] Möchtest du …?; Würdest du gern …? I

wrecked [rekt] demoliert; zerstört;
zertrümmert IV U1, 21

***to write** [raɪt] schreiben I

writing ['raɪtɪŋ] Schreiben <I>
  writing skills ['raɪtɪŋ ,skɪlz] Fertigkeit Schreiben <II>
wrong [rɒŋ] falsch I
wrote [rəʊt] simple past von *to write*
  II

Y

year [jɪə] Klasse; Jahrgangsstufe;
  Jahr I
yellow ['jeləʊ] gelb I
yes [jes] ja I
yesterday ['jestədeɪ] gestern I
yet [jet] schon III
  not … yet [nɒt … 'jet] noch nicht
  III
you [ju:] du; Sie; ihr; dich; euch; dir;
  Ihnen I
  You're welcome. [jɔː 'welkəm] Gern
  geschehen. <IV U1, 15>
young [jʌŋ] jung II
your [jɔː] dein; euer; Ihr I
yours [jɔːz] deine; eure; Ihre III
  Yours sincerely, [jɔːz sɪn'sɪəli] Mit
  freundlichen Grüßen IV U4, 76
  Yours, [jɔːz] Dein *(Grußformel in
  Briefen oder E-Mails)* II
yourself [jɔː'self] dich; selbst III; dir;
  dir selbst; sich; sich selbst IV U2, 32
yourselves [jɔː'selvz] selbst; euch;
  euch selbst; sich; Sie sich; Sie sich
  selbst IV U2, 32
youth [ju:θ] Jugend- I

Z

zero ['zɪərəʊ] null I
zip line ['zɪp ,laɪn] Seilrutsche III
zoo [zu:] Zoo; Tierpark IV U1, 16
to zoom in ['zu:m ,ɪn] heranzoomen
  <I>

Boys' names

Aman ['æmən] IV U3, 56
Brian ['braɪən] IV U3, 66
Chris [krɪs] IV U2, 32
Greg [greg] IV U3, 51
Huck [hʌk] IV U3, 60
Jacob ['dʒeɪkəb] IV U3, 52
Jian [dʒæn] IV U1, 16
José [həʊ'zeɪ] IV U1, 12
Josh [dʒɒʃ] IV U4, 70

Marc [mɑːk] IV U4, 79
Martin ['mɑːtɪn] IV U4, 77
Matt [mæt] <IV U4, 82>
Nikolai ['nɪkəʊlaɪ] IV U1, 16
Pete [pi:t] <IV U4, 82>
Raheem [rə'hi:m] IV U3, 57
Ronan ['rəʊnən] <IV U1, 23>
Scott [skɒt] IV U4, 71
Shamar [ʃə'mɑː] IV U3, 57
Steve [sti:v] IV U2, 34
Wesley ['wezli] <IV U1, 23>

Girls' names

Alice ['ælɪs] IV U1, 20
Ally ['æli] IV U1, 20
Amy ['eɪmi] IV U4, 76
Angela ['ændʒlə] IV U1, 16
Brenda ['brendə] IV U3, 52
Carrie ['kæri] IV U2, 37
Danielle [dæn'jel] IV U3, 58
Florence ['flɒrns] IV U3, 66
Helen ['helən] IV U4, 79
Jade [dʒeɪd] IV U4, 77
Jessica ['dʒesɪkə] <IV U1, 23>
Jill [dʒɪl] <IV U4, 82>
Lara ['lɑːrə] IV U4, 71
Laura ['lɔːrə] IV U2, 31
Layla ['leɪlə] IV U3, 56
Malee ['mæli] IV U1, 13
Mandy ['mændi] IV U1, 21
Mia ['mi:ə] IV U4, 77
Sherrie ['ʃeri] IV U3, 52
Sonia ['sɒnjə] <IV U4, 82>
Sophie ['səʊfi] IV U2, 35
Susan ['su:zn] IV U2, 37
Tamila [tə'mɪlə] IV U1, 16
Tara ['tɑːrə] IV U3, 56
Taylor ['teɪlə] IV U4, 77
Vicky ['vɪki] IV U4, 78

Surnames

Blanco ['blæŋkəʊ] IV U1, 12
Carter ['kɑːtə] <IV U4, 82>
Clarke [klɑːk] IV U3, 56
Dawson ['dɔːsn] IV U1, 20
Dickens ['dɪkɪnz] <IV U4, 82>
Finn [fɪn] IV U3, 60
Henderson ['hendəsn] IV U4, 77
Jolly ['dʒɒli] <IV U4, 82>
Ling [lɪŋ] IV U1, 21
Mancini [mæn'si:ni] IV U1, 21

Miller ['mɪlə] IV U3, 52
Roberts ['rɒbəts] IV U4, 76
Walker ['wɔːkə] IV U4, 77
Watson ['wɒtsn] IV U3, 60
Wilson ['wɪlsn] IV U3, 66
Wynner ['wɪnə] IV U4, 76

Place names

Africa ['æfrɪkə] Afrika II
Alaska [ə'læskə] *Bundesstaat in den
  USA* II
America [ə'merɪkə] Amerika III
American South [ə,merɪkən 'saʊθ]
  Südstaaten Amerikas IV U3, 50
Anchorage ['æŋkrɪdʒ] *Stadt in den
  USA* II
Antarctica [æn'tɑːktɪkə] Antarktis II
Australia [ɒs'treɪliə] Australien I
Barbados [bɑː'beɪdɒs] Barbados
  (Inselstaat in der Karibik) IV U3, 51
Boston ['bɒstn] *Stadt in den USA*
  IV U1, 26
Britain ['brɪtn] Großbritannien II
The British Isles [ðə ,brɪtɪʃ 'aɪlz] die
  Britischen Inseln III
The Bronx [ðə 'brɒŋks] *Stadtteil von
  NYC* IV U1, 10
Brooklyn ['brʊklɪn] *Stadtteil von NYC*
  IV U1, 10
California (CA) [,kælɪ'fɔːniə] Kalifor-
  nien IV U2, 31
Canada ['kænədə] Kanada I
Cape Cod [,keɪp 'kɒd] *Halbinsel in den
  USA* IV U1, 26
The Caribbean [ðə ,kærɪ'bi:ən] die
  Karibik IV U3, 51
Chicago [ʃɪ'kɑːgəʊ] *Großstadt in den
  USA* II
Cork [kɔːk] *Stadt in Irland* III
Cuba ['kju:bə] Kuba IV U1, 12
England ['ɪŋglənd] England I
Europe ['jʊərəp] Europa II
Florida ['flɒrɪdə] *Bundesstaat in den
  USA* II
France [frɑːns] Frankreich IV U1, 10
Germany ['dʒɜːməni] Deutschland I
Great Britain [,greɪt 'brɪtn] Großbri-
  tannien I
Harlem ['hɑːləm] *Stadtviertel in NYC*
  IV U1, 16

Harlem

Houston ['hju:stn] *Großstadt in den USA* <IV U1, 24>

Illinois (IL) [ˌɪlɪ'nɔɪ] *Bundesstaat in den USA* <IV U1, 22>

India ['ɪndɪə] Indien I

Ireland ['aɪələnd] Irland III

Istanbul [ˌɪstæn'bʊl] *Großstadt in der Türkei* I

Italy ['ɪtli] Italien IV U1, 11

Jackson's Island [ˌdʒæksns ̩'aɪlənd] *Flussinsel in den USA* IV U3, 60

Jamaica [dʒə'meɪkə] Jamaika II

Kingston ['kɪŋstən] *Hauptstadt von Jamaika* IV U3, 56

Little Italy [ˌlɪtl 'ɪtli] *Stadtviertel in NYC* IV U1, 11

London ['lʌndən] *Hauptstadt von England* I; *Stadt in Kanada* IV U4, 76

Los Angeles (LA) [lɒs'ænʒɪli:z] *Großstadt in den USA* III

Manchester ['mæntʃɪstə] *Stadt in Nordengland* II

Manhattan [mæn'hætn] *Stadtteil von NYC* IV U1, 10

Massachusetts [ˌmæsə'tʃu:sɪts] *Bundesstaat in den USA* IV U1, 26

Memphis ['memfɪs] *Stadt in den USA* IV U3, 52

Mexico ['meksɪkəʊ] Mexiko IV U2, 31

Moscow ['mɒskəʊ] Moskau I

Munich ['mju:nɪk] München IV U4, 79

New Orleans [ˌnju:'ɔ:liənz] *Stadt in den USA* IV U3, 50

New York City (NYC) [ˌnju: jɔ:k 'sɪti (ˌenwɑ'si:)] *Großstadt in den USA* IV U1, 10

Northern Ireland [ˌnɔ:ðn ̩'aɪlənd] Nordirland III

Nunavut [nʊ'nʌvʌt] *Territorium im Norden Kanadas* IV U4, 71

Ontario [ɒn'teəriəʊ] *Provinz in Kanada* IV U4, 72

Ottawa ['ɒtəwə] *Hauptstadt von Kanada* IV U4, 80

Philadelphia [ˌfɪlə'delfiə] *Stadt in den USA* <IV U1, 22>

Poland ['pəʊlənd] Polen II

Quebec [kwɪ'bek] *Provinz in Kanada* IV U4, 71; *Stadt in Kanada* <IV U4, 87>

Queens [kwi:nz] *Stadtteil von NYC* IV U1, 10

The Republic of Ireland [ðə rɪˌpʌblɪk ̩əv ̩'aɪələnd] Irland III

Russia ['rʌʃə] Russland I

San Francisco [ˌsæn frən'sɪskəʊ] *Stadt in den USA* IV U2, 31

Scotland ['skɒtlənd] Schottland I

St Petersburg [sn'pi:təzbɜ:g] *Romanhandlungsort* IV U3, 60

Staten Island [ˌstætn ̩'aɪlənd] *Stadtteil von NYC* IV U1, 10

Texas ['teksəs] *Bundesstaat in den USA* IV U3, 56

Thailand ['taɪlænd] Thailand I

Toronto [tə'rɒntəʊ] *Stadt in Kanada* IV U4, 70

Turkey ['tɜ:ki] Türkei I

UK (United Kingdom) [ˌju:'keɪ (ˌju:ˌnaɪtɪd 'kɪŋdəm)] Vereinigtes Königreich von Großbritannien und Nordirland II

United States [ju:ˌnaɪtɪd'steɪts] Vereinigte Staaten II

USA (United States of America) [ˌju:es'eɪ (ju:ˌnaɪtɪd ̩steɪts ̩əv ə'merɪkə)] USA (Vereinigte Staaten von Amerika) I

Vancouver [væn'ku:və] *Großstadt in Kanada* I

Wales [weɪlz] Wales III

Washington, D.C. [ˌwɒʃɪŋtən ̩di:'si:] *Hauptstadt der USA* III

Wilmington ['wɪlmɪŋtən] *Stadt in den USA* IV U3, 66

Other names

American Dream [əˌmerɪkən 'dri:m] *der amerikanische Traum* IV U1, 12

Banff National Park ['bænf ˌnæfnl 'pɑ:k] *Nationalpark in Kanada* IV U4, 72

Black Friday [ˌblæk 'fraɪdeɪ] *Einkaufstag mit vielen Sonderangeboten* IV U3, 55

Brooklyn Bridge [ˌbrʊklɪn 'brɪdʒ] *Brücke in NYC* <IV U1, 23>

Central Park [ˌsentrl 'pɑ:k] *Park in NYC* IV U1, 11

Chelsea Hotel [ˌtʃelsi hə'tel] *Hotelname* IV U4, 76

Chinatown ['tʃaɪnətaʊn] *chinesisches Stadtviertel* IV U1, 16

Denali [də'nɑ:li] *höchster Berg in Nordamerika (neuer Name)* IV U2, 30

Denali National Park [də'nɑ:li ˌnæfnl 'pɑ:k] *Nationalpark in den USA* IV U2, 30

Huckleberry Finn [ˌhʌklbri 'fɪn] *Buchcharakter* IV U3, 60

The Golden Gate Bridge [ðə ˌgəʊldn ˌgeɪt 'brɪdʒ] *berühmte Brücke in San Francisco* IV U2, 31

Hollywood ['hɒliwʊd] *Zentrum der amerikanischen Filmindustrie (in Los Angeles)* IV ZI, 8

Hotel Luxor [hə,tel 'lʌksɔ:] *Hotelname* <IV U2, 42>

Hurricane Katrina [ˌhʌrɪkən kə'tri:nə] *Name eines Hurrikans* <IV U3, 62>

Labor Day ['leɪbə ˌdeɪ] *Tag der Arbeit* IV U1, 16

Bob Marley [bɒb 'mɑ:li] *jamaikanischer Sänger* IV U3, 51

Mississippi River [ˌmɪsɪsɪpi 'rɪvə] *Fluss in den USA* IV U3, 50

Monroe Street [mən,rəʊ 'stri:t] *Straßenname* IV U1, 20

Monte Carlo Restaurant [ˌmɒnti'kɑ:ləʊ ˌrestrɒnt] *Restaurantname* IV U4, 77

Park Hotel [ˌpɑ:k hə'tel] *Hotelname* IV U4, 76

Romero Fashions [rə,meərəʊ 'fæʃnz] *Firmenname* IV U1, 20

Tom Sawyer [ˌtɒm 'sɔ:jə] *Buchcharakter* IV U3, 60

Silverley [ˌsɪlvə'li] *Name eines Feriencamps* <IV U4, 83>

Statue of Liberty [ˌstætʃu: ̩əv 'lɪbəti] *Freiheitsstatue in NYC* IV U1, 10

Tillary Street [ˌtɪləri 'stri:t] *Straßenname* IV U1, 20

Times Square ['taɪm ̩skweə] *Platz in NYC* IV U1, 10

Toronto Maple Leafs [tə,rɒntəʊ meɪpl 'li:fs] *Name der Toronto Eishockeymannschaft* IV U4, 70

Venice Beach [ˌvenɪs 'bi:tʃ] *Strand bei Los Angeles* IV U2, 32

p pen • **b** bed • **t** ten • **d** dad • **k** cat • **g** grey • **tʃ** chair • **dʒ** job • **f** fan • **v** very • **θ** three • **ð** the

A

abbiegen to turn II
Abend evening I
Abendessen dinner; tea I
abends in the evening I
Abenteuer adventure III
aber but I
abfahren to leave II; to depart
    IV U2, 36
Abfall rubbish I
abfliegen to depart; to leave IV U2, 36
abgeschlossen locked I
Abschieds- leaving II
Abschluss qualification IV U4, 80
acht eight I
Achterbahn roller coaster II
achtzehn eighteen I
achtzig eighty I
Adresse address IV U4, 81
Afroamerikaner African American
    IV U3, 50
Afroamerikanerin African American
    IV U3, 50
Aktivität activity I
Aktualisierung update IV U4, 72
aktuelle Information update IV U4, 72
Akzent accent III
Alaska- Alaskan IV U2, 48
alaskisch Alaskan IV U2, 48
albern silly II
alle all I; everyone; every II
    von allen Staaten of all the states
    IV U2, 31
alles everything II
    Alles Gute Best wishes, I; All the
    best, II
Alligator alligator II
als as; than; when II
    als Nächstes next II
    als ob like IV U2, 32
also so I
Also … Well, … II
alt old I
am in; on I
    am Ende at the end II
Amerikaner American II
Amerikanerin American II
Amerikanisch American II
amerikanisch American II
amüsant fun III

sich **amüsieren** to enjoy oneself
    IV U2, 32
an on; at I; to II; about; by III; in
    IV U2, 40
anbauen to produce IV U2, 31
anbieten to offer IV U4, 76
andauern to last II
Andenken souvenir II
andere other II; different III; another
    IV U2, 36
    anderen others II
    ein anderer another IV U2, 36
    anderer Meinung sein to disagree
    IV U3, 56
ändern to change II
anders different I
Anfang beginning II
anfangen to start I
Anfrage request IV U4, 81
sich **anfühlen** to feel III
angeln gehen to go fishing IV U3, 60
Angestellte worker IV U2, 31;
    employee IV U2, 36
Angestellter worker IV U2, 31;
    employee IV U2, 36
Angst haben to be scared I
anhaben to wear I
anhalten to stop II
Anhänger follower IV U4, 72
Anhängerin follower IV U4, 72
anhören to listen (to) I
ankommen to arrive I
Ankömmling arrival IV U1, 12
Anleitung tutorial IV U4, 72
anprobieren to try on II
Anruf phone call I
anrufen to phone II; to call III
anschauen to look at; to watch I
ansehen to watch I
anspornen to motivate III
Antwort answer II
antworten to answer II
Anzeichen sign IV U1, 16
Anzeige ad(vert) (= advertisement) III
anziehen to put on II
Apartment apartment (AE) IV U1, 16
Apfel apple I
App app IV U4, 72
April April I
Arbeit work II
arbeiten to work I

Arbeiter worker IV U2, 31
Arbeiterin worker IV U2, 31
Arbeitnehmer employee IV U2, 36
Arbeitnehmerin employee IV U2, 36
Arbeitszeit working hours (pl)
    IV U4, 80
Arbeitszeugnis reference IV U4, 81
Areal area IV U2, 41
Arm arm II
arm poor IV U1, 12
Art kind II
    Art und Weise way III
Artikel item IV U2, 41
Arzt doctor II
Ärztin doctor II
Assistent assistant IV U3, 56
Assistentin assistant IV U3, 56
auch too; also I
    auch nicht not … either III
auf in; on; at I; to III
    auf einmal suddenly I
    Auf Wiedersehen. Goodbye. I
    auf der linken Seite on the left II
    auf der rechten Seite on the right
    II
Geld **aufbringen** to raise money II
Aufführung show I
Aufgabe job III
aufgeregt excited II
aufhören to finish; to stop II
aufmachen to open I
aufpassen auf to look after II
aufräumen to tidy II
aufregend exciting I
aufstehen to get up I
jmdm. etw. **auftragen** to tell sb to do
    sth III
aufwachen to wake up III
Aufwärmen warm-up II
Aufwärmtraining warm-up II
aufwecken to wake up III
Aufzug lift II
Auge eye I
August August I
aus from I; of III
    aus dem Weg gehen to avoid
    IV U3, 56
ausbilden to train IV U2, 48
Ausbildung training IV U4, 76; qualifi-
    cation IV U4, 80; education IV U4, 81

eine Ausbildung machen to train
IV U2, 48

sich **ausdenken** to think of III

Auseinandersetzung argument II

Ausflug trip I

den Hund **ausführen** to take the dog
for a walk I

ausgeben *(Geld)* to spend II

ein **ausgefüllter** Tag a busy day II

Aushang lost and found notice III

(sich) **ausleihen** to borrow II

ausliefern to deliver IV U1, 20

auslösen to cause IV U2, 40

ausprobieren to try III

die Spülmaschine **ausräumen** to
empty the dishwasher II

aussehen to look I

außen outside II

außerhalb outside II

aussprechen to say III

etw. nicht **aussstehen** können can't
stand + -ing III

aussteigen to get off II; to get out
IV U1, 20

Ausstellung exhibition III

auswählen to choose III

ausweichen to avoid IV U3, 56

Auto car I

B

Bad(ezimmer) bathroom II

Bahn railway IV U4, 80

Bahnhof station III; railway station
IV U4, 80

bald soon II

Balkon balcony I

Ball ball I

Banane banana I

Band band II

Bär bear II

Base base III

Baseball baseball III

Basketball basketball II

Basketballkorb basket III

basteln to make II

bauen to build II

Bauer farmer I

Bäuerin farmer I

Bauernhof farm I

Baum tree I

Baumstamm caber III

Baumstammwerfen caber toss III

Bauwerk building II

beängstigend scary I

beantworten to answer II

beben to shake IV U2, 40

bedeuten to mean IV U4, 72

Bedeutung sense IV U2, 48

beeindruckend awesome III

beenden to finish; to stop II

befördern to transport IV U2, 48

Befrager interviewer IV U1, 12

Befragerin interviewer IV U1, 12

Befragung interview IV U3, 66

Begabung talent I

begeistert excited II

Beginn beginning II

beginnen to start I

bei at I; with II; to III; in IV U2, 40;
during IV U2, 41

beibringen to teach IV U2, 32

beide both IV U4, 71

Bein leg II

beinahe nearly II

Beispiel example III
zum Beispiel for example III

sich **beklagen** to complain IV U2, 36

bekommen to get I

bekommen (Bus/Zug) to catch (bus/
train) III

beliebt popular III

bellen to bark II

bemalen to paint II

benutzen to use III

beobachten to watch II

bereit ready I

bereits already III

Berg mountain II; hill IV U2, 31

Beruf career IV U1, 12

Berufspraktikum internship IV U4, 76

berühmt famous I

Beschädigung damage IV U2, 40

beschäftigt busy I

beschließen to decide III

sich **beschweren** to complain
IV U2, 36

besitzen to have I; to have got II; to
own III

besonders special I

besorgt worried II

besser better II

beste best II

am besten best II

besteigen to climb II

Besuch visit III

besuchen to visit I

Besucher visitor II

Besucherin visitor II

Betreff subject III

Bett bed I
ins Bett gehen to go to bed I

Bettdecke blanket IV U2, 41

beunruhigt worried II

Bevölkerung population *(no pl)*
IV U1, 11

bevor before II

(sich) **bewegen** to move IV U2, 40

Bewegung movement IV U3, 66

beweisen to prove IV U1, 21

sich **bewerben** (für/um) to apply (for)
IV U4, 76

Bewerbung application IV U4, 76

Bewerbungsschreiben letter of application IV U4, 76

bewölkt cloudy II

Bezirk borough IV U1, 10

bieten to offer IV U4, 76

Bild picture I

Bildung education IV U4, 81

billig cheap II

Biologie Biology I

bis until; to III
Bis bald. See you soon. I; See you. II

ein (kleines) **bisschen** a little (bit) II

bitte please I
Bitte schön. Here you are. I

blau blue I

bleiben to stay I
in Verbindung bleiben staying
connected III
stecken bleiben to be stuck I

Bleistift pencil I

blinken to signal IV U1, 20

Blog blog I

Bonbon sweet I

Boom boom IV U3, 60

Boot boat IV U2, 30

Bordkarte boarding card IV U2, 36

böse angry II

Boss boss III

Bote messenger IV U1, 11

Botin messenger IV U1, 11

Box box I

brauchbar useful III
brauchen to need I; to take III
braun brown I
Brief letter IV U4, 76
Brieffreund penfriend III
Brieffreundin penfriend III
bringen to bring II; to get IV U1, 20
Broschüre brochure III
Brot bread I
   belegtes Brot sandwich I
Brücke bridge II
Bruder brother I
Bub boy I
Buch book I
buchen to book III
Buchstabe letter IV U4, 76
Bude stall I
Bühne stage II
Bühnenbild scenery III
Bundesstaat state III
Burg castle III
Bus bus I
Butter butter I

C

Café snack bar I; café III
Cafeteria cafeteria I
Camp camp III
campen gehen to go camping III
Campingplatz campsite III
Cent (Währung) cent III
Center centre; center (AE) III
Chance chance III; opportunity
   IV U1, 12
chatten to chat II
Check-in-Mitarbeiter check-in agent
   IV U2, 36
Check-in-Mitarbeiterin check-in
   agent IV U2, 36
Cheerleader cheerleader III
Cheerleaderin cheerleader III
Cheerleading cheerleading III
Chef boss III
Chefin boss III
Chinese Chinese II
Chinesin Chinese II
Chinesisch Chinese II
chinesisch Chinese II
circa about II
Cola cola I
Comic(heft) comic II

Computer computer I
cool cool I
Copyright copyright IV U4, 72
Cousin cousin II
Cousine cousin II

D

da there; because I
Dach roof III
Dachboden attic I
daheim at home I
dahin there I
Dame lady IV U1, 21
damit so that IV U3, 60
Dampfer steamboat IV U3, 50
Dampfschiff steamboat IV U3, 50
danach then; after that I
dankbar thankful IV U3, 52
Danke. Thanks.; Thank you. I
dann then I
Darsteller actor III
Darstellerin actor III
das the; this; that I; which; who III
dass that II
Datum date IV U4, 81
dauern to last II; to take III
davor in front of I
Decke blanket IV U2, 41
dein your I
   Dein (Grußformel in Briefen oder
   E-Mails) Yours, II
deine yours III
demoliert wrecked IV U1, 21
denken to think II
   denken an to think about III
   denken an/über to think of III
der the; which; that; who III
dermaßen so II
derselbe the same II
deshalb so I
Design design II
Detektiv detective I
Detektivin detective I
deutlich clear III
Deutsch German I
deutsch German II
Deutsche German II
Deutscher German II
Dezember December I
Dialog dialogue II
dich you I; yourself III

die the I; which; that; who III
Dienstag Tuesday I
dies this I
diese these II
dieses that I
Ding thing I; item IV U2, 41
dir you I; yourself IV U2, 32
   dir selbst yourself IV U2, 32
Dollar (amer. Währungseinheit) dollar
   ($) IV ZI, 9
Donner boom IV U3, 60
Donnerstag Thursday I
Dorf village I
dort there I
dorthin there I
Dose can IV U2, 41
Drama drama III
draußen outside II
dreckig dirty I
drei three I
dreißig thirty I
dreizehn thirteen I
dritte third II
Droge drug IV U3, 56
drüben over III
du you I
Dudelsack bagpipes (pl) III
Duft smell IV U2, 48
dunkel dark I
durch around; through III
Durcheinander mess I
Durchmesser diameter II
(etw. tun) dürfen to be allowed to
   (do sth) IV U3, 52

E

effizient efficient IV U4, 80
Ei egg I
eiförmig oval III
eigene own II
eigentlich really I
ein one; a; an I
   ein paar a few IV U3, 52
einander each other III
eine a; an I
einfach easy I; just III
   einfache Fahrkarte single ticket III
   die einfachste the least difficult III
sich einfallen lassen to think of III
einhundert a/one hundred I
einige some I; a few IV U3, 52

Einkaufen shopping I

Einkaufspassage mall II

Einkaufszentrum shopping centre I; mall II

Einkaufszettel shopping list I

einladen to invite II

Einladung invitation I

einmal once II
   schon einmal ever III

einpacken to pack III

die Spülmaschine **einräumen** to load the dishwasher II

eins one I

einsam lonely III

einst once II

einsteigen to get in IV U1, 21
   in etw. einsteigen to get on sth IV U3, 50

Einsteigezeit boarding time IV U2, 36

eintausend a/one thousand II

Eintrittskarte ticket II

einundzwanzig twenty-one I

nicht **einverstanden** sein to disagree IV U3, 56

Einwanderer immigrant IV U1, 10

Einwanderin immigrant IV U1, 10

Einwohner population (no pl) IV U1, 11

Einwohnerzahl population (no pl) IV U1, 11

Eis ice cream II

Eiscreme ice cream II

Eisenbahn railway IV U4, 80

Eishockey ice hockey; hockey IV U4, 70

Elch moose IV U4, 71

elf eleven I

Eltern parents (pl) I

E-Mail e-mail II

Empfangschef receptionist IV U4, 76

Empfangsdame receptionist IV U4, 76

Empfehlung reference IV U4, 81

Ende end II
   am Ende at the end II
   oberes Ende top II

enden to finish II

die **Engländer** the English III

Englisch English I

englisch English III

entfernt away II

entfliehen to escape IV U3, 60

entkommen to escape IV U3, 60

(sich) **entscheiden** to decide III

Entscheidung decision IV U1, 12

Entschuldigung. Sorry. I; I'm sorry.; Excuse me. II

entwerfen to design IV U2, 41

entwickeln to design IV U2, 41

Entwurf design II

Episode episode IV U4, 72

er it; he I

Erdbeben earthquake IV U2, 31

Erdbeere strawberry I

Erde earth III

Erdteil continent II

sich **ereignen** to happen IV U2, 40

Ereignis event II

erfahren von to hear about IV U3, 60

Erfahrung experience IV U4, 76

erfolgreich successful IV U1, 12

erforschen to explore IV U3, 61

erhältlich available IV U4, 81

sich **erinnern** (an) to remember III

Erkältung cold II

erklettern to climb II

erkunden to explore IV U3, 61

sich **erkundigen** nach to ask about II

Erlebnis adventure III; experience IV U4, 76

erledigen to finish II

ernst serious II

Erntedankfest Thanksgiving IV U3, 52

erraten to guess I

erschießen to shoot IV U3, 60

erstaunlich amazing II

erste first I
   das erste Mal the first time I

Erste-Hilfe- first-aid IV U2, 41

als **Erstes** first II

etw. nicht **ertragen** can't stand + -ing III

erwachen to wake up III

erzählen to tell I

Erzähler narrator I

Erzählerin narrator I

erzeugen to produce IV U2, 31

Erziehung education IV U4, 81

erzielen to score III

es it I
   Es macht nichts. I don't mind. IV U3, 52
   Es tut mir leid. I'm sorry. II
   es war einmal once upon a time II

Essen food I; meal II

essen to eat; to have I

Etage floor II

etwa about II

etwas something; some I; anything III

euch you I; yourselves IV U2, 32
   euch selbst yourselves IV U2, 32

euer your I

eure yours III

Euro (Währung) euro III

Europäer European III

Europäerin European III

europäisch European III

ewig forever IV U3, 56

Experiment experiment II

F

Fabrik factory III

(zu etw.) **fähig** sein (Ersatzform für can) to be able to (do sth) IV U3, 52

Fähigkeit skill IV U4, 76

fahren to go; to ride I; to run; to travel II; to drive IV U1, 21
   Fahrrad fahren to go bike riding II
   Tandem fahren to go tandem bike riding II

Fahrer driver IV U1, 21

Fahrerin driver IV U1, 21

Fahrgeschäft ride II

einfache **Fahrkarte** single ticket III

Fahrplan timetable III

Fahrrad bike I
   Fahrrad fahren to go bike riding II

Fahrschein ticket II

Fahrt trip I; ride II; journey III

fair fair IV U4, 72

Fakt fact II

fallen to fall I

falls if IV U2, 32

falsch wrong I

Familie family I

Fan fan I

fangen to catch II

fantastisch fantastic II

Farbe colour I; color (AE) III

Fasching carnival I

fast nearly II

Februar February I

Feier party I

feiern to celebrate III
   eine Party feiern to have a party I

Feiertag holiday *(AE)* IV U3, 52
Feld field III
Fenster window I
Ferien holiday II; vacation *(AE)* III
fernhalten to keep away IV U2, 48
Fernseh- TV IV U4, 72
Fernsehen television III; TV IV U4, 72
  im Fernsehen on TV III
fernsehen to watch TV I
Fernseher TV I; television III
fertig ready I
  fertig machen to finish II
Fertigkeit skill IV U4, 76
fertigstellen to finish I
Fest fair II; festival III
festhalten to hold II
Festival festival III
feststecken to be stuck I
Festzug procession II
Feuer fire III
Figur figure II
Film film I; movie *(AE)* III
finden to find I
  Gefallen finden an to enjoy
  IV U3, 51
Firma company II
Fisch fish I
fischen gehen to go fishing IV U3, 60
fit fit III
Flagge flag IV ZI, 9
eine **Flasche** ... a bottle of II
Fledermaus bat I
Fleisch meat IV U3, 52
flexibel flexible IV U4, 80
Fliegen flying III
fliegen to fly II
fliehen to escape IV U3, 60
Floh flea I
Flohmarkt flea market I
Floß raft III
flüchten to escape IV U3, 60
Flug flight IV U2, 32
  Guten Flug! Have a good flight!
  IV U2, 36
Flughafen airport IV U2, 32
Flugsteig gate IV U2, 36
Flugzeug plane IV U2, 30
Fluss river I
Folge episode IV U4, 72
Follower follower IV U4, 72
Followerin follower IV U4, 72

Foto photo I
  Fotos machen to take photos (of)
  II
fotografieren to take photos (of) II
Frage question I
fragen to ask I
  fragen nach to ask about II
Französisch French IV U4, 71
französisch French IV U4, 71
Frau woman I; lady IV U1, 21
Frau *(Anrede)* Mrs I; Miss IV U3, 60
frei free III
im **Freien** outside II
Freitag Friday I
Freizeit free time I
Freizeitpark theme park II
Freude fun I
sich **freuen** auf to look forward to
  (+ -ing) IV U2, 32
Freund friend I
Freundin friend I
freundlich friendly IV U4, 80
Freundschaft(en) schließen to make
  friends II
Frisbee frisbee I
Frisbeescheibe frisbee I
Friseur hairdresser IV U3, 56
Friseurin hairdresser IV U3, 56
Friseursalon hairdressing salon
  IV U3, 56
froh happy IV U3, 52
Frohe Weihnachten! Merry Christ-
  mas! I
fröhlich happy IV U3, 52
Frucht fruit I
früh early II
Frühling spring II
Frühstück breakfast I
frühstücken to have breakfast I
Frühstückspension bed and break-
  fast (B & B) III
(sich) **fühlen** to feel II
Führer guide IV U1, 26
Führerin guide IV U1, 26
Führung tour III
Füller pen I
fünf five I
fünfzehn fifteen I
fünfzig fifty I
für for I; to IV U3, 56
  für immer forever IV U3, 56

furchtbar awful I
Fuß foot II
  zu Fuß on foot I
  zu Fuß gehen to walk IV U1, 16
Fußball football I; soccer *(AE)* II
füttern to feed I

G

ganz all I; all of; quite II
  in ganz all over II
Ganztages- all-day III
Garten garden I
Gast guest IV U4, 76
Gate gate IV U2, 36
Gebäude building II
geben to give I
Gebiet field III; area IV U2, 41
geboren werden to be born IV U1, 16
gebratener Reis mit Hühnerfleisch
  chicken fried rice II
gebraucht second-hand I
Geburtsdatum date of birth IV U4, 81
Geburtstag birthday I
Gedicht poem III
gefährlich dangerous III
Gefallen finden an to enjoy IV U3, 51
jmdn. **gefangen** halten to keep sb
  prisoner IV U3, 60
Gefangene prisoner IV U3, 60
Gefangener prisoner IV U3, 60
gegen against III
Gegend area IV U2, 41
gegenseitig each other III
Gegenstand item IV U2, 41
gegenüber opposite II
Gehalt salary IV U4, 76
gehen to go I; to walk IV U1, 16; to
  leave IV U2, 36
  aus dem Weg gehen to avoid
  IV U3, 56
  campen gehen to go camping III
  fischen gehen to go fishing
  IV U3, 60
  inlineskaten gehen to go skating II
  ins Bett gehen to go to bed I
  raften gehen to go rafting III
  Schlittschuhlaufen gehen to go
  skating II
  zelten gehen to go camping III
Gehör hearing II
Geist ghost IV U3, 61

gelb yellow I

Geld money I

    Geld aufbringen to raise money II

    Geld sammeln to raise money II

Gelegenheit chance III; opportunity
    IV U1, 12

gelegentlich occasionally III

Gemüse vegetable (veg) IV U2, 31

genauso the same II

genießen to enjoy IV U3, 51

genug enough III

genügend enough III

geöffnet open I

gerade (eben) just III

geradeaus straight on II

Geräusch noise I

gerecht fair IV U4, 72

ich hätte **gern** … I'd love (to) …
    (= I would love to) IV U2, 32

ich würde sehr **gern** … I'd love
    (to) … (= I would love to) IV U2, 32

… **gerne** like + -ing I

gernhaben to like I

Geruch smell IV U2, 48

Geruchssinn sense of smell IV U2, 48

Geschäft shop I; store (AE) III

Geschäftsführer manager IV U3, 56

Geschäftsführerin manager IV U3, 56

geschehen to happen II

Geschenk present I

Geschichte story I

Geschick skill IV U4, 76

geschlossen closed I

Gesellschaft company II

Gesicht face I

Gespenst ghost IV U3, 61

Gespräch dialogue II; interview
    IV U3, 66

Gestalt figure II

gestalten to design IV U2, 41

Gestaltung design II

gestern yesterday I

gesund healthy III

Getränk drink I

Getreide corn IV U3, 52

Gewalt violence (no pl) IV U3, 56

Gewinn prize II

gewinnen to win I

Gewinner winner I

Gewinnerin winner I

Gewinnspiel raffle II

sich **gewöhnen** an (etw.) to get used
    to (sth) IV U1, 12

gewöhnlich usually II

glauben to think; to believe II

gleich the same II

der **gleiche** the same II

gleichzeitig at the same time II

Glocke bell II

Glück bringend lucky II

Glück haben to be lucky II

Viel **Glück!** Good luck! IV U1, 12

glücklich happy I; lucky II

Glückstag lucky day II

Glückwunsch! Congratulations! II

Gold gold III

Gold- gold III

golden gold III

grau grey I

Grenze border IV U4, 70

Grill barbecue I

Grillfest barbecue I

Grizzlybär grizzly bear IV U2, 32

groß big I; large; high; tall II; great III

großartig great I; fantastic II; awe-
    some III

Größe size II

Großeltern grandparents (pl) II

Großstadt city I

Großvater grandfather II

grün green I

Grundschule primary school IV U4, 81

Gruppe team I; group IV U4, 71

gruselig scary I

Viele **Grüße** Best wishes, I

Mit freundlichen **Grüßen** Yours sin-
    cerely, IV U4, 76

günstig cheap II

gut fine; good I; well II

    gut sein in to be good at I

    Gut gemacht! Well done! II

    gut sein bei to be good at I

    Guten Flug! Have a good flight!
    IV U2, 36

    Mir geht es gut. I'm fine. I

Alles **Gute!** Best wishes, I; All the
    best, II; Good luck! IV U1, 12

H

haben to have I; to have got II

    Angst haben to be scared I

    Glück haben to be lucky II

Hähnchen chicken I

Hai shark I

halb half III

    halb (acht) half past (seven) II

    eine halbe Million half a million III

Hallen- indoor III

Hallo. Hello.; Hi. I

Hals neck II

Halsband collar I

Halt stop II

halten to hold; to keep II

    jmdn. gefangen halten to keep sb
    prisoner IV U3, 60

Haltestelle stop II; station III

Hamburger burger I

Hammer hammer III

Hammerwerfen hammer throwing III

Hamster hamster I

Hand hand II

    aus zweiter Hand second-hand I

Handschuh glove II

Handy phone I

hart hard II

hassen to hate I

häufig often II

häufiger more often IV U2, 40

Hauptstadt capital (city) I

Haus house I

    nach Hause home I

    zu Hause at home I

Hausaufgabe(n) homework I

    Hausaufgabe(n) machen to do
    homework I

Hausmeister caretaker I

Hausmeisterin caretaker I

Haustier pet I

Heft book I

Heim home I

Heimat home country IV U1, 12

Heimatland home country IV U1, 12

Heimweh haben to be homesick
    IV U1, 12

heiß hot I

Ich **heiße** … My name is … I

helfen to help I

Helfer assistant IV U3, 56

Helferin assistant IV U3, 56

Helm helmet I

Hemd shirt I

herausfallen to fall out III

herausfinden to find I; to find out IV U1, 26

herauskommen to get out IV U1, 20

Herberge hostel II

Herbst autumn II; fall *(AE)* III

Herr *(Anrede)* Mr I

herstellen to produce IV U2, 31

herüber over III

herumhängen to hang about I

herunter down III

herunterfallen to fall off II

Herzliche Grüße Love, I

heute today I
   heute Morgen this morning II

hier here I

hierher here III

hierhin here III

hiesig local II

Hilfe help I

hilfreich useful III

Himmel sky IV U3, 60

Hin- und Rückfahrkarte return ticket III

hinauf up II

hinausbringen to take out II

hinbringen to take II

in … **hinein** into II

hinfallen to fall I

sich **hinsetzen** to sit (down) I

hinter behind I

Hintergrund background III

hinterlassen to leave III

hinunter down III

hinunterfallen to fall off II

Hinweis clue I

hispanisch Hispanic IV U2, 31

Hispanoamerikaner Hispanic IV U2, 31

Hispanoamerikanerin Hispanic IV U2, 31

Hobby hobby II

hoch high; up; tall II

hochladen to upload II

Hockey hockey IV U4, 70

hoffen (auf) to hope (for) II

Höhe height II

Höhle cave IV U3, 61

holen to get IV U1, 20

Holz wood I

hören to listen (to) I; to hear II
   hören von to hear about IV U3, 60

kurze **Hose** shorts *(pl)* II

Hostel hostel II

Hotdog hot dog II

Hotel hotel IV U3, 56

hübsch pretty II; beautiful III

Hügel hill IV U2, 31

Huhn chicken I

gebratener Reis mit **Hühnerfleisch** chicken fried rice II

Hund dog I
   den Hund ausführen to take the dog for a walk I

hundert a/one hundred I

hungrig hungry I

hüpfen to bounce III

Hurrikan hurricane IV U3, 66

Husky *(Schlittenhunderasse)* husky IV U2, 48

Hut hat II

hüten to look after II

I

ich I; me I
   ich hätte gern I'd (= I would) I
   ich hätte gern … I'd love (to) … (= I would love to) IV U2, 32
   ich möchte … I'd like (to) … (= I would like to) I
   ich würde I'd (= I would) I
   ich würde gerne … I'd like (to) … (= I would like to) I
   ich würde nicht gerne … I wouldn't like (to) … I
   ich würde sehr gern … I'd love (to) … (= I would love to) IV U2, 32

Idee idea I

ihm it; him II

ihn it; him II

Ihnen you I

ihnen them II

ihr you; her; their; its I

Ihr your I

Ihre yours III

ihre hers; theirs III

im in I
   im Fernsehen on TV III
   im Freien outside II
   im Jahr a year IV U2, 40
   im Moment at the moment II
   im Norden von in the north of III

Imbissstube snack bar I

immer always I
   für immer forever IV U3, 56
   immer noch still II
   schon immer always III

Immigrant immigrant IV U1, 10

Immigrantin immigrant IV U1, 10

in to; in; at I; into II
   in der Schule at school I
   in ganz all over II
   in Ordnung fine I

Indianer Native American III

Indianerin Native American III

indianisch Native American III

Industrie industry III

aktuelle **Information** update IV U4, 72

Information(en) information II

Ingenieur engineer II

Ingenieurin engineer II

inlineskaten to skate II
   inlineskaten gehen to go skating II

Innen- indoor III

Insel island IV U1, 10

interessant interesting I

Interesse interest IV U4, 81

sich **interessieren** für to be interested in III

interessiert sein an to be interested in III

Internetseite website III

Internettagebuch blog I

Interview interview IV U3, 66

Interviewer interviewer IV U1, 12

Interviewerin interviewer IV U1, 12

irgendeine any I

irgendeiner anyone IV U3, 61

irgendetwas anything III

irgendjemand someone; anybody III; anyone IV U3, 61

irgendwelche any I

Irisch Irish III

irisch Irish III

Italiener Italian IV U1, 11

Italienerin Italian IV U1, 11

Italienisch Italian IV U1, 11

italienisch Italian IV U1, 11

J

ja yes I

Jacke coat I

Jahr year I
   im Jahr a year IV U2, 40

pro Jahr a year IV U2, 40
Jahreszeit season II
Jahrgangsstufe year I; grade *(AE)* II
Jahrhundert century IV U3, 60
Jahrmarkt fair II
Januar January I
Japaner Japanese IV U1, 16
Japanerin Japanese IV U1, 16
Japanisch Japanese IV U1, 16
japanisch Japanese IV U1, 16
jede every I
jeder everyone II; anybody III
jemals ever III
jemand somebody I; someone;
    anybody III
jene that I; those II
jetzt now I
Job job I
Jugend- youth I; teen II
Jugendliche teen II
Jugendlicher teen II
Juli July I
jung young II
Junge boy I
Juni June I

K

Käfig cage II
Kajak kayak IV U1, 26
Kajakfahren kayaking IV U1, 26
Kalender planner II
kalt cold I
Kälte cold II
kämpfen to fight II
Kanadier Canadian IV U4, 71
Kanadierin Canadian IV U4, 71
kanadisch Canadian IV U4, 71
Kanal canal III
Kaninchen rabbit I
Kanone cannon III
Kanonenkugel cannon ball III
Kanu canoe IV U3, 60
Kanufahren canoeing I
Kapitän captain II
Kapitänin captain II
Karibe Caribbean IV U3, 56
Karibin Caribbean IV U3, 56
karibisch Caribbean IV U3, 56
Karneval carnival I
Karriere career IV U1, 12
Karte map II; card III

Kartoffel potato IV U3, 52
Käse cheese I
Katze cat I
kaufen to buy I
kein no I; not … any III
keine no I; not … any III
Keks biscuit; cookie *(AE)* III
kennen to know I
kennenlernen to meet I
Kenntnis skill IV U4, 76
Kette chain III
Kilo (kg, Kilogramm) kilo (kg, kilo-
    gram) I
Kilometer (km) kilometre (km)
    IV U4, 88
Kilt kilt III
Kind kid I
Kinder children *(pl)* I
Kinderzimmer bedroom II
Kino cinema I
Kirche church II
Kiste box I
klar clear III
Klasse year; class I; grade *(AE)* II
Klassenfahrt school trip II
Klassenzimmer classroom I
Kleeblatt shamrock III
Kleid dress I
Kleider clothes *(pl only)* I
Kleiderschrank wardrobe II
Kleidung clothes *(pl only)* I
klein little; small I
Klettern rock climbing I
klettern to climb II
Klima climate IV U3, 51
klingeln to ring I
klingen to sound III
Klub club I
Koch chef II
Koch- cooking II
Kochen cooking II
kochen to cook II
Koffer suitcase IV U2, 36
Kohlenbergwerk coal mine III
Kohlengrube coal mine III
Kolonie colony IV U4, 71
komisch funny I
kommen to come; to get I
    zu spät kommen to be late II
Kommentar comment IV U3, 56

kommentieren to comment (on)
    IV U4, 72
kompliziert difficult III
König king II
Königin queen II
können can I
    (etw. tun) können *(Ersatzform für
    can)* to be able to (do sth) IV U3, 52
    nicht können can't I
konnte could III
konstruieren to design IV U2, 41
Kontakt contact I
    in Kontakt bleiben to keep in
    touch II
Kontinent continent II
kontrollieren to check II
Konzert concert I
Kopf head II
Kopfschmerzen headache II
Kopfweh headache II
Korb basket III
Korbball netball I
Korn corn IV U3, 52
Körper body IV U3, 60
korrekt right I
korrigieren to correct II
kosten to cost III
kostenlos free III
Kostüm costume; fancy dress I
Krankenhaus hospital II
Krankenpfleger nurse IV U3, 56
Krankenschwester nurse IV U3, 56
Kratzer scratch IV U1, 20
Kricket cricket II
Kronjuwelen crown jewels *(pl)* II
Kruste crust IV U2, 40
Küche kitchen II
Kuchen cake I
Küchenchef chef II
Kugel ball III
Kuh cow III
Kulissen scenery III
Kultur culture III
sich **kümmern** um to look after II
Kunde customer I
Kundenbetreuung customer service
    IV U4, 76
Kundendienst customer service
    IV U4, 76
Kundenservice customer service
    IV U4, 76

Kundin customer I
Kunst Art I
Künstler artist III
Künstlerin artist III
Kunststück trick I
Kurier messenger IV U1, 11
Kurierin messenger IV U1, 11
Kurs class IV U1, 26
kurz short II
    kurze Hose shorts *(pl)* II
Küste coast III

L

lachen to laugh II
Laden shop I; store *(AE)* III
Lager camp III
Lampe lamp II
Land country I; nation III
landen to land IV U2, 36
ländliche Gegend country I
Landwirt farmer I
Landwirtin farmer I
lang long III
länger longer I
langsam slow IV U1, 16
langweilig boring I
Laptop laptop I
lassen to leave II
    lass(t) uns let's (= let us) I
Laterne lantern II
Laufbahn career IV U1, 12
laufen to run II; to walk IV U1, 16
    Schlittschuh laufen to skate II
laut loud I; noisy III
läuten to ring I
Leben life II
leben to live I
Lebenslauf CV (curriculum vitae)
    IV U4, 76
Lebensmittel food I
legen to put I
lehren to teach IV U2, 32
Lehrer teacher I
Lehrerin teacher I
Leiche body IV U3, 60
leicht easy I
Es tut mir **leid**. I'm sorry. II
Tut mir **leid**. Sorry. I
leider I'm afraid IV U2, 36
leise quiet II
leistungsfähig efficient IV U4, 80

Leiter ladder I; leader III
Leiterin leader III
lernen to learn II
lesen to read II
letzte last I
Leute people; persons *(pl)* I
Liebe(r) …, *(Anrede in Briefen)*
    Dear …, I
    Liebe Grüße Love, I
lieben to love I
Lieblings- favourite I; favorite *(AE)* III
am **liebsten** best II
Lied song I
liefern to deliver IV U1, 20
Lieferwagen van IV U1, 20
Lineal ruler I
Linie line III
links on the left; left II
Loch hole I
lokal local II
Luft air III
lügen to lie IV U1, 21
lustig funny I; fun III

M

machen to do, to make I
    eine Ausbildung machen to train
    IV U2, 48
    Fotos machen to take photos (of)
    II
    Hausaufgabe(n) machen to do
    homework I
    Mach die Musik leiser. Turn the
    music down. I
    Mach dir keine Sorgen. Don't
    worry. I
    Mach dir nichts draus. Never mind.
    II
    Macht nichts. Never mind. II
Mädchen girl I
Mahlzeit meal II
Mai May I
Mais corn IV U3, 52
Mal time I; base III
    das erste Mal the first time I
    zum 200. Mal for the 200th time III
malen to paint II
Mama mum I; mom *(AE)* III
Manager manager IV U3, 56
Managerin manager IV U3, 56
manchmal sometimes I

Mann man I
Mannschaft team I
Mannschaftsführer captain II
Mannschaftsführerin captain II
Markt market I
März March I
Match match I
Mathe Maths I; Math *(AE)* III
Mathematik Math *(AE)* III
Matsch mud I
Mauer wall II
Maus mouse I
Medaille medal II
soziale **Medien** social media III
Meer sea I
    am Meer at the seaside I
Meerschweinchen guinea pig II
mehr more II
    nicht mehr not … any more III
die **Mehrheit** most III
meiden to avoid IV U3, 56
Meile mile III
mein my I
meine mine III
meinen to mean IV U4, 72
anderer **Meinung** sein to disagree
    IV U3, 56
einer **Meinung** sein (mit) to agree
    (with) II
die **meisten** most III
am **meisten** most III
eine **Menge** a lot of I
Mensa cafeteria I
Mensch person *(sg)* II
Menschen people; persons *(pl)* I
Menschenhändler slave trader
    IV U3, 61
sich **merken** to remember III
merkwürdig funny I
Messe fair II
Metall- metal III
metallen metal III
Meter metre II; meter *(AE)* III
mich me I; myself III
    mich selbst myself IV U2, 32
mild mild II
Million million I
    eine halbe Million half a million III
Minute minute I
mir me I; myself IV U2, 32
mit with I; on II; of III

mit (dem Zug) by (train) I

Mitarbeiter employee IV U2, 36; assistant IV U3, 56

Mitarbeiterin employee IV U2, 36; assistant IV U3, 56

mitbringen to bring II

mitmachen (bei) to take part (in) II

mitnehmen to take I

mitspielen to act III

Mittagessen lunch; dinner I

Mittagspause lunchtime I

Mittagszeit lunchtime I

Mitte centre; middle; center *(AE)* III

Mittelschule secondary school IV U4, 81

mitten in in the middle of II

mittlerer Schulabschluss secondary school leaving certificate IV U4, 80

Mittwoch Wednesday I

Mode fashion IV U1, 20

modern modern I

mögen to like; to want (to) I

gern mögen to love I

nicht mögen to hate I

ich möchte nicht … I wouldn't like (to) … I

ich möchte … I'd like (to) … (= I would like to) I

Möchtest du …? Would you like (to) …? I

Möglichkeit chance III; opportunity IV U1, 12

im **Moment** at the moment II

momentan at the moment II

Monat month II

Montag Monday I

Morgen morning I

heute Morgen this morning II

morgen tomorrow II

motivieren to motivate III

müde tired I

Muffin muffin II

Müll rubbish I

multikulturell multicultural IV U1, 11

Mund mouth II

Museum museum II

Musik music I

Musikgruppe band II

Muslim Muslim I

Muslimin Muslim I

müssen to have to; must II; to need to III

mutig brave III

Mutter mother I

Mutti mum I

Mütze hat II

N

Na ja, … Well, … II

nach to; after I

nach *(bei Uhrzeitangaben)* past II

nach Hause home I

Nachbar neighbour I

Nachbarin neighbour I

nachdem after IV U3, 61

nachdenken über to think about III

Nachmittag afternoon I

nachmittags *(Uhrzeit)* p.m. III

Nachricht message II

Nachricht(en) news II

nachschauen to look I

nächste next I

als Nächstes next II

Nacht night I

nachts at night IV U1, 16

Nacken neck II

nah near II

in der **Nähe** von near I

Name name I

Nase nose II

die Nase voll haben (von) to be fed up (with) III

nass wet I

Nation nation III

national national III

National- national III

Nationalität nationality IV U1, 16

Nationalpark national park III

natürlich of course II

Naturwissenschaft science III

neben next to I; by III

nebenher at the same time II

nehmen to take I; to use III

nehmen (Bus/Zug) to catch (bus/train) III

Nehmen Sie Platz. Take a seat. IV U3, 52

Nimm Platz. Take a seat. IV U3, 52

nein no I

nennen to call III

nett nice I

neu new I

Neuigkeit(en) news II

neun nine I

neunzehn nineteen I

neunzig ninety I

nicht not I

auch nicht not … either III

nicht können can't I

nicht mögen to hate I

nicht einverstanden sein to disagree IV U3, 56

nicht mehr not … any more III

nichts nothing II; not … anything III

nie never II

niemals never II

niemand no one I; nobody II

noch still II

immer noch still II

noch ein another IV U2, 36

noch einmal again I

noch nicht not … yet III

Nord- north III

Norden north III

im Norden von in the north of III

normalerweise usually II

Note grade *(AE)* II

November November I

null zero I

Null *(bei Uhrzeiten und Telefonnummern)* oh III

Nummer number I

nun now I

nur only I; just III

nutzen to use III

nützlich useful III

O

ob if IV U2, 32

als ob like IV U2, 32

oben up II

oberer Teil top II

oberes Ende top II

oberhalb above II

Obst fruit I

oder or I

öffentliche Verkehrsmittel public transport III

öffnen to open I

oft often II

öfter more often IV U2, 40

ohne without II

okay OK (okay) I
Oktober October I
Öl oil II
Oma grandma I
Onkel uncle I
online online II
   online stellen to post III
Online- online II
Orange orange I
orange orange I
in **Ordnung** fine I
   in Ordnung bringen to tidy II
organisieren to organize I
Orkan hurricane IV U3, 66
Ort place I
örtlich local II
Ost- east III
Osten east III
oval oval III

P

ein **paar** some I; a few IV U3, 52
packen to pack III
Paket package IV U1, 20
Papa dad I
Papier paper III
Parade parade IV U1, 16
Park park I
Partner partner I
Partnerin partner I
Partnerstadt twin town III
Party party I
   eine Party feiern to have a party I
Pass passport IV U2, 36
Passagier passenger IV U2, 36
Passagierin passenger IV U2, 36
passieren to happen II
   Das ist passiert. That's what hap-
   pened. II
Pause break I
Pausenhof playground I
Person person (sg) II
Pferd horse I
Pflanze plant III
Pflaume plum I
Pfund (brit. Währungseinheit) pound
   (£) I
Picknick picnic I
Pier pier II
pink pink I
Pistole gun IV U3, 56

Pizza pizza I
Plan map II; plan IV U1, 12
planen to plan IV U4, 80
Planer planner II
Platte plate IV U2, 40
Platz place I
plaudern to chat II
plötzlich suddenly I
Polizei police IV U1, 20
Polizeibeamter police officer I
Polizeibeamtin police officer I
Pommes frites chips (pl) I
Pop (Musik) pop II
positiv positive III
posten to post III
Poster poster II
Postkarte postcard I
Praktikum internship IV U4, 76
Präsentation presentation III
Präsident president III
Präsidentin president III
Preis price I; prize II
prellen to bounce III
pro Jahr a year IV U2, 40
probieren to try III
Problem problem I
Profil profile III
Programm programme III
Projekt project II
Prospekt brochure III
Prozent percent (%) III
Prozession parade IV U1, 16
prüfen to test II
Pullover pullover I
Puma mountain lion II
Punkt point III
Pute turkey IV U3, 52
putzen to clean II

Q

Qualifikation qualification IV U4, 80
Quiz quiz IV ZI, 8

R

Rad wheel II
Radiergummi rubber I
Radio radio III
Raft raft III
raften gehen to go rafting III
Rafting rafting III
Rakete rocket III

Ranger ranger (AE) IV U2, 48
Rangerin ranger (AE) IV U2, 48
Rap rap I
Rat advice III
raten to guess I
Ratespiel quiz IV ZI, 8
Ratschlag advice III
Rauch smoke IV U3, 60
Raum room I
Raumfahrt space III
Realschulabschluss secondary
   school leaving certificate IV U4, 80
Du hast **recht**. You're right. I
rechte right II
rechts on the right; right II
Rechtschreibung spelling I
reden (mit) to talk (to) I
Referat presentation III
Referenz reference IV U4, 81
Regal shelf II
Regalbrett shelf II
Regenbogen rainbow III
Reggae (Musik) reggae IV U3, 51
regnen to rain I
regnerisch rainy II
Reihenhaus townhouse III
Reis rice II
   gebratener Reis mit Hühnerfleisch
   chicken fried rice II
Reise trip I; tour; journey III
Reisebüro travel agent's IV U4, 76
Reisebürokauffrau travel agent
   IV U4, 80
Reisebürokaufmann travel agent
   IV U4, 80
reisen to travel II
Reisepass passport IV U2, 36
Reiten horse riding I
reiten to ride I
Rennen race II
rennen to run II
reparieren to repair IV U4, 72
Reservat reservation III
reservieren to book III; to make
   reservations IV U4, 80
Reservierung reservation III
Rest rest II
Restaurant restaurant II
retten to save II
Richterskala Richter scale (no pl)
   IV U2, 41

richtig right I
richtigstellen to correct II
Riesenrad big wheel II
riesig great III
Rinde crust IV U2, 40
Ritt ride II
Rock skirt III
Rolle part II
Rollstuhl wheelchair I
rosa pink I
rot red I
Hin- und **Rückfahrkarte** return ticket
   III
rufen to shout I; to call III
Rugby rugby III
ruhig quiet II
Russe Russian IV U4, 81
Russin Russian IV U4, 81
Russisch Russian IV U4, 81
russisch Russian IV U4, 81

S

Sache thing I
Sack bag I
Sackhüpfen sack race II
Saft juice I
sagen to say; to tell I
Saison season II
Salat salad I
Geld **sammeln** to raise money II
Sammlung collection III
Samstag Saturday I
samstags on Saturdays I
Sandwich sandwich I
Sänger singer I
Sängerin singer I
sauber machen to clean II
Saxofon saxophone I
Schachtel box I
Schade! That's too bad. II
Schäden damage IV U2, 40
Schaden damage IV U2, 40
Schaf sheep I
Schal scarf II
Schatzsuche treasure hunt II
schauen to look I
Schauspieler actor III
Schauspielerei drama III
Schauspielerin actor III
Schauspielworkshop acting work-
   shop III

schenken to give I
schicken to send I
schieben to push I
schießen to kick III; to shoot IV U3, 60
Schiff ship I; boat IV U2, 30
Schild sign IV U1, 16
Schimpanse chimpanzee II
schlafen to sleep II
Schlafzimmer bedroom II
schlagen to hit III
Schläger stick III
Schlagfrau batter III
Schlagmann batter III
Schlamm mud I
schlecht bad I
schlechter worse II
schlechteste worst II
schließen to close I
   Freundschaft(en) schließen to
   make friends II
schlimm bad II
schlimmer worse II
schlimmste worst II
Schlitten sled IV U2, 48
Schlittschuh laufen to skate II
Schlittschuhlaufen gehen to go
   skating II
Schloss castle III
Schlumpf smurf I
Schluss end II
Schlüssel key III
Schminken face painting II
schmutzig dirty I
Schnee snow II
schneereich snowy II
schnell fast II; quick IV U1, 16
Schnitzeljagd treasure hunt II
Schokolade chocolate I
schön fine; nice I; beautiful III
schon already; yet III
   schon einmal ever III
   schon immer always III
   Schon gut. Never mind. II
Schottenrock kilt III
schottisch Scottish III
schrecklich awful I
Schreiben letter IV U4, 76
Schreibtisch desk II
schreien to shout I
Schritt step II
Schuh shoe I

Schulabschluss qualification IV U4, 80
   mittlerer Schulabschluss secon-
   dary school leaving certificate
   IV U4, 80
Schul-AG club I
Schulausflug school trip II
Schule school I
   in der Schule at school I
   weiterführende Schule secondary
   school IV U4, 81
Schüler student I
Schülerin student I
Schulfach subject I
Schulhof playground I
Schulstunde lesson I
Schusswaffe gun IV U3, 56
schütteln to shake IV U2, 40
schützen to protect III
Schwanz tail I
schwarz black I
schwenken to swing III
schwer hard; serious II; heavy;
   difficult III
Schwert sword III
Schwester sister I
schwierig hard II; heavy; difficult III
Schwimmbad swimming pool I
schwimmen to swim I
   schwimmen gehen to go swimming I
schwingen to swing III
Science-Fiction science fiction I
sechs six I
sechzehn sixteen I
sechzig sixty I
secondhand second-hand I
See lake IV U1, 11
sehen to spy; to see; to look I
   Wir sehen uns. See you. II
Sehenswürdigkeit sight II
sehr very I
Sehr geehrte(r) …, Dear …, IV U4, 76
Seilbahn cable car IV U2, 31
seilgezogene Straßenbahn cable car
   IV U2, 31
Seilrutsche zip line III
sein his; to be; its I
   einer Meinung sein (mit) to agree
   (with) II
   weit weg sein to be a long way
   away II

seine his III

seit for; since IV U1, 12

seitdem since IV U1, 12

Seite side II

selbst myself; themselves; yourself III; himself; ourselves; yourselves; herself IV U2, 32

selbstbewusst confident IV U4, 76

selbstsicher confident IV U4, 76

selbstverständlich of course II

Selfie selfie IV U4, 72

selten rarely III

Seminar workshop III

senden to send I

Sendung programme III

September September I

Serie series (no pl) IV U4, 72

Servus. Goodbye. I

setzen to put I

sich setzen to sit (down) I

Setz dich. Take a seat. IV U3, 52

Setzen Sie sich. Take a seat. IV U3, 52

Shirt shirt I

Shorts shorts (pl) II

Show show I

sich each other; themselves III; himself; yourselves; herself; yourself IV U2, 32

sich selbst himself; herself; themselves; yourself IV U2, 32

sicher sure II; safe IV U1, 16; confident IV U4, 76

in Sicherheit safe IV U1, 16

sie it; she I; her II

Sie you I

Sie sich yourselves IV U2, 32

Sie sich selbst yourselves IV U2, 32

sie (Pl.) they; them I

sie selbst themselves III

sieben seven I

siebzehn seventeen I

siebzig seventy I

siegen to win I

Sieger winner I

Siegerin winner I

singen to sing I

Sinn sense IV U2, 48

Sitz seat III

sitzen to sit IV U2, 32

Sitzplatz seat III

Skateboard skateboard I

Skater skater I

Skaterin skater I

Sklave slave IV U3, 60

Sklavenhändler slave trader IV U3, 61

Sklavin slave IV U3, 60

SMS message II

Snowboard snowboard I

so so II

so … wie as … as III

sodass so that IV U3, 60

soeben just III

Software software IV U4, 72

Sohn son IV U3, 52

sollte should III

Sommer summer II

Sonne sun II

sonnig sunny II

Sonntag Sunday I

sich Sorgen machen to worry I

Mach dir keine Sorgen. Don't worry. I

sorgfältig careful III

Sorte kind II

Souvenir souvenir II

sowohl … als auch … … as well as … II

soziale Medien social media III

Spanisch Spanish IV U1, 16

spanisch Spanish IV U1, 16

spannend exciting I

sparen to save II

Spaß fun I

Spaß haben to enjoy oneself IV U2, 32

Spaß machen to be fun II

spaßig fun III

(zu) spät late II

zu spät kommen to be late II

später later I

Spaziergang walk I

Speck bacon I

speziell special I

Spiel game; match I

spielen to play I; to act III

Spieler player II

Spielerin player II

Spielfeld field III

Spielplatz playground I

Spitze top II

Sport sport III

Sportarten sports (pl only) I

Sportfest sports day II

Sportgeschäft sports shop II

Sportplatz playing field II

Sportunterricht PE (Physical Education) I

Sportzentrum sports centre I

Sprache language IV U4, 71

sprechen to say; to speak I

sprechen (mit) to talk (to) I

springen to jump III

spülen to wash II

die Spülmaschine ausräumen to empty the dishwasher II

die Spülmaschine einräumen to load the dishwasher II

Spur clue I

Staat state; nation III

von allen Staaten of all the states IV U2, 31

Staatsangehörige citizen IV U1, 12

Staatsangehöriger citizen IV U1, 12

Staatsangehörigkeit nationality IV U1, 16

Staatsbürger citizen IV U1, 12

Staatsbürgerin citizen IV U1, 12

stabil strong IV U2, 41

Stadion stadium I

Stadt city; town I

Stadtmitte city centre II

Stadtteil borough IV U1, 10

Stadtzentrum city centre II

Stand stall I

Star star I

stark heavy; strong III

starten to start I

Station station III

Statue statue IV U1, 10

staubsaugen to hoover II

Steckbrief profile III

stecken to put II

stecken bleiben to be stuck I

stehen to stand II

stehen für to stand for III

steigen to climb II

in etw. steigen to get on sth IV U3, 50

Stein stone III

Steinstoßen stone put III

Stell dir vor! Guess what? II

Stelle place I

stellen to put I
    online stellen to post III
Stellt euch vor! Guess what? II
sterben to die III
Stift pen I
Stiftung charity II
still quiet II
Stimmt etwas nicht? Is something
    wrong? II
Stock stick III
Stockwerk floor II
stolz (auf) proud (of) IV U3, 50
jmdn. von etw. **stoßen** to knock sb off
    sth IV U1, 20
Strand beach I
Straße street; road I
Straßenbahn tram I
    seilgezogene Straßenbahn cable
    car IV U2, 31
Streich trick II
streichen to paint II
Streit argument II
(sich) **streiten** to fight II
Stromschnelle rapid III
Strömung current III
ein **Stück** … a piece of II
Stufe step II
Stuhl chair I
Stunde hour II
Stundenplan timetable I
Sturm storm I
von etw. **stürzen** to fall off II
suchen (nach) to look for IV U4, 76
Suchplakat lost and found notice III
Süd- south III; southern IV U3, 50
Süden south III
südlich southern IV U3, 50
Südstaaten- southern IV U3, 50
super cool I
Supermarkt supermarket I
Surf- surfing IV U2, 31
Surfen surfing IV U2, 31
surfen gehen to go surfing III
Süßigkeit sweet I
Symbol symbol III
sympathisch friendly IV U4, 80

T

Tafel blackboard I
Tag day I
    ein ausgefüllter Tag a busy day II

    eines Tages one day I
Tagebuch diary I
Tal valley III
Talent talent I
Talentwettbewerb talent show I
Tandem tandem II
    Tandem fahren to go tandem bike
    riding II
Tante aunt I
Tanz dancing; dance III
Tanzen dancing III
tanzen to dance I
Tänzer dancer I
Tänzerin dancer I
tapfer brave III
Tasche bag I
Taschenlampe torch I
Taschenrechner calculator I
eine **Tasse** … a cup of II
Tätigkeit job III
Tatsache fact II
tausend a/one thousand II
Team team I
Technik DT (Design Technology) I;
    technology III
Techniker engineer II
Technikerin engineer II
Technologie technology III
Teddybär teddy I
Tee tea I
Teenager teen II
Teenagerin teen II
Teil part II
    oberer Teil top II
teilen to share III
teilnehmen (an) to take part (in) II
Telefon phone I
Telefonanruf phone call I
telefonieren to phone II
Telefonzelle telephone box II
Teller plate IV U2, 40
Tennis tennis I
Teppich carpet II
testen to test II
teuer expensive I
Theater theatre; theater (AE) III
Theater- drama III
Theaterstück play III
Thema topic IV U4, 88
Ticket ticket II
Tier animal I

Tierarzt vet IV U3, 56
Tierärztin vet IV U3, 56
Tierheim animal rescue shelter I
Tierpark zoo IV U1, 16
Tisch table I; desk II
Tochter daughter I
toll great I; amazing II; awesome III
Tomate tomato I
Tombola raffle II
Topf pot III
Tor goal III
Torpfosten goalpost III
Torstange goalpost III
tot dead IV U3, 60
Tour tour III
Tourismus tourism IV U4, 80; tourist
    industry IV U3, 51
Tourist tourist II
Touristin tourist II
Tradition tradition III
tragen to wear I
trainieren to train IV U2, 48
Training practice I; training
    IV U4, 76
Transport transport II
Transporter van IV U1, 20
transportieren to transport
    IV U2, 48
Traum dream I
traurig sad I; unhappy II
Treff club I
treffen to meet I; to hit III
    (sich) treffen to meet II
Treffer goal III
treiben to drive IV U1, 21
treten to kick III
Trick trick I
trinken to have I; to drink II
trocken dry II
Trompete trumpet II
Truthahn turkey IV U3, 52
Tschüss. Bye. I; See you. II
T-Shirt T-shirt II
Tsunami (durch Seebeben ausgelöste
    Flutwelle) tsunami IV U2, 41
Tuch scarf II
tun to do; to make I
    Tut mir leid. Sorry. I
Tür door II
Türkisch Turkish IV U1, 16
türkisch Turkish IV U1, 16

Türklingel doorbell I
Turm tower II
Turnschuh trainer II
Tüte bag I
Tutorial tutorial IV U4, 72

U

U-Bahn underground I
über about I; above; across II; over III
überall all over; everywhere II
überallhin everywhere II
sich **übergeben** to be sick I
überhaupt ever III
überlegen to guess I
    sich **überlegen** to think about III
übernachten to stay I
überprüfen to check II
überrascht surprised II
Überraschung surprise III
übrig left III
Übung exercise; practice I
Übungsheft exercise book I
Uhr clock II
Uhr *(Zeitangabe bei vollen Stunden)*
    o'clock I
Uhrzeit time I
um at I; around III
    um zu to II
    um … herum around II
(sich) **umdrehen** to turn over III
Umgebung environment II
umkippen to turn over III
umsteigen to change III
Umwelt environment II
umziehen to move II
Umzug procession II; parade
    IV U1, 16
Unabhängigkeit independence
    IV ZI, 9
und and I
    Und …? What about …? II
Unfall accident I
ungefähr about II
ungefährlich safe IV U1, 16
unglaublich amazing II
unglücklich unhappy II
unheimlich scary I
Uniform uniform I
unmöglich impossible IV U3, 66
Unordnung mess I
uns us II; ourselves IV U2, 32

uns selbst ourselves IV U2, 32
unser our I
unsere ours III
unter under I
Unternehmen company II
Unterricht lesson I; class IV U1, 26
unterrichten to teach IV U2, 32
Unterrichtsstunde class IV U1, 26
unterschiedlich different I
unterwegs out and about III
unversehrt safe IV U1, 16
Update update IV U4, 72
Ureinwohner Amerikas Native American III
Ureinwohnerin Amerikas Native American III
Urheberrecht copyright IV U4, 72
Urlaub holiday II; vacation *(AE)* III
Ururopa great-great-grandad I
US-amerikanisch US III

V

Vater father I
Vati dad I
Vegetarier vegetarian I
Vegetarlerin vegetarian I
verändern to change II
Veranstaltung event II
verärgert angry II; annoyed IV U3, 52
verbessern to correct II
in **Verbindung** bleiben staying connected III
verbringen *(Zeit)* to spend II
verfügbar available IV U4, 81
Vergangenheit past III
vergessen to forget II; to leave III
sich **verirren** to get lost IV U2, 36
verkaufen to sell I
Verkäufer assistant I
Verkäuferin assistant I
Verkehr transport II; traffic III
öffentliche **Verkehrsmittel** public transport III
Verkleidung fancy dress I
verlassen to leave II
    sich **verlassen** (auf) to rely (on)
    IV U3, 56
verlässlich reliable IV U4, 76
verletzen to hurt II
verletzt hurt III
verlieren to lose II

verloren gehen to get lost IV U2, 36
vermeiden to avoid IV U3, 56
vermissen to miss II
verpassen to miss II
verschieden different I
verschneit snowy II
verspätet delayed IV U2, 36
verstehen to understand II
Versuch experiment II
versuchen to try III
vertrauen (auf) to rely (on) IV U3, 56
vertrauenswürdig reliable IV U4, 76
verursachen to cause IV U2, 40
vervollständigen to finish I
verwenden to use III
Video video III
viel a lot of; lots of; much I
    Viel Glück! Good luck! IV U1, 12
viele a lot of; lots of; many I
    Viele Grüße Best wishes, I
vielleicht maybe II
vier four I
Viertel vor/nach quarter to/past II
vierzehn fourteen I
vierzig forty I
Vogel bird IV U2, 32
Volk nation III
völlig quite II
von from; of I; by III
vor in front of I; before; ago II; of III
vorbei (an) past I
Vordergrund foreground III
vorher before III
vorkommen to happen IV U2, 40
vorlesen to read II
Vormittag morning I
vormittags *(Uhrzeit)* a.m. III
vorn in front II
Vorräte supplies *(pl)* IV U2, 48
vorsichtig careful III
jmdn. jmdm. **vorstellen** to introduce
    sb to sb III
Vortrag presentation III

W

Wachs wax II
Waffe gun IV U3, 56
wählen to choose III
während while IV U2, 32; during
    IV U2, 41
Wahrheit truth IV U1, 21

Wahrheit

wahrscheinlich probably IV U3, 60
Wahrzeichen landmark IV U2, 31
Wal whale IV U1, 26
Walbeobachtungs- whale-watching
    IV U1, 26
Wald wood IV U2, 32
Walisisch Welsh III
walisisch Welsh III
Wand wall II
Wanderung walk I
Wandmalerei wall painting II
wann when I
warm warm II
warten (auf) to wait (for) II
Warteschlange queue II
warum why I
was what I; which II
    Was ist mit …? What about …? II
    Was kann ich für euch/dich tun?
    How can I help you? I
Waschbär raccoon I
Wäsche wash II
(sich) **waschen** to wash II
Wasser water I
Website website III
Wechselgeld change I
wechseln to change II
Weg way I
    aus dem Weg gehen to avoid
    IV U3, 56
weg away II
    weit weg sein to be a long way
    away II
wegen about IV U2, 36
wegfahren to drive off IV U1, 21
weggehen to leave II
weglaufen to run away II
wehtun to hurt II
Weihnachten Christmas I
    Frohe Weihnachten! Merry Christ-
    mas! I
weil because I
Art und **Weise** way III
weiß white I
weit far II
    weit weg sein to be a long way
    away II
weitere more II
Weitsprung long jump II
welche what I; which II
Welle wave III

Wellenreiten surfing IV U2, 31
Welt world I; earth III
    in aller Welt all around the world II
Weltraum space III
ein (klein) **wenig** a little (bit) II
wenige a few IV U3, 52
weniger less III
wenn when II; if IV U2, 32
wer who I
Werbung ad(vert) (= advertisement)
    III
werden to get I; will II
    etw. tun werden to be going to do
    sth III
    nicht werden won't (= will not) II
    (zu etw.) werden to become II
werfen to throw II
Werk factory III
West- west III
Westen west III
Wetter weather II
Wettlauf race II
Wettrennen race II
wichtig important III
wie how; like I; as II
    so … wie as … as III
    Wie alt bist du? How old are you? I
    Wie geht es dir? How are you? I
    Wie heißt du? What's your name? I
    Wie ist das Wetter? What's the
    weather like? II
    wie man … how to … IV U2, 32
    Wie spät ist es? What time is it? I
    Wie viel (kostet/kosten) …? How
    much (is/are) …? I
    Wie viel Uhr ist es? What time is
    it? I
wieder again I
wiederaufbauen to rebuild IV U3, 66
Auf **Wiedersehen.** Goodbye. I
wild wild IV U2, 30
Wildnis wilderness IV U4, 71
willkommen (bei/in) welcome (to) I
Wind wind I
windig windy II
Winter winter I
wir we I; us II
Wirbelsturm hurricane IV U3, 66
wirklich really I
wissen to know I
    Ich weiß (es) nicht! I don't know. I

Wissenschaft science III
Witterung weather II
witzig sein to be fun II
wo where I
Woche week I
Wochenende weekend I
woher where I
    Woher kommst du? Where are you
    from? I
wohin where I
wohltätige Zwecke charity II
Wohltätigkeits- charity II
Wohltätigkeitsorganisation charity II
wohnen to live I
Wohnung flat I; apartment
    (AE) IV U1, 16
Wohnzimmer living room II
Wolf wolf II
Wolke cloud II
wolkig cloudy II
Wolldecke blanket IV U2, 41
Wolle wool I
wollen to want (to) I
Workshop workshop III
Wort word II
wunderschön beautiful III
ich **würde** I'd (= I would) I
    ich würde gerne … I'd like (to) …
    (= I would like to) I
    ich würde nicht gerne … I
    wouldn't like (to) … I
    ich würde sehr gern … I'd love
    (to) … (= I would love to) IV U2, 32
    Würdest du gern …? Would you
    like (to) …? I
wütend angry II

Z

Zahl number I
Zahn tooth II
Zauberer wizard II
Zauberkünstler magician II
Zauberkünstlerin magician II
zaubern to do magic II
zehn ten I
Zeichen sign IV U1, 16
zeigen to show II
Zeit time I
Zeiten hours (pl) IV U4, 80
Zeitpunkt date IV U4, 81
Zeitschrift magazine IV U1, 12

Zeitung newspaper III
Zeitungsstand newspaper kiosk II
Zelt tent II
zelten gehen to go camping III
Zeltplatz campsite III
Zentrum centre; center *(AE)* III
zerstören to destroy IV U2, 41
zerstört wrecked IV U1, 21
zertrümmert wrecked IV U1, 21
Zeuge witness IV U1, 20
Zeugin witness IV U1, 20
Ziege goat III
ziehen to pull I; to move IV U2, 40
Ziel goal III
ziemlich quite II

Zimmer room I
zittern to shake IV U2, 40
Zoo zoo IV U1, 16
zornig angry II
zu to; at; too I
  zu Fuß on foot I
zuerst first II
Zug train I
Zuhause home I
zuhören to listen (to) I
Zukunft future IV U1, 12
zum 200. Mal for the 200th time III
zum Beispiel for example III
zumachen to close I
zurück back II

zusammen together I; everyone II
zuschauen to watch II
zusehen to watch II
zustimmen to agree (with) II
zuverlässig reliable IV U4, 76
zuvor before III
zwanzig twenty I
wohltätige Zwecke charity II
zwei two I
zweit- second IV U4, 70
zweite second II
  aus zweiter Hand second-hand I
zwischen between III
zwölf twelve I

Instructions
Arbeitsanweisungen mit Operatoren

Act the dialogue with your partner.	**Spiele** den Dialog mit deinem Partner / deiner Partnerin.
Answer the questions.	**Beantworte** die Fragen.
Ask questions.	**Stelle** Fragen.
Ask your partner.	**Frage** deinen Partner / deine Partnerin.
Ask for feedback.	**Bitte um** Rückmeldung.
Check the sentences • your draft.	**Überprüfe** die Sätze • deinen Entwurf.
Choose one of the tasks • the right answers • the right words.	**Wähle** eine der Aufgaben • die richtigen Antworten • die richtigen Wörter aus.
Collect ideas • pictures.	**Sammle** Ideen • Bilder.
Compare the people • the activities • the things.	**Vergleiche** die Leute • die Aktivitäten • die Dinge.
Complete the sentences • the dialogue.	**Vervollständige** die Sätze • den Dialog.
Correct the wrong words • sentences.	**Verbessere** die falschen Wörter • Sätze.
Describe the picture.	**Beschreibe** das Bild.
Discuss in groups.	**Besprecht** euch in Gruppen.
Draw a picture.	**Zeichne** ein Bild.
Find the names • the words • the answers • the four true statements.	**Finde** die Namen • die Wörter • die Antworten • die vier richtigen Aussagen.
Find out about the country.	**Finde** etwas über das Land **heraus**.
Finish the sentences.	**Vervollständige** die Sätze.
Give a presentation.	**Halte** eine Präsentation.
Give feedback.	**Gib Rückmeldung.**
Guess.	**Überlege.**
Interview your partner.	**Interviewe** deinen Partner / deine Partnerin.
Listen, **read** and **say.**	**Höre zu**, **lies mit** und **sprich nach.**
Listen to the dialogue • the interview • the announcements.	**Höre** dir den Dialog • das Gespräch • die Durchsagen **an.**
Look at the photos • the pictures (again).	**Schaue** dir die Fotos • die Bilder (noch einmal) **an.**
Make sentences • questions.	**Bilde** Sätze • Fragen.
Make a dialogue with your partner.	**Erstelle** einen Dialog mit deinem Partner / deiner Partnerin.
Make a list • a poster • a mind map • a table • a chart.	**Erstelle** eine Liste • ein Poster • ein Wörternetz • eine Tabelle • ein Diagramm.
Make notes.	**Mache** dir Notizen.
Match the words • the sentences.	**Ordne** die Wörter • die Sätze **zu.**
Match the sentences with the pictures.	**Ordne** die Sätze den Bildern **zu.**
Organize your information.	**Ordnet** eure Informationen.
Practise with a partner.	**Übe** mit einem Partner / einer Partnerin.
Prepare a presentation.	**Bereite** eine Präsentation **vor.**
Present your poster to your class.	**Stellt** euer Poster der Klasse **vor.**
Put in the right word • the right form • the right verbs.	**Setze** das richtige Wort • die richtige Form • die richtigen Verben **ein.**

Put the pictures • the words • the sentences **in the right order**.	**Bringe** die Bilder • die Wörter • die Sätze **in die richtige Reihenfolge**.
Put the words into groups.	**Sortiere** die Wörter in Gruppen.
Read the story • the dialogue • the text.	**Lies** die Geschichte • den Dialog • den Text.
Read your sentences • your text to your class.	**Lies** deine Sätze • deinen Text der Klasse **vor**.
Report in class.	**Berichte** der Klasse.
Are the sentences **right or wrong**?	Sind die Sätze **richtig oder falsch**?
Say the names • the numbers.	**Nenne** die Namen • die Zahlen.
Show your brochure • your report to your group.	**Zeige** deiner Gruppe deine Broschüre • deinen Bericht.
Take notes.	**Mache dir Notizen**.
Talk about the photos • the film • your free time.	**Sprich über** die Fotos • den Film • deine Freizeit.
Talk to your partner.	**Sprich mit** deinem Partner / deiner Partnerin.
Tell the class.	**Erzähle** der Klasse davon.
Tell your partner **about** what you do at home.	**Erzähle** deinem Partner / deiner Partnerin, was du zu Hause machst.
Think about these questions.	**Denke über** diese Fragen **nach**.
Think of questions.	**Denke** dir Fragen **aus**.
Use your own ideas.	**Benutze** deine eigenen Ideen.
Watch the film.	**Schaue** den Film **an**.
What are the words?	**Wie** heißen die Wörter?
What (else) can you see in the photo?	**Was** kannst du **(noch)** auf dem Foto sehen?
Where are the things?	**Wo** sind die Dinge?
Which sentences are right?	**Welche** Sätze sind richtig?
Who is • says it?	**Wer** ist • sagt das?
Why (not)?	**Warum** (nicht)?
Work with the text.	**Arbeite** mit dem Text.
Write sentences • an e-mail • a message • a text.	**Schreibe** Sätze • eine E-Mail • eine Nachricht • einen Text.

Classroom phrases

Before or after the lesson

Good morning, Mr/Mrs/Miss ….	Guten Morgen, Herr/Frau ….
I'm sorry I'm late.	Tut mir leid, dass ich mich verspätet habe.
I'm sorry I don't have my exercise book / my homework with me.	Tut mir leid, ich habe mein Heft / meine Hausaufgaben nicht dabei.
What's for homework?	Was haben wir als Hausaufgabe auf?

Asking for help

What page are we on?	Auf welcher Seite sind wir?
Can you help me, please?	Können Sie / Kannst du mir bitte helfen?
What does … mean?	Was heißt …?
Can you say that again, please?	Können Sie / Kannst du das bitte wiederholen?
Can you write that on the board?	Können Sie das an die Tafel schreiben?
Can I go to the toilet, please?	Kann ich bitte auf die Toilette gehen?
Mr/Mrs/Miss …, I don't feel well.	Herr/Frau …, mir geht es nicht gut.

Asking for information

What page is it on, please?	Auf welcher Seite ist das?
What's the homework?	Was haben wir als Hausaufgabe auf?
What's the German/English word for …?	Was ist das deutsche/englische Wort für …?
How do you spell …?	Wie schreibt man …?
What's this in English, please?	Was heißt das bitte auf Englisch?
What does that mean?	Was heißt/bedeutet das?
Sorry, I don't understand.	Tut mir leid, ich verstehe das nicht.
Sorry, I don't know.	Tut mir leid, ich weiß es nicht.

Working together

Can we work in pairs/groups?	Können wir zu zweit / in Gruppen arbeiten?
Do you want to work with me/us?	Willst du / Wollt ihr mit mir/uns arbeiten?
Let's make/draw a ….	Lass(t) uns ein … machen/zeichnen.
Whose turn is it?	Wer ist dran?
It's my/your turn.	Ich bin dran. / Du bist dran.
Who is going to do our presentation?	Wer macht unsere Präsentation?

Your teacher can say …

Listen, please.	Hört bitte zu.
Listen to the dialogue.	Höre dir / Hört euch den Dialog an.
Open your books at page ….	Öffnet eure Bücher auf Seite ….
Turn to page ….	Schlagt Seite … auf.
Read the text on page ….	Lest den Text auf Seite ….
Look at line ….	Schaue/Schaut in Zeile ….
Take out your pens.	Holt eure Stifte raus.

Show me your homework, please.	Zeigt mir bitte eure Hausaufgaben. / Zeige mir bitte deine Hausaufgaben.
Where's your homework?	Wo sind deine/eure Hausaufgaben?
Get into pairs/groups.	Bildet Paare/Gruppen.
Learn these words for homework.	Lernt diese Wörter als Hausaufgabe.
Look at the board.	Schaut an die Tafel.
Who can do number …?	Wer kann Nummer … machen?
Put your hands up, please.	Meldet euch, bitte.
Try again.	Versuche es noch einmal. / Versucht es noch einmal.
Sit down, please, and be quiet.	Setz dich bitte und sei ruhig. / Setzt euch bitte und seid ruhig.
Talk to your partner.	Sprecht mit eurem Partner / eurer Partnerin.
Talk about the pictures.	Redet über die Bilder.
Please speak up.	Bitte sprich lauter.
Well done.	Gut gemacht.

Lösungen

Zoom in – The USA, p. 8

1 Do the USA quiz with a partner.

1. They celebrate.
2. the president of the USA
3. Washington, D.C.
4. dollars and cents
5. the Native Americans
6. in California
7. alligators
8. the Rocky Mountains

Bildquellennachweis

Cover.1 ShutterStock.com RF (Little_Desire), New York, NY; **Cover.2** Alamy stock photo (Russ Bishop), Abingdon, Oxon; **8.1** ShutterStock.com RF (jdross75), New York, NY; **8.2** Getty Images Plus (Steve Debenport/E+), München; **9.1** Getty Images Plus (iStock Editorial / Roberto Galan), München; **9.2** Ullstein Bild GmbH (imagestate), Berlin; **9.3** Getty Images Plus (Image Source), München; **9.4** Alamy stock photo (Feije Riemersma), Abingdon, Oxon; **10.1** Alamy stock photo (JOHN KELLERMAN), Abingdon, Oxon; **10.2** Fotolia.com (mshch), New York; **11.1** ShutterStock.com RF (JoeSAPhotos), New York, NY; **11.2** ShutterStock.com RF (Olha Tytska), New York, NY; **11.3** Alamy stock photo (Ted Pink), Abingdon, Oxon; **12.1** Avenue Images GmbH (ponton), Hamburg; **12.2** Getty Images Plus (iStock / sonofpioneer), München; **12.3** Thinkstock (claudiodivizia/iStock), München; **13.1** Getty Images Plus (prizela_ning), München; **16.1** Getty Images Plus (iStock / bo1982), München; **16.2** Getty Images Plus (iStock / fstop123), München; **16.3** Alamy stock photo (Muskopf Photography, LLC), Abingdon, Oxon; **16.4** stock.adobe.com (ashtproductions), Dublin; **16.5** Thinkstock (claudiodivizia/iStock), München; **17.1** stock.adobe.com (Tarik GOK), Dublin; **17.2** Geoatlas, Hendaye; **17.5** stock.adobe.com (Tarik GOK), Dublin; **18.1** stock.adobe.com (PhotoSpirit), Dublin; **19.1** Getty Images Plus (HaizhanZheng), München; **22.1** Thinkstock (claudiodivizia/iStock), München; **23.1** Getty Images Plus (Matteo Colombo), München; **23.2** ShutterStock.com RF (Vacclav), New York, NY; **23.3** Thinkstock (iStockphoto), München; **23.4** ShutterStock.com RF (Stuart Monk), New York, NY; **24.1** Getty Images (Lonely Planet/jean pierre lescourret), München; **25.1** Klett-Archiv, Stuttgart; **25.2** iStockphoto (Liu), Calgary, Alberta; **26.1** Getty Images Plus (LagunaticPhoto), München; **26.2** Alamy stock photo (Madeleine Jettre/dbimages), Abingdon, Oxon; **26.3** ShutterStock.com RF (stephenallen75), New York, NY; **26.4** iStockphoto (kickstand), Calgary, Alberta; **30.1** Getty Images Plus (Robert Postma / Design Pics), München; **30.2** Alamy stock photo (Beth Dixson, 2016), Abingdon, Oxon; **31.1** ShutterStock.com RF (LagunaticPhoto), New York, NY; **31.2** iStockphoto (RudyBalasko), Calgary, Alberta; **31.3** ShutterStock.com RF (David Litman), New York, NY; **32.1** Alamy stock photo (Beth Dixson, 2016), Abingdon, Oxon; **32.2** Thinkstock (Jack Hollingsworth), München; **32.3** Thinkstock (claudiodivizia/iStock), München; **33.1** ShutterStock.com RF (Hof), New York, NY; **33.2** stock.adobe.com (gans340), Dublin; **33.3** stock.adobe.com (rouda100), Dublin; **33.4** stock.adobe.com (Andreas Edelmann), Dublin; **33.5** ShutterStock.com RF (Matej Kastelic), New York, NY; **33.6** Getty Images Plus (ianmcdonnell), München; **34.1** Getty Images Plus (bbtomas), München; **34.2** Getty Images Plus (iStock / DenKuvaiev), München; **34.3** Getty Images Plus (Fertnig), München; **34.4** Thinkstock (Comstock), München; **34.5** stock.adobe.com (sianc), Dublin; **34.6** Getty Images Plus (kali9), München; **35.1** Thinkstock (yenwen), München; **36.1** Thinkstock (Stockbyte/Jupiterimages), München; **37.1** Thinkstock (claudiodivizia/iStock), München; **40.1** ShutterStock.com RF (yankane), New York, NY; **40.2** Getty Images (Spencer Sutton), München; **41.1** ShutterStock.com RF (think4photop), New York, NY; **41.2** Alamy stock photo (Doug Houghton), Abingdon, Oxon; **42.1** Alamy stock photo (Igor Stevanovic), Abingdon, Oxon; **42.2** Thinkstock (claudiodivizia/iStock), München; **43.1** JDM Productions Inc, New York; **43.2** Thinkstock (claudiodivizia/iStock), München; **45.1** Getty Images Plus (Thinkstock), München; **45.2** imago images, Berlin; **45.3** ShutterStock.com RF (maxpro), New York, NY; **46.1** ShutterStock.com RF (Daboost), New York, NY; **46.2** ShutterStock.com RF (Popartic), New York, NY; **46.3** ShutterStock.com RF (Nicku), New York, NY; **46.4** ShutterStock.com RF (Nicku), New York, NY; **46.5** Thinkstock (claudiodivizia/iStock), München; **47.1** Thinkstock (claudiodivizia/iStock), München; **48.1** ShutterStock.com RF (Michael Kuijl), New York, NY; **48.2** stock.adobe.com (Reinhard Tiburzy), Dublin; **48.3** Alamy stock photo (imageBROKER / Stefan Wackerhagen), Abingdon, Oxon; **50.1** Getty Images (Corbis Documentary), München; **50.2** Getty Images (Blend Images), München; **51.1** Getty Images Plus (Preto_perola), München; **51.2** Alamy stock photo (Pictorial Press Ltd), Abingdon, Oxon; **51.3** Getty Images (Nikada), München; **52.1** Getty Images Plus (YinYang/E+), München; **52.2** Thinkstock (claudiodivizia/iStock), München; **53.1** ShutterStock.com RF (pixelheadphoto digitalskillet), New York, NY; **53.2** ShutterStock.com RF (pixelheadphoto digitalskillet), New York, NY; **53.3** ShutterStock.com RF (pixelheadphoto digitalskillet), New York, NY; **53.4** ShutterStock.com RF (pixelheadphoto digitalskillet), New York, NY; **53.5** ShutterStock.com RF (pixelheadphoto digitalskillet), New York, NY; **55.1** ShutterStock.com RF (Everett Historical), New York, NY; **56.1** stock.adobe.com (PhotoSpirit), Dublin; **56.2** ShutterStock.com RF (Daniel M Ernst), New York, NY; **56.3** ShutterStock.com RF (Globe Turner), New York, NY; **58.1** stock.adobe.com (Andrey Popov), Dublin; **58.2** Getty Images Plus (neirfy), München; **58.3** ShutterStock.com RF (Claudio Divizia), New York, NY; **58.4** Getty Images Plus (inxti), München; **58.5** ShutterStock.com RF (Pawel Michalowski), New York, NY; **58.6** Getty Images Plus (Dzevoniia), München; **60.1** Thinkstock (claudiodivizia/iStock), München; **62.1** Alamy stock photo (RSBPhoto), Abingdon, Oxon; **62.2** Getty Images (Sean Gardner), München; **62.3** Thinkstock (claudiodivizia/iStock), München; **63.1** JDM Productions Inc, New York; **63.2** Thinkstock (claudiodivizia/iStock), München; **66.1** Alamy stock photo (Bob Collet), Abingdon, Oxon; **69.1** Getty Images Plus (iStock Editorial / Sasha-Photography), München; **69.2** Getty Images Plus (iStock / Blacqbook), München; **69.3** stock.adobe.com (Pictures news), Dublin; **69.4** stock.adobe.com (k5hu), Dublin; **69.5** stock.adobe.com (WavebreakMediaMicro), Dublin; **70.1** stock.adobe.com (Sergey Novikov), Dublin; **70.2** Getty Images (EyeEm), München; **71.1** plainpicture GmbH & Co. KG (Minden Pictures/Jim Brandenburg), Hamburg; **71.2** Getty Images Plus (bakerjarvis), München; **71.3** Getty Images Plus (RyersonClark), München; **72.1** ShutterStock.com RF (cheapbooks), New York, NY; **72.2** stock.adobe.com (dusanpetkovic1), Dublin; **72.3** stock.adobe.com (Shooter Bob), Dublin; **72.4** iStockphoto (David Sucsy), Calgary, Alberta; **72.5** Fotolia.com (vospalej), New York; **73.1** Getty Images Plus (istock/DMEPhotography), München; **75.1** ShutterStock.com RF (Vibrant Image Studio), New York, NY; **75.2** BigStockPhoto.com (AISPIX), Davis, CA; **75.3** stock.adobe.com (grafikplusfoto), Dublin; **75.4** Getty Images Plus (Carso80 / iStock), München; **75.5** ShutterStock.com RF (Pixel-Shot), New York, NY; **75.6** stock.adobe.com (Martina Berg), Dublin; **76.1** ShutterStock.com RF (Dmitry Kalinovsky), New York, NY; **79.1** Getty Images Plus (iStock / yacobchuk), München; **79.2** ShutterStock.com RF (Iakov Filimonov), New York, NY; **79.3** Thinkstock (Pixland), München; **82.1** stock.adobe.com (Daniel Ernst), Dublin; **83.1** Fotolia.com (vospalej), New York; **83.2** Thinkstock (claudiodivizia/iStock), München; **83.3** JDM Productions Inc, New York; **86.1** Getty Images Plus (DigitalVision / Hero Images), München; **86.2** stock.adobe.com (Jessica), Dublin; **86.3** ShutterStock.com RF (Dan Breckwoldt), New York, NY; **86.4** Getty Images Plus (twildlife), München; **86.6** Getty Images Plus (AdonisVillanueva), München; **87.1** Getty Images Plus (iStock / carterdayne), München; **87.2** Getty Images Plus (iStock / MoreISO), München; **87.3** ShutterStock.com RF (BigAlBaloo), New York, NY; **87.4** ShutterStock.com RF (Tory Kallman), New York, NY; **87.5** Getty Images Plus (eyfoto/iStock), München; **87.6** ShutterStock.com RF, New York, NY; **88.1** iStockphoto (Eugene

Choi), Calgary, Alberta; **88.2** ShutterStock.com RF (JJFarq), New York, NY; **88.3** Getty Images Plus (Andrew Bertuleit), München; **90.1** Avenue Images GmbH (ponton), Hamburg; **90.2** Getty Images Plus (iStock / sonofpioneer), München; **92.1** Getty Images Plus (iStock / bo1982), München; **92.2** Getty Images Plus (iStock / fstop123), München; **92.3** Alamy stock photo (Muskopf Photography, LLC), Abingdon, Oxon; **92.4** stock.adobe.com (ashtproductions), Dublin; **94.1** ShutterStock.com RF (Hof), New York, NY; **94.2** stock.adobe.com (gans340), Dublin; **94.3** stock.adobe.com (rouda100), Dublin; **94.4** stock.adobe.com (Andreas Edelmann), Dublin; **94.5** ShutterStock.com RF (Matej Kastelic), New York, NY; **94.6** Getty Images Plus (ianmcdonnell), München; **94.7** Getty Images Plus (iStock / DenKuvaiev), München; **94.8** Getty Images Plus (Fertnig), München; **94.9** Thinkstock (Comstock), München; **94.10** stock.adobe.com (sianc), Dublin; **94.11** Getty Images Plus (kali9), München; **95.1** Thinkstock (Stockbyte/Jupiterimages), München; **98.1** stock.adobe.com (PhotoSpirit), Dublin; **98.2** ShutterStock.com RF (Daniel M Ernst), New York, NY; **99.1** stock.adobe.com (Andrey Popov), Dublin; **99.2** Getty Images Plus (neirfy), München; **99.3** ShutterStock.com RF (Claudio Divizia), New York, NY; **99.4** Getty Images Plus (inxti), München; **99.5** ShutterStock.com RF (Pawel Michalowski), New York, NY; **99.6** Getty Images Plus (Dzevoniia), München; **101.1** Getty Images Plus (istock/DMEPhotography), München; **101.2** ShutterStock.com RF (Sergei Bachlakov), New York, NY; **101.3** ShutterStock.com RF (Mark Byer), New York, NY; **101.4** Alamy stock photo (Torontonian), Abingdon, Oxon; **101.5** iStockphoto (ferlistockphoto), Calgary, Alberta; **101.6** iStockphoto (monkeybusinessimages), Calgary, Alberta; **101.7** ShutterStock.com RF (Ed Dods), New York, NY; **102.1** ShutterStock.com RF (Vibrant Image Studio), New York, NY; **102.2** BigStockPhoto.com (AISPIX), Davis, CA; **102.3** stock.adobe.com (grafikplusfoto), Dublin; **102.4** Getty Images Plus (Carso80 / iStock), München; **102.5** ShutterStock.com RF (Pixel-Shot), New York, NY; **102.6** stock.adobe.com (Martina Berg), Dublin; **103.1** Getty Images Plus (iStock / yacobchuk), München; **103.2** ShutterStock.com RF (Iakov Filimonov), New York, NY; **103.3** Thinkstock (Pixland), München; **130.1** Thinkstock (Owat Tasai), München; **131.1** ShutterStock.com RF (Anna Mandrikyan), New York, NY; **131.2** ShutterStock.com RF (Iryna Denysova), New York, NY; **131.3** ShutterStock.com RF (Troscha), New York, NY; **131.4** ShutterStock.com RF (stocksolutions), New York, NY; **131.5** ShutterStock.com RF (Aleksandra Duda), New York, NY; **131.6** stock.adobe.com (sonne_fleckl), Dublin; **131.7** ShutterStock.com RF (hlphoto), New York, NY; **131.8** ShutterStock.com RF (stockcreations), New York, NY; **131.9** ShutterStock.com RF (Visionsi), New York, NY; **131.10** ShutterStock.com RF (Aleksandar Mijatovic), New York, NY; **131.11** ShutterStock.com RF (Various-Everythings), New York, NY; **131.12** ShutterStock.com RF (ArpornSeemaroj), New York, NY; **131.13** ShutterStock.com RF (Irina Rumyantseva), New York, NY; **131.14** ShutterStock.com RF (Various-Everythings), New York, NY; **131.15** ShutterStock.com RF (Daboost), New York, NY; **131.16** ShutterStock.com RF (Niyazz), New York, NY; **131.17** ShutterStock.com RF (Daboost), New York, NY; **131.18** ShutterStock.com RF (Various-Everythings), New York, NY; **131.19** ShutterStock.com RF (Various-Everythings), New York, NY; **131.20** ShutterStock.com RF (Niyazz), New York, NY; **131.21** ShutterStock.com RF (NAN SKYBLACK), New York, NY; **131.22** ShutterStock.com RF (Anchiy), New York, NY; **131.23** ShutterStock.com RF (Daboost), New York, NY; **131.24** ShutterStock.com RF (Steve Allen), New York, NY; **131.25** ShutterStock.com RF (Niyazz), New York, NY; **131.26** ShutterStock.com RF (PhotoStockImage), New York, NY; **131.27** ShutterStock.com RF (Campre83), New York, NY; **132.1** Fotolia.com (Markus Mainka), New York, NY; **132.2** Thinkstock (Jupiterimages), München; **132.3** Foto-Geuther, Rötha; **132.4** Thinkstock (Comstock), München; **132.5** Thinkstock (Lifesize), München; **132.6** Thinkstock (istockphoto), München; **132.7** ShutterStock.com RF (Fotokostic), New York, NY; **132.8** Fotolia.com (Steve Lovegrove), New York, NY; **132.9** iStockphoto (Alex Bramwell), Calgary, Alberta; **132.10** stock.adobe.com (lunamarina), Dublin; **132.11** iStockphoto (David Mathies), Calgary, Alberta; **132.12** dreamstime.com (Marcel De Grijs), Brentwood, TN; **132.13** iStockphoto (kodachrome25), Calgary, Alberta; **132.14** 123rf Germany, c/o Inmagine GmbH (Andrey Volokhatiuk), Nidderau; **132.15** 123rf Germany, c/o Inmagine GmbH (footoo), Nidderau; **132.16** 123rf Germany, c/o Inmagine GmbH (Allan Wallberg), Nidderau; **132.17** stock.adobe.com (apfelweile), Dublin; **132.18** stock.adobe.com (NICOLAS LARENTO), Dublin; **132.19** 123rf Germany, c/o Inmagine GmbH (Jaroslav Silhan), Nidderau; **132.20** stock.adobe.com (Lioneska), Dublin; **132.21** 123rf Germany, c/o Inmagine GmbH (Cindy Fischer), Nidderau; **132.22** Fotolia.com (Joachim Neumann), New York; **132.23** Okapia (Hans Reinhard), Frankfurt; **132.24** Von Gibe, CC BY-SA 3.0, https://commons.wikimedia.org/w/index.php?curid=29948 (Gibe), siehe *3; **132.25** stock.adobe.com (faustyna), Dublin; **133.1** ShutterStock.com RF (Mikko Hyvärinen), New York, NY; **133.2** ShutterStock.com RF (asiandelight), New York, NY; **133.3** ShutterStock.com RF (asiandelight), New York, NY; **133.4** Alamy stock photo (Antonio Saba), Abingdon, Oxon; **133.5** Getty Images Plus (iStock/humonia), München; **135.1** stock.adobe.com (ajr_images), Dublin; **135.1** 123rf Germany, c/o Inmagine GmbH (olegdudko), Nidderau; **135.2** stock.adobe.com (Jashin), Dublin; **135.3** Fotolia.com (basin_stock), New York; **135.4** dreamstime.com (Norman Pogson), Brentwood, TN; **135.5** Getty Images Plus (Wavebreakmedia Ltd), München; **135.6** ShutterStock.com RF (Kzenon), New York, NY; **135.7** Alamy stock photo (Mint Images Limited), Abingdon, Oxon; **135.8** ShutterStock.com RF (CandyBox Images), New York, NY; **135.9** 123rf Germany, c/o Inmagine GmbH (Jens Brggemann), Nidderau; **135.10** iStockphoto (andresr), Calgary, Alberta; **135.11** Alamy stock photo (Hero Images), Abingdon, Oxon; **135.12** MEV Verlag GmbH, Augsburg; **135.13** ShutterStock.com RF (pio3), New York, NY; **135.14** stock.adobe.com (contrastwerkstatt), Dublin; **135.15** stock.adobe.com (Blue Jean Images), Dublin; **136.1** ShutterStock.com RF (Standard Studio), New York, NY; **136.2** ShutterStock.com RF (Beny1), New York, NY; **136.3** ShutterStock.com RF (Mr.Creative), New York, NY; **136.4** ShutterStock.com RF (HN Works), New York, NY; **136.5** ShutterStock.com RF (Alice July), New York, NY; **136.6** ShutterStock.com RF (Aliyev1), New York, NY; **137.1** Thinkstock (iStock/Michael Braun), München; **137.2** Thinkstock (Comstock), München; **137.3** Fotolia.com (Steve Lovegrove), New York; **137.4** Thinkstock (Lifesize), München; **137.5** Thinkstock (istockphoto), München; **137.6** Fotolia.com (Ints), New York; **137.7** Thinkstock (istockphoto), München; **137.8** ShutterStock.com RF (RF / McNally), New York, NY; **137.9** ShutterStock.com RF (FlashStudio), New York, NY; **137.10** ShutterStock.com RF (bodrumsurf), New York, NY; **137.11** Corbis RF (RF), Berlin; **137.12** Thinkstock (Comstock), München; **137.13** ShutterStock.com RF (gorillaimages), New York, NY; **137.14** Thinkstock (mavrek), München; **137.15** iStockphoto (Liz Leyden), Calgary, Alberta; **137.16** ShutterStock.com RF (PrinceOfLove), New York, NY; **137.17** Getty Images Plus (E+ / Vertigo3d), München; **137.18** ShutterStock.com RF (Stefan Schurr), New York, NY; **137.19** dreamstime.com (Denyskuvaiev), Brentwood, TN; **137.20** iStockphoto (technotr), Calgary, Alberta; **137.21** Getty Images RF (PhotoDisc), München; **137.22** Avenue Images GmbH (Ingram Publishing), Hamburg; **137.23** iStockphoto (Webphotographeer), Calgary, Alberta; **137.24** Thinkstock (iStockphoto), München; **137.25** creativ collection Verlag GmbH, Freiburg; **137.26** Avenue Images GmbH (image source), Hamburg; **137.27** Ingram Publishing, Tattenhall Chester; **137.28** Thinkstock (iStock/Ljupco), München; **137.29** Fotolia.com (mustgo), New York; **137.30** ShutterStock.com RF

(Cathleen A Clapper), New York, NY; **137.31** Thinkstock (Jupiterimages), München; **138.1** ShutterStock.com RF (SpeedKingz), New York, NY; **138.2** Studio Silberzahn, Stuttgart; **138.3** Fotolia.com (Dan Race), New York; **138.4** iStockphoto (Louis-Paul St-Onge), Calgary, Alberta; **138.5** Kliemann, Sabine, Krefeld; **138.6** 123rf Germany, c/o Inmagine GmbH (Mark Bowden), Nidderau

*3 Lizenzbestimmungen zu CC-BY-SA-4.0 siehe: http://creativecommons.org/licenses/by-sa/4.0/legalcode

Textquellennachweis
49.1 PONS Schülerwörterbuch Englisch, Stuttgart 2016; **60.2** © 2016 Black Cat – A brand of De Agostini Scuola Spa. Written by Mark Twain. Adapted by Gina D.B. Clemen

Sollte es in einem Einzelfall nicht gelungen sein, den korrekten Rechteinhaber ausfindig zu machen, so werden berechtigte Ansprüche selbstverständlich im Rahmen der üblichen Regelungen abgegolten.

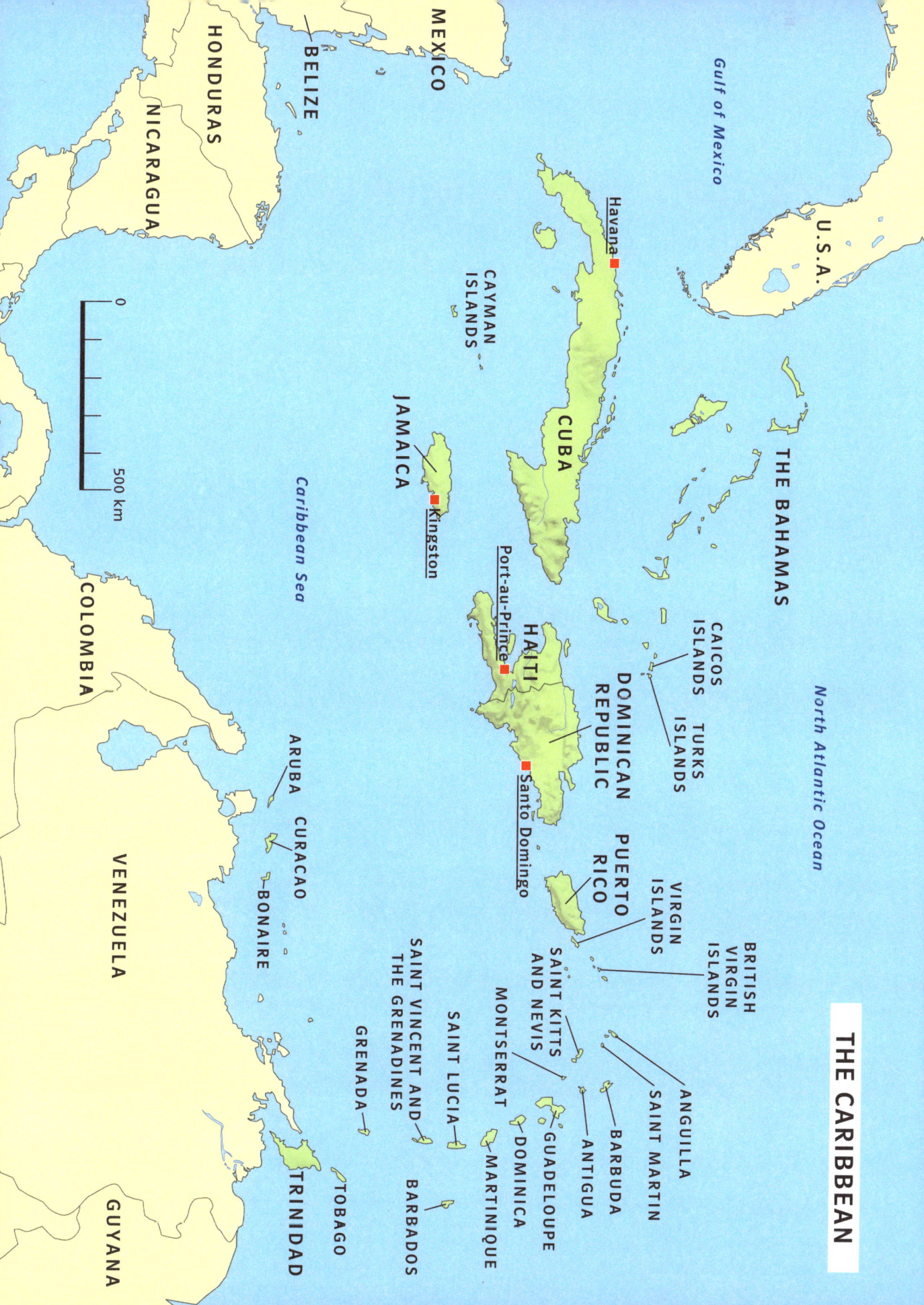

THE CARIBBEAN

HONDURAS

NICARAGUA

BELIZE

MEXICO

COLOMBIA

VENEZUELA

GUYANA

U.S.A.

Gulf of Mexico

Havana

CUBA

CAYMAN
ISLANDS

JAMAICA

Kingston

Caribbean Sea

500 km

0

THE BAHAMAS

North Atlantic Ocean

CAICOS
ISLANDS

TURKS
ISLANDS

Port-au-Prince

HAITI

DOMINICAN
REPUBLIC

Santo Domingo

PUERTO
RICO

VIRGIN
ISLANDS

BRITISH
VIRGIN
ISLANDS

ANGUILLA

SAINT MARTIN

SAINT KITTS
AND NEVIS

BARBUDA

ANTIGUA

MONTSERRAT

GUADELOUPE

DOMINICA

MARTINIQUE

SAINT LUCIA

SAINT VINCENT AND
THE GRENADINES

BARBADOS

GRENADA

ARUBA

CURACAO

BONAIRE

TRINIDAD

TOBAGO

MANHATTAN

THE BRONX

W 155th St.

W 145th St.

Harlem River Dr.

W 125th St.

HARLEM

Broadway

7th Avenue

Lenox Avenue

Park Avenue

2nd Avenue

1st Avenue

MANHATTAN

Henry Hudson Pkwy.

Amsterdam Ave.

Central Park

E 106th St.

E 96th St.

Hudson River

UPPER WEST SIDE

W 81st St.

5th Avenue

E 86th St.

E 84th St.

UPPER EAST SIDE

Metropolitan Museum of Art

Lincoln Center

Broadway

E 79th St.

Park Avenue

3rd Avenue

2nd Avenue

1st Avenue

10th Avenue

E 66th St.

9th Avenue

Central Park S.

QUEENS

Museum of Modern Art

Rockefeller Center

Lexington Avenue

Avenue of the Americas

Queensboro Bridge

Lincoln Tunnel

12th Avenue

W 42nd St.

Times Square

5th Avenue

Grand Central Station

W 34th St.

E 42nd St.

Chrysler Building

High Line

MIDTOWN

United Nations

Empire State Building

Queens Midtown Tunnel

9th Avenue

8th Avenue

7th Avenue

Broadway

NEW JERSEY

W 14th St.

E 23rd St.

E 14th St.

Greenwich Village

Avenue D

West Side Highway

Bleecker St.

Broadway

East River

Holland Tunnel

Hudson St.

Soho

Little Italy

E Houston St.

LOWER WEST SIDE

Broome St.

Canal St.

LOWER EAST SIDE

Chinatown

Bowery

Williamsburg Bridge

One World Trade Center

Wall St. Drive

FDR Drive

Manhattan Bridge

Brooklyn Bridge

ELLIS ISLAND

Brooklyn Battery Tunnel

LIBERTY ISLAND

Statue of Liberty

BROOKLYN

NEW YORK CITY

Van Cortlandt Park

THE BRONX

NY Botanical Garden

The Cloisters • Bronx Zoo

Teterboro Airport

Hudson River

Yankee Stadium

Harlem

Long Island Sound

Bronx-Whitestone Bridge
Throgs Neck Bridge

East River

MANHATTAN

Central Park

Rikers Island

La Guardia Airport

Flushing

Metropolitan Museum of Art

Rockefeller Center
Grand Central Station

Long Island City

Louis Armstrong House

Citi Field
Flushing Meadow
New York Hall of Science
Amphitheater

NEWARK

JERSEY CITY

One World Trade Center

Ellis Island

Newark Airport

Statue of Liberty

Governor's Island

Williamsburg

Brooklyn Bridge

Forest Hills Tennis Stadium

Corona Park

Forest Park

Golf Course

QUEENS

Jamaica

Flatbush

East New York

Newark Bay

Brooklyn Museum

Prospect Park

Spring Creek Park

Upper Bay

Postcards 9/11 Memorial

Children's Museum

Clove Lakes Park

The Narrows

Dyker Beach Park

BROOKLYN

Jamaica Bay

John F. Kennedy International Airport

Richmond

Verrazano-Narrows Bridge
Lower Bay

Brooklyn Marine Park

US Naval Air Station

STATEN ISLAND

Richmondtown

Coney Island

Long Beach

Great Kills Park

Crooke's Point

Rockaway Inlet

Rockaway Point

Conference House

Atlantic Ocean

Raritan Bay

0 1 2 3 4 5 km

0 1 2 3 miles

NORTH

WEST   EAST

SOUTH